# Touring the Screen:
## Tourism and New Zealand Film Geographies

# Touring the Screen:
## Tourism and New Zealand Film Geographies

by Alfio Leotta

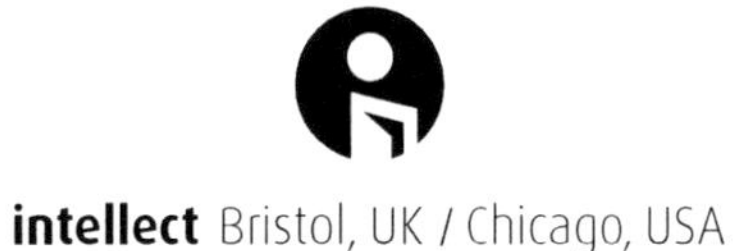

**intellect** Bristol, UK / Chicago, USA

First published in the UK in 2011 by Intellect,
The Mill, Parnall Road, Fishponds, Bristol, BS16 3JG, UK

First published in the USA in 2011 by Intellect, The University of Chicago Press,
1427 E. 60th Street, Chicago, IL 60637, USA



Library of Congress Cataloging-in-Publication Data

Leotta, Alfio.
   Touring the screen: tourism and New Zealand film geographies / Alfio Leotta.
        p.  cm.
   Includes bibliographical references.
   Includes filmography.
   ISBN 978-1-84150-475-9 (alk. paper)

1. New Zealand—In motion pictures.  2. Tourism and motion pictures.  3. Travelogues (Motion
pictures)—New Zealand—History and criticism.  4. Tourism—Social aspects —New Zealand.  5.
Motion picture industry—New Zealand—History—20th century.  I. Title.
   PN1995.9.N494L46 2011
   791.43'65893--dc22

                                                                                  2011011406



A catalogue record for this book is available from the British Library.


Cover design: Holly Rose
Cover photo: David Scott
Typesetting: John Teehan

ISBN  9781841504759

Printed and bound by Gutenberg Press, Malta.

# Contents

# Acknowledgements

This undertaking would have not been possible without the unvaluable support offered by Professor Nick Perry and Associate Professor Laurence Simmons of the Department of Film, Television and Media Studies at the University of Auckland.

I would also like to thank those peers, colleagues and friends who offered to share their knowledge and erudition during various long and insightful conversations about the topic of my book. I am particularly grateful to Professor Tom O'Regan, Associate Professor Bernadette Luciano, Dr. Amy West, Dr. Stephen Turner, Dr. Cherie Lacey, David Williams, Line Hazer, Jenny Leitheiser, Antonio Orlino and Marion Nouvel for their suggestions and invaluable encouragement over the last four years. Special thanks also to David Scott for generously providing the photo for the cover of the book and to Melanie Marshall for her crucial support during the editing process.

For the extraordinary contribution they made to this study my gratitude goes to Vincent Ward, Owen Hughes, Sue Radcliff from Samurai Village Tours, Joanna Cheok from Tourism New Zealand, the staff of Lord of the Rings Tours Queenstown and Gary from Minareth Lodge in Wanaka.

Finally, I would like to express my love and recognition to my family for their incommensurable practical and moral support throughout my studies and my whole life.

My first memory of New Zealand is associated with a 1988 Japanese computer game called *New Zealand Story*[1] (Nyū Jīrando Sutōrī). In *New Zealand Story* the player controls a sneaker-wearing kiwi called Tiki, and the aim of the game is to rescue several of his kiwi friends who have been trapped in various parts of New Zealand by a leopard seal. Over the course of the game the player can use improbable weapons such as arrows, laser guns or bombs to destroy his enemies. The main appeal of the game for me was the interaction it offered with the exotic and magical space of New Zealand. In the game, the country was constituted as a maze of platforms, a playground within which Tiki moved using vehicles as diverse as balloons, flying saucers and ducks.

As the years went by, other encounters with media products, from films to guidebooks as well as articles and TV programmes, slowly combined to form my personal virtual image of 'New Zealand'. Of course, its geographical position as the antipodean equivalent of Italy has always exerted a great fascination on the Italian imaginary, and this certainly influenced my own perception of Aotearoa. While the history of migration has made equally distant places such as America and Australia eerily familiar to Italians, New Zealand has been relatively untouched by the traditional routes of the Italian diaspora, and it has therefore kept an aura of mystery. Because of its unfamiliarity and geographical distance from Europe, New Zealand features in Italian popular culture as a synonym for 'ends of the earth'.

The release of *The Lord of the Rings* trilogy at the beginning of the millennium offered a great opportunity for a more extensive simulated journey to the country, particularly for devoted Tolkien fans like myself. My graduation in Communication Studies at the University 'La Sapienza' of Rome in 2003 offered a serendipitous opportunity to take a sabbatical year to visit New Zealand. After my working-holiday experience in Aotearoa I returned to Europe where I continued my studies, undertaking a European Master in Tourism Communication at the University of Nice in France. This course stimulated my interest in Tourism Studies and further augmented my passion for academic research. When I subsequently decided to continue my studies at a doctoral level it seemed logical to combine my Film and Communication Studies background with my new interest in tourism. *The Lord of the Rings* craze that was raging at the time made New Zealand famous all around the world as a potential tourist destination, thus offering a perfect case study for my research into film tourism. The possibility of returning to New Zealand gradually materialised and my previous experience of the country proved to be crucial in helping me defining my research project. A pre-doctoral six-month study period at the EHESS of Marseille, under the supervision of Professor Serge Tcherkezoff, head of the CREDO (Centre de recherche et documentation sur l'Océanie), anticipated my relocation to New Zealand and deepened my knowledge of the country's colonial history. In 2006 I returned to Auckland again, this time to investigate the tourist drive that had originally brought me here.

During the three and a half years that it has taken to assemble this book I have embarked on a triple journey. Firstly, it has been an exciting voyage through New Zealand cinema. Since the beginning of my research my personal collection of local films has flourished and both the Auckland Film Archive and University Audio Visual Library have become very familiar places. The second journey has been the one that took me through my doctoral research. The challenge of working in a different language and dealing with a different academic tradition has energised and motivated me throughout this research. Finally, at a more personal level, the last few years have also represented a thrilling opportunity to discover New Zealand culture and society. I believe my initial status of 'tourist' gradually shifted as I immersed myself in the local cultural milieu. I hope that this research has benefited from my multiple and overlapping identities as Italian, migrant and prospective New Zealander.

Twenty years after my first media encounter with New Zealand, through Tiki the kiwi, I am grateful that I have had the privilege of accessing a more complex picture of the country. I hope that this work, inspired by the filmic journey which has directly influenced my personal 'New Zealand Story', will be of some use to the reader.


**Notes**

1.  *New Zealand Story* is defined in technical terms as an arcade game. The main characteristics of arcade games are very short levels, simple and intuitive control schemes and rapidly increasing difficulty.

# Introduction

This book examines the relation between cinematic representations of New Zealand and the tourist imagery of the country. The histories of cinema and tourism are deeply interconnected, since both these cultural activities provide different but overlapping answers to the modern desire for temporal and spatial mobility. As forms of modern symbolic production, tourism and cinema are also responsible for the emergence of new myths and their collective representations. Recent film features that have represented New Zealand, both as an imaginary fantasyland and as a 'real' place, have served to reinforce the myth of a wild, pure and 'natural' New Zealand. This myth, in turn, has been exploited by the local tourism board, which, during the last two decades, has been able to create a successful travel brand destination. Globalisation has boosted competition between international destinations, previously unaffordable to the average tourist. This global competition has, in turn, obliged countries and tourist destinations to position themselves in order to cover different market niches. From this point of view, the production of *The Lord of the Rings* (dir. Peter Jackson, 2001–03), which associated the country with adventure and other-worldly scenery over a period of three years, has been a serendipitous development for New Zealand's tourist authorities. During the time this research has been conducted, more than 40 local tour operators around the country have offered *Lord of the Rings*-related products, some of which specifically target hardcore fans and foreign tourists. Several destination marketing organisations, such as Tourism New Zealand and Air New Zealand, have used the film to promote the country as a tourist destination. In fact, since the launch of the '100% Pure New Zealand' campaign in 1999, Tourism New Zealand has tried to capitalise on the possibilities of non-conventional publicity tools, particularly film-induced tourism. As Glenn Croy points out, "this image building and promotion process effectively utilises TNZ's [Tourism New Zealand] limited financial resources by using other groups' resources to provide the images and then creating association to New Zealand" (Croy, 2004: 7).

Research commissioned by Tourism New Zealand at the beginning of the 2000s identified the country as rich in four assets: landscape, people, adventure and culture

(Morgan et al., 2003: 292). The tourist authorities consequently designed a new promotional strategy which positioned New Zealand as "an adventurous new land and an adventurous new culture on the edge of the Pacific Ocean" (Piggott cited in Morgan et al., 2003: 292). The essence of the New Zealand brand, as conceived by New Zealand Tourism, is the landscape and in particular a landscape imbued with sophisticated, innovative and spirited values which allow tourists to express themselves through activities and experiences. Landscape plays a crucial role in tourism as a function of commodification which orientates space towards the selling of tourist destinations and experiences. Similarly, landscape has an equally central function in the cinematic medium. Early films privileged the representation of the natural world, and the subsequent emergence of narrative cinema relied on a spatial background to accompany the depiction of actions and events. Landscape seems to have an even more prominent role in New Zealand national cinema, to the extent that several critics have stressed its structural importance in local feature films. As Bob Harvey, the Mayor of Waitakere City, puts it, "for many years New Zealand film production was without major facilities and studios were unknown. Sets were difficult, so location was everything, both an asset and a challenge" (Harvey and Bridge, 2005: 17). Roger Horrocks goes even further, arguing that "in almost all New Zealand films the physical landscape makes its presence strongly felt not only as scenic background, but as an influence shaping the lives of the characters. Certain emotions seem to grow and flourish in this landscape" (Horrocks, 1989: 102). Others have celebrated the uniqueness of the New Zealand cinematographic landscape, allegedly characterised by a dark, gloomy and edgy look (Neill and Rymer, 1995; Harvey and Bridge, 2005).[1] Landscape is an artificial construct, one which cannot be divorced from the real and imaginary relation human beings entertain with space. This notion is crucial to the relation between film and tourism in New Zealand. In order to understand this interaction it is necessary to investigate the ways in which space is constructed in both film and tourist texts and how it is invested with symbolic and ideological meaning.


## Scope of the study

As suggested by the title of this book, the geographical scope of my research is limited to the New Zealand context. Like most of the recent academic work on film-induced tourism, my book cannot ignore the significant dimensions of this phenomenon in New Zealand. Expectations about the potential of film-induced tourism have engendered considerable enthusiasm among stakeholders and local authorities alike (Walker, 2001; Yeabsley and Duncan, 2002) making New Zealand a particularly interesting case study.

This book will focus on the textual analysis of four films shot in New Zealand:

*The Piano* (dir. Jane Campion, 1993)
*Whale Rider* (dir. Niki Caro, 2002)
*The Last Samurai* (dir. Edward Zwick, 2003)
*The Lord of the Rings* (*The Fellowship of the Ring*, 2001;
    *The Two Towers*, 2002; *The Return of the King*, 2003)

I believe these primary texts are particularly relevant to the study of film-induced tourism in Aotearoa. These four films have all been used as marketing tools to attract tourists to New Zealand or specific locations within the country. Furthermore, each film boasts a different representation of New Zealand, which ultimately leads to different types of film-tourist practices. *The Piano* represents a nineteenth century, colonial New Zealand. The film induced essentially on-location tourism (visits to the actual outdoor film locations) to the Auckland West Coast, where most of the famous beach scenes were shot. *Whale Rider* is set entirely in a remote coastal town, a contemporary 'lost paradise' where the Māori community can still escape the logic of globalisation. The film is believed to have contributed to the revitalisation of tourism in the Gisborne region and generated interest in Māori traditions. In *The Last Samurai* New Zealand is a blank canvas in which a fictional Japan is reconstructed and where Mount Taranaki in New Plymouth stands in for Mount Fuji. The film has attracted tourist interest in the 'aura' of the celebrities involved in the film. The attempts to market the film location as the fictional setting (Japan) have failed overall. *The Lord of the Rings* (here after *LOTR*) transforms New Zealand into the imaginary land of Middle Earth. The movie has induced 'on-location tourism' all around the country. There also exists a minor form of 'off-location tourism' (visits to the film studios, *LOTR* exhibitions) to specific locations associated with the films. Of the four case studies, the tourist impact of *LOTR* has been by far the most significant. However, analysed in relation to each other these films map the different kinds of film-induced tourism in New Zealand.

This work draws upon an approach based on the theoretical premises of structuralist semiotics, to investigate the way in which the selected films construct viewers as textual tourists. The representation of space and characters in these texts can, in fact, generate an imaginative activity that may in turn interpellate the physical and simulated mobility typical of tourist practice. This approach is based, in particular, on the theoretical premises of Greimasian generative semiotics. Greimas is, along with Claude Levi-Strauss, Michel Foucault and Jacques Lacan, one of the main exponents of French structuralism. Drawing on Saussurean linguistics, Greimas attempts to detect the basic semantic principles, the 'elementary structure of signification'. A consequence of this is the formulation of a 'narrative grammar', which implies the development of a syntactic analysis of discourse (Greimas and Courtes, 1982). In the last step of his theoretical enterprise, Greimas turns to the language act, or enunciation, attempting to outline the means by which semiotic possibilities are transformed into real words with real consequences (Greimas and Courtes, 1982).

Greimasian semiotics have been developed and applied by other scholars to the analysis of cultural texts very different from each other, such as commercial advertisements, novels and films. Francesco Casetti, in particular in his *Inside the Gaze: The Fiction Film and its Spectator* (1998), draws upon Greimas' theory of enunciation in an effort to satisfactorily explain the complicated web of cinematic spectatorship. Casetti locates an intersection between the filmic text and the empirical spectator and attempts to understand the textually constructed avatar of the spectator which is, in other words, the figure addressed by the film text (Sellors, 2000).

In this study, the textual and semiotic analysis of selected film features is complemented by a historiographical overview of New Zealand cinema, which emphasises the influence of the cultural, social and historical specificity of Aotearoa/ New Zealand in the development of a 'national' film landscape. This perspective foregrounds the significance of the colonial past of the country for contemporary New Zealand society. Thus, I argue that the conflation of a tourist gaze with a filmic one, which is a characteristic of my main four case studies, is rooted in the colonial history of New Zealand cinema.

The book also investigates the strategies and the forms of co-operation adopted by film producers and local film and tourism authorities, in order to promote the film and the film locations. This is supported by the analysis of selected local tourist products such as tourist guidebooks, brochures, tourist circuits and sites that are related to the four case studies. The examination of the specific features of this material is linked to a broader discussion of the relationship between film and tourist discourses. Before moving onto the discussion of the structure of this book, it is necessary to review the main theoretical references concerning the relation between film and tourism.

## Film, tourism and postmodernism

A theoretical approach to the relationship between film and tourism has to be framed within the cultural paradigm of postmodernism. Acknowledging the irritating elusiveness of this notion, Featherstone attempts to define it both as a break with the modernist era and as a shift of emphasis from modern social institutions and technologies (factories, mass production, representative democracy) towards new ones (Internet, post-Fordist consumption) (Featherstone, 1988).

For Lash, postmodernism is "a regime of signification whose fundamental trait is de-differentiation" (Lash, 1990: 5). One of the main features of postmodernism is the blurring of boundaries between high and low cultures and between different cultural forms such as tourism, education, art and sport. Postmodernism is also a cultural framework for the processes of globalisation, as it recognises the existence of multiple realities and changing meanings without attempting to provide a meta-discourse to explain all language forms, meanings and realities (Lyotard, 1984). Furthermore, the dissolution of the boundaries between categories means a change in the relationship between the cultural object and the audience. On the one hand, the audience participates increasingly in the production of the cultural object itself. On the other hand, cultural consumption is no longer contemplative, but rather playful, distracted and anti-auratic.

Postmodernism also problematises the relationship between reality and representation. The ability to distinguish reality from its images has gradually disappeared, leading to the fictionalisation of reality. In order to explain this phenomenon, Baudrillard employs the notion of 'simulacra': representations of material reality that substitute that very material reality, to the extent that so many copies have been made of copies that an original no longer exists (Baudrillard, 1983). Similarly, Umberto Eco uses the term 'hyperreality' to describe those situations in which the copy is constructed as more real and more desirable than the original. Eco's analysis refers in particular to the theme park, a space in which authenticity and illusion merge, creating hyper-real experiences (Eco, 1986). His 'travels in hyperreality' are mainly inspired by American cultural locations such as Disneyland, even though, in his definition of this notion, Eco looks back to Europe, detecting examples of proto-hyperreality in the Old Continent (Perry, 1998: 43).

The theme park is the ultimate postmodern construct. The extension of feature films and their characters into the built environment is a clear example of de-differentiation of cultural forms and activities, namely tourism, cinema and television. In his description of the 'Fantasy City' Hannigan points out some of the theme park's established features: they are based around a single or multi-theme; they are modular, mixing different components, like restaurants and attractions; and they are constructed around simulations and the virtual. Furthermore, the theme parks encourage the notion of playfulness, but in a strongly engineered setting and within a well-ordered commercial organisation (Hannigan, 1998). The strong tendencies towards commercialisation of the theme parks, along with their perceived association with a wider cultural imperialist process (the so called 'McDisneyization' of tourism), has attracted particular criticism (Ritzer, 1996).

The academic discourse on theme parks, however, has contributed strongly to the emergence of a broader debate around the issue of 'authenticity'. Some authors argue that tourists of 'hyperreal' attractions such as theme parks no longer look for authenticity, but rather for a playful consumption of the cultural object; the tourist seldom likes authenticity, rather preferring his or her own expectations (Eco, 1986;

Boorstin, 1962). Such views have been strongly criticised by other scholars, who instead suggest the existence of different types of authenticity (Shaw and Williams, 2004). Dean MacCannell sees authenticity in two different ways, as a feeling and as knowledge, and suggests that the tourist experience often involves authenticity as a feeling, even in absence of an 'objective authenticity'. In this way, the tourist's search could be satisfied by a 'staged authenticity', a kind of authenticity simulated just for tourist purposes (MacCannell, 1999: 98).[2]

In turn, the negotiated meaning of the notion of authenticity in the postmodern era is inextricably linked to the emergence of the 'post-tourist'. This term was employed for the first time by Maxine Feifer, to describe the new type of tourist arising out of the shift from mass consumption to post-Fordist consumption (Feifer, 1985). The post-tourists are increasingly home-focused, as media technology allows them to gaze at virtual tourist sites. They possess a greater range of choices for tourism opportunities and they have a playful approach to the tourist experience. As Williams and Shaw put it "For such (post)tourist there is no separately authentic experience, since all experiences may be viewed as authentic or real" (Shaw and Williams, 2004: 151). Similarly, Rojek highlights the post-tourist acceptance of the commodification of tourism and the importance given to signs and signifiers (Rojek, 1993).

In his analysis of the tourist perception of the USA in the global media age, Campbell has partially redefined the concept of post-tourism. For him, the post-tourist moves in a different way, adopts different strategies, crossing boundaries, shifting between experiences without necessarily having to travel in any conventional manner. S/he constructs his or her own tourist experience and destination, combining these into a package of overlapping and disjunctive elements: the imagined (dreams, screen cultures), the real (actual travels, guides) and the virtual (myths, internet) (Campbell, 2005: 203). Campbell argues that "the nomadic post-tourist dwells and travels, moving and 'poaching' between the arrays of experiences that constitute 'America', actively constructing a hybrid sense of place and identity in the process" (Campbell, 2005: 204).

The increased number of overlaps between tourism and film has gradually become apparent to the academic world after the recent recognition of the economic and cultural potential of film-induced tourism, particularly in New Zealand. John Urry was one of the first scholars to highlight the interdependence between tourism and the media, elaborating the concept of the 'tourist gaze'. Urry argues that the gaze dominates tourism, which is primarily concerned with the commodification of images and visual consumption. A prevalent mode of the tourist gaze is the 'mediatised gaze', shaped by movies and television; this is "a collective gaze where particular sites, famous for their 'mediated' nature are viewed" (Urry, 2002: 151). In this mode, the tourist compares what is gazed at with the familiar. The tourist experience represents a break with everyday life and the tourist gaze searches for the peculiarities of the visited destination, while judging and comparing these features with those with which s/he is familiar. The tourist tries to reproduce his or her own expectations, which have been "constructed and sustained through a variety of non-tourist practices, such as film, TV, literature, records, and videos" (Urry, 2002: 3). Even if, recently, Urry has partially redefined the concept of tourist gaze by recognising that tourism is a multisensorial activity, he still claims that the most important component of the tourist activity is concerned with viewing and gazing.[3]

Attempting to investigate the relationship between visual media and travel, Rhona Jackson has integrated the notion of the tourist gaze with Metz's theory of the film gaze, drawn from Freudian psychoanalysis. Metz argues that Freud's analysis of the child's relationship to 'the imaginary' and symbolic stages of development could explain the relationship of the spectator to the images on the cinema screen (Metz, 1975; Jackson, 2005). Metz points to the analogy between the screen and the mirror, suggesting that the activity of movie watching replays the primary instances of perception and recognition, namely the understanding of the difference between the Self and the image. The cinema provides the spectator with the ideal Self of the mirror image so s/he is at once involved and distanced from the cinema screen. Looking at the screen involves the quest for the always absent self-image and the desire of identification with the Other. The pleasure gained by looking at films could be explained by the pleasures Freud originally associated with looking: narcissism, voyeurism, exhibitionism and fetishism. According to Jackson, integrating Urry's and Metz's theories could explain how, in terms of narcissism for example, "the tourist, like the film spectator, seeks a familiar image, someone like themselves, or one with whom they wish to identify" (Jackson, 2005: 193). Similarly, the process of objectification by looking, that is at work in both tourism and film-viewing activities, might be better understood in light of the notion of voyeurism. For Jackson, tourism and film viewing might therefore be considered as converging practices, for they are both predicated on the desire to look and possess the object of the gaze (Jackson, 2005).

Urry's tourist gaze is also the main theoretical reference in Crouch, Jackson and Thompson's ground-breaking study of the relationship between tourism and the media (2005). In particular, they use Urry's theory to elaborate the notion of 'tourist imagination'. The 'tourist imagination' is a bridging construct that explains the sense of global mobility engendered by the daily consumption of the media, as well as actual travel. As Crouch, Jackson and Thompson put it, "the activity of tourism itself makes sense only as an imaginative process which involves a certain comprehension of the world and enthuses a distinctive emotional engagement with it" (Crouch et al., 2005: 1). The post-tourist crosses boundaries and shifts between experiences of everyday life, either through the actual or the simulated mobility allowed by the omnipresence of signs and electronic images in the contemporary age. The importance of the connection between media and mobility is expressed by growing interest in the phenomenon of film-induced tourism.

Evans has been one of the first scholars to define film-induced tourism as "tourist visits to a destination or attraction as a result of the destination being featured on television, video or the cinema screen" (Evans, 1997: D35). In their pioneering study of film-induced tourism, Riley and Van Doren compare this phenomenon to a hallmark event. The authors highlight the way in which a movie relies on its uniqueness and status to create attention (Riley and Van Doren, 1992: 268). In the most complete academic contribution to the study of the subject, Sue Beeton raises some major criticisms of this definition, pointing out that a film is seldom consumed at the tourist destination and it is not primarily produced in order to enhance or reshape the image of the destination. Beeton redefines film-induced tourism as "visitation to sites where movies and TV programmes have been filmed as well as to tours to production studios, including film-related theme parks" (Beeton, 2005: 11). Film-induced tourism could, therefore, be more loosely defined as tourist activity associated with the film industry.

Recently, an increasing number of academic studies have analysed the actual benefits and effects of film-induced tourism. Most of the literature on movie tourism has focused on the increase in visitor numbers to destinations depicted in films (Riley and Van Doren, 1992; Riley et al., 1998; Tooke and Baker, 1996; Busby and Klug 2001; Hudson and Ritchie, 2005; Beeton, 2005). All the studies have revealed that television films or movies attract tourists to the locations where they are filmed or set. Another branch of the literature on film-induced tourism (Kim and Richardson, 2003; Hahm, 2004; Croy, 2004; Tzanelli, 2007) has focused on the effects of feature films on the construction of destination image. Some of the studies cited above established that different forms of film-induced tourism exist. Beeton (2005), for example, drawing on the general notion of movie tourism, elaborates a more complex schema aiming at categorising different forms of film-induced tourism.[4]

Even though the study of film-induced tourism is progressing quickly, generating increasing interest in the academic field, this subject, as suggested by Beeton (2005), is still relatively unexplored. While the great majority of the academic studies in this field originate from Tourism Studies, this book is instead anchored by a Film and Media studies perspective. This does not mean that my research excluded a priori a confrontation with studies conceived by scholars coming from other disciplines. On the contrary, within the scope of my research, I have attempted to create interdisciplinary connections that reinforce my arguments. In particular, my study is motivated by the issue raised by Sue Beeton at the end of her seminal work about film induced-tourism: "what are the elements that make a film 'create' film-induced tourism and how are they combined?" (Beeton, 2005: 244). The rest of this book attempts to answer this crucial research question.

## Chapter outline

This book begins with an overview of the association between film and tourism in New Zealand in the first part of the twentieth century. In Chapter 1 I note how the country's settler culture played a crucial role in the establishment of this strong connection, which in turn led to the production of those 'empty landscapes' typical of early New Zealand film. The representation of both indigenous subjects and space, which is characteristic of these colonial productions, directly influenced the more recent use by runaway productions of New Zealand as a "transposable 'otherness'" (Jutel, 2004: 55). In this way, the emptying of the country, which began at the beginning of the last century, eventually prepared the terrain for the branding of the country as Middle Earth.

Chapter 2 focuses on the 50-year period between 1940 and 1990 that was characterised by the emergence of an established film industry in New Zealand. Here, through a consideration of the most important film features of the time, I attempt to formulate a semiotic categorisation of New Zealand filmic places. The recurring patterns of landscape representation become part of a New Zealand film tradition, which, in turn, influenced the construction of space in the main four case studies of this research. In this chapter, I also consider how changed historical, social and cultural conditions impact upon the relation between film and tourist imagery.

In Chapter 3 the centre of attention shifts to the first case study: Jane Campion's *The Piano*. In particular, I look at the way in which the film text suggests the identification of the spectator with both the protagonist and the camera, and the consequence of this on the development of a 'tourist imagination'. In these pages I also consider Campion's use of traditional European artistic conventions and their contribution to the tourist appeal of the film. The semiotic analysis of a '100% Pure New Zealand' advertisement that uses *The Piano* to promote Karekare beach sheds more light on the interconnection between film and tourist languages. The end of the chapter looks at the legacy of *The Piano*, both in terms of its landscape representational modes and on the process of national identity formation. A serendipitous example of the influence of *The Piano* on the New Zealand film tradition is represented by *Memory and Desire* (dir. Niki Caro, 1997). The intertextual reference to Campion's film in *Memory and Desire* concerns, on the one hand, the representation of the beach and, on the other, the construction of New Zealand as a 'sublime' tourist destination whose existence depends on its status of commodity for global consumers.

*Memory and Desire* and Niki Caro constitute the bridge to Chapter 4, which focuses on the second case study of the research, *Whale Rider*, Caro's most successful film. *Whale Rider* deals with the issue of representation of indigenous people, which I partially considered in Chapter 1. In Chapter 4 I contravene the chronological order that characterises the earlier parts of the book, to look back at films made by Māori directors. *Whale Rider* borrows some of the tropes of films made by Māori film-makers, particularly *Ngati* (dir. Barry Barclay, 1987) and *Mauri* (dir. Merata Mita, 1988), adapting them to the demand of the global market. The tourist and ethnographic gaze which characterises the film, in fact, may satisfy the desire of urban audiences for 'otherness'. From this point of view the commodification of an 'authentic' Māori culture in *Whale Rider* draws from another cinematic tradition: the early tourist films which supported the imperialist rhetoric about a mythical Maoriland on the verge of extinction.

Chapter 5 deals with the use of New Zealand as an interchangeable setting in runaway productions. *The Last Samurai* represents a very useful case study because of the interest generated by its potential tourist spin-off. Tourist authorities and stakeholders hoped to capitalise at once on the association of the film locations with Hollywood celebrity and their resemblance to a primeval Japan. Even though *The Last Samurai* ultimately failed to generate the anticipated tourist flows, the analysis of both the film and the tourist discourses associated with it help to uncover some of the socio-historical processes which eventually led to the spectacular success of the rebranding of New Zealand as Middle Earth.

In the final chapter of the book I discuss *LOTR* and its decisive impact on the tourist image of New Zealand at a global level. The relation between Jackson's films and tourism in New Zealand has generated a significant number of academic responses and ignited a renewed interest in the very phenomenon of film-induced tourism. In this chapter I attempt to review the main contributions on this subject. The stunning tourist spin-off of the *LOTR* trilogy can be explained by factors as different as the economic mode of production typical of the film franchise, the style of the film based on an aesthetic of spectacle that largely exploited the New Zealand landscape and the importance of the notion of journey and mobility in the film narrative. I also argue that the complex interplay of factors as different as the context of reception of the trilogy, the films' conservative narrative subtext and the colonial history of New Zealand played a crucial role in determining the success of New Zealand/Middle Earth as a film-tourist destination.


**On the notes**

I have made extensive use of footnotes to create interconnections between the different chapters and refer the reader to other sections of the document when certain arguments mentioned in the text are further developed elsewhere.

In order to avoid confusion between films, essays and books I have used italics for film titles, italics and single quotation marks for essays and I have underlined the titles of printed works.

**Notes**

1. Similarly, some art critics have claimed that the work of local painters is determined by the distinctive 'harsh clarity' of New Zealand light. According to Gordon Brown and Hamish Keith, in New Zealand painting "two patterns emerge: a general orientation towards landscape [...] and a positive response on the part of a number of more important New Zealand painters to the distinctive qualities of New Zealand light" (Brown and Keith, 1982: 9). The thesis of a geographic determinism was later criticised by Francis Pound, who argued that an immediate response to the landscape is impossible as nature is always seen through the eyes of culture (Pound, 1982). Landscape is also a crucial theme in much twentieth-century New Zealand literature. Literary critics have pointed out how the popularity of the trope of a 'haunted landscape' in New Zealand literature reflects the alienation of European settlers from a land they wanted to possess, but failed to relate to (McNaughton, 1986; Schafer, 1998). For a more extensive discussion of the 'hauntedness' of New Zealand landscape see Chapter 6.

2. A typical example of 'staged authenticity' are the film studio tours reconstructed for tourist visits, even though these 'simulated backstages' have never actually been used for film production purposes.

3. This stand has been criticised, with many academic commentators troubled by Urry's "oversimplification [that] neglects other sensual dimensions of being a tourist and dematerialises places so that the concentration on the visual and semiotic features of attractions overwhelms their tactile, sonic and odorous qualities" (Edensor, 2005: 115).

4. For Beeton there are six kinds of film-induced tourism: on location (visits to the actual outdoor film locations); commercial (the location is [re]constructed after the filming to attract tourists); mistaken identities (visits to places where the film is set but not filmed and vice versa); off-location (theme parks and industrial tours of working film studios); one-off events (movie premieres and film festivals); armchair travels (TV travel programmes and documentaries) (Beeton, 2005: 10).

**1**

# Early New Zealand Films and Western Voy(ag)eurs

## Introduction

A wide shot of a small town beneath the hills reveals a four-horse-drawn coach coming up the valley and rushing past the camera. The opening shot of *Across the Mountain Passes of New Zealand* (dir. Franklyn Barrett, 1910), a four-minute-long film produced by Pathé Frères, is one of the first moving images of New Zealand offered up to the gaze of the European spectators. The fixed gaze of photography turned the modern Western subject into a voyeur. Emphasising the film's spatio-corporeal kinetics, the stagecoach that inhabits and traverses the New Zealand landscape reminds us that the spectator is also a *voyageur* or rather a voy(ag)eur (Bruno, 1997a). The constant reinvention of space, typical of cinematic technology, has made film a modern cartography. *Across the Mountain Passes* was, therefore, one of the first films to put New Zealand on this new mobile map. Later in the film we see people on horseback, a man riding a bike, tourists on a motorboat travelling along the riverbank and women walking along a bush track. Inscribing the simulacra of the spectator (the tourists) within the moving image, the film becomes an aesthetic tourist practice of spatial consumption. As Giuliana Bruno puts it:

> Film creates space for viewing, perusing and wandering about. As in all forms of journey, space is physically consumed as a vast commodity. [...] Attracted to vistas, the spectator turns into a visitor. The film viewer is a practitioner of viewing space—a tourist. (Bruno, 1997a:11)

In her analysis of the emergence of the cinematic apparatus, Anne Friedberg defines the new aesthetic of reception found in cinematic spectatorship as the "'mobilised' and 'virtual' gaze" (Friedberg, 1993: 37). In this reading, movie-going activity has been prepared, on the one hand, by the mobilised scopophilia of the flaneur and the tourist, and, on the other hand, by the virtual gaze promoted by pre-cinematic apparatuses such as the panorama and the diorama (Friedberg, 1993). Thus, the technological innovations of the nineteenth century have deeply altered the subjectivity of the traveller. The train window permitted a 'mobilised immobility' in which the mobility of the gaze framed by the window is associated with the bodily absence of movement. These are also some of the conditions peculiar to cinematic spectatorship: physical immobility, the presence of the frame, moving images. The temporal displacement offered by the cinema not only contributed to a conceptual reshaping of the measure of space and time but also the role of memory and history (Schivelbusch, 1986; Simmons, 1995b).

The strict interconnection between cinema and tourism, exemplified by the early film's obsession with exotic views and travel images, should be placed within the larger context of colonial expansion and technological innovation. This relation seems particularly prominent in the history of New Zealand cinema. The New Zealand governments of the first half of the twentieth century were, in fact, pioneers in the use of film as a means of national publicity. Since 1917 tourist promotions, including moving pictures, were produced by the Department of Tourism and Health Resources and targeted tourists from America, Britain and other British colonies (NZOYB, 1976). By 1930 the Government Publicity Office, responsible for government film-making activities, was, significantly, transferred from the Internal Affairs Department to the Tourist Department (Dennis, 1981: 8). More importantly, the use of film for tourist promotion by early New Zealand governments was underpinned by a deeply rooted settler culture which framed the landscape within established European conventions (Pound, 1983). A critical examination of New Zealand tourist imagery at the beginning of the twentieth century reveals the government's policy of linking tourism and immigration. In particular, the mythology of a scenic wonderland and the depiction of an untouched 'Maoriland' were deployed to attract potential settlement by what a 1930s New Zealand Trade Commissioner defined as "good-type Europeans" (Taylor cited in Hillyer, 1997: 15). The term 'Maoriland' was a literary synonym for late colonial New Zealand. Stafford and Williams highlight the paternalist and colonialist connotations embedded within a concept which combined tourist images of Māori warriors and maidens with the convenient notion that the indigenous people were a 'dying race'. At the heart of the concept of Maoriland there is a deep contradiction, for "its archaism cohabits with and compensates for the colony's sense of its own modernity" (Stafford and Williams, 2006: 11). This is particularly apparent in the tourist advertisements of the country, which often integrated romantic images of Maoriland with symbols of progress, such as hotels and railways. This, in turn, was meant to demonstrate, as Martin Blythe puts it, that "contemporary Māori had abandoned Maoriland's 'barbaric' ways, and now the rest of New Zealand could be subjected to the system of property acquisition and ownership that arrived with colonisation" (Blythe, 1994: 52).

This chapter examines the role of early New Zealand films in shaping the country's official tourism imagery in the first half of the twentieth century. The deconstruction of those discourses of tourism, within a wider social and political context, is critical to an understanding of the more contemporary emphasis of local tourist authorities on film-induced tourism. The juxtaposition of New Zealand film-tourism imagery of the first decades of the twentieth and twenty-first centuries will uncover a historical shift in tourist practices and ideologies. Furthermore, the analysis of early films explicitly or implicitly produced for tourism-promotion purposes will shed new light on the process of forging New Zealand nationhood. The rhetorical strategy adopted by contemporary tourism advertisers is evidently woven into the historical, cultural and social fabric of the nation. The analysis of the nation's political economy of identity is, therefore, crucial for examining the selling of places for tourism consumption. More precisely, this chapter will argue that there is a direct connection between the branding of New Zealand as Middle Earth and the depiction of the country as a series of empty landscapes in the early films of the Publicity Office. Both processes are based on "a logic of franchise capital that is constitutive of the business of settlement" (Kavka and Turner, 2009: 231), for, in order to succeed, the tourist-settler enterprise has to remove the place from its people (scenic views) and transpose its history into a timeless past (Maoriland or Middle Earth).

## New Zealand, or the "world in a nutshell"

The opening credits of *Romantic New Zealand* (dir. Filmcraft Studios, 1934), the first feature-length New Zealand sound film, introduced the country as "a world in a nutshell". This description is particularly meaningful within the context of the film's production. During the 1930s, the very modern obsession with processing the world as a series of images, to be made available through a range of visual devices, was already in its advanced stages. The consumption of the world through projected images, postcards and actual tourism had boomed at the beginning of the twentieth century in the context of industrial and colonial expansion. The curiosity for new geographic realms, brought on by the photographic medium, is aptly dissected by Martin Heidegger in his definition of the "Age of the World Picture":

> Where the world becomes picture, what is in its entirety, is juxtaposed as that for which man is prepared and which correspondingly, he therefore intends to bring before himself and have before himself, and consequently intends in a decisive sense to set in place before himself. Hence world picture, when understood essentially, does not mean a picture of the world but the world conceived and grasped as a picture. (Heidegger, 1977: 129)

The travel images so popular during the nineteenth and twentieth centuries brought distant places closer and made them ready for consumption. Western photographers and spectators took possession of the world through pictures of it, while colonialism played an essential role in the commodification of 'foreign views'. Geoffrey Batchen locates the social origin of the photographic medium within the reproduction of certain forms of power, in his words: "power inhabits the very grain of photography's existence as a modern Western event" (Batchen, 1997: 202). Similarly, Bernard Smith notices how the emergence of a modern observer, which is the main precondition for the invention of photography, coincides with the observation of the Western colonial expansion into the Pacific (Smith, 1960: 337).

Thus, there is a strict interrelation between colonialism, tourism and photography, for colonial discourses were reinforced by tourist practices of observation, particularly the use of the camera, which dealt with recording and consuming. Photography, as a practice of observation, stages the privileging of the observing subject (often male, white and colonialist), thus reproducing the relationships of power in a given colonial context. Hayes aptly describes this interconnection, pointing out how the tourist economy of representation, evident in the construction of stereotypical images of the colonised people and land, functioned to validate the political, economic and cultural ambitions of colonialism (Hayes, 2002: 173). In this vein, he argues that the presence of a photographer, Alfred Burton, on the first Pacific cruise in 1884, was not a fortuitous episode but rather a symptom of a changing epistemology of representation that conflated new modes of vision with imperialist expansion.

Similarly, the very science of topography was developed in the eighteenth century in correlation with the expansion of the Western empires in the rest of the world. Along with other institutions of power, such as the census and the museum, topography worked on the basis of a totalising classification. By the end of the eighteenth century, the surface of the planet had been subjected to a geometrical grid which squared off unexplored regions in measured boxes. As Anderson puts it: "The task of, 'filling in' the boxes was to be accomplished by explorers, surveyors and military forces" (Anderson, 1991: 176). In her book *Boundary Markers* (2001) Giselle Byrnes examines the role of land surveying in the process of colonisation of New Zealand. Under nineteenth-century international law, a European state could legally claim any land not possessed by another state. The process of naming and measuring the land played a crucial role in this regard, averting wars between imperial powers by providing an orderly way of divvying up unclaimed land. In New Zealand, the European techniques of surveying ignored boundaries, place names and territories established by the Māori over several centuries (Byrnes, 2001).

The Western representation of colonised landscapes is strictly connected to the logic of legal inheritance and legal transferability of geographic space. Thus, representation is inextricably part of the process of commensuration and commodification of the land.

This could explain why the notion of image as appropriation dominates the nineteenth-century image-making industry. As Tom Gunning points out: "Images fascinate the world obsessively, and this modern sense of images comes from a belief that images can somehow deliver what they portray" (Gunning, 2006: 30). Since the eighteenth century, the illustrated travel book, written by explorers and military officers, had become an extremely popular literary genre. Travel images supplied the most frequent subjects of early cinema, as they had earlier for panoramas and dioramas. In these early films travel curiosity often overlapped with an interest in colonial wars shown by early American producers. One of the Biograph catalogues, for example, claims that "in every case our operators worked under the direct patronage and with the most perfect co-operation of the respective Governments involved" (Musser, 1985: 138). From this point of view, the slogan used by several early film companies—'the whole world within reach'—could be read as a way of establishing routes of power and appropriation, from the gazer (coloniser) to the object of the gaze (colonised). Thanks to travel and ethnographic films, the most popular genres of early cinema, even the most remote places of the planet were no longer inaccessible.

New Zealand film of this period, of every genre, shows some affinity with the act, or experience, of travelling. The fictional *Under the Southern Cross* (dir. Lew Collins, 1929) and *Hei Tiki* (dir. Alexander Markey, 1935), both based on Māori legends, for example, are punctuated by shots of scenic attractions and scenes of Māori life closer to ethnographic or tourist films rather than classical narrative movies. Both productions are characterised by the involvement of the eccentric film-maker Alexander Markey. In his *Hei Tiki*, one of the most controversial productions of New Zealand film history,[1] Markey himself introduces the fictional story in the manner of the lecturer-traveller of the turn of the century. From the outset, the narration defines the film consumption as an escapist pleasure: "Forget your cares and troubles for a brief interlude, and join me on a voyage to the isle of ghosts. You will feast your eyes on a sight no living white man has ever seen before" (Markey cited in Blythe, 1988: 62).

Eyes and images are essential media which allow to structure travel and appropriate the world. The passage from the civilised world of New York into primitive Maoriland is mediated by the narrator's guidance, as every stop is accompanied by images and Markey's comments:

> We leave the miracle city of the modern age behind us, and sail down the Caribbean Sea, through the Panama canal [...]. On past the myriad islands of the South Seas, miniature paradises of tranquillity, to the strange fuzzy-haired people of the Fiji Islands. On still further in the direction of the South Pole until we come to Aotearoa, the long white cloud at the bottom of the world. (Markey cited in Blythe, 1988: 63)

Markey's directional finger, tracing his itinerary on a map of the globe, carries out the appropriation of the world implicit in Heidegger's theorisation of the world picture. The famous dictum of the travelogue film-maker Burton Holmes aptly summarises this notion: "To travel is to possess the world" (Holmes, 1953: ix). The mechanical eye of the camera operating in symbiosis with the modern technologies of mobility delivers a new perception of the world. The gaze is freed from human immobility and ready to impose its power over space.

Significantly, *Hei Tiki* makes explicit the direction of this gaze, literally defining New Zealand as a function of its distance from the civilised world. Three dashed lines on the map connect Aotearoa to the centres or sub-centres of the Empire: Britain, America and Australia. Markey informs the spectator of the precise distance in miles that separates New Zealand from the three other countries which are potential sources of other voy(ag)eurs. On the one hand, this information reinforces the heroic character of the traveller/film-maker, and the presence of a questing hero provides the audience with the possibility of identification and vicarious pleasure in the romantic journey. On the other hand, even if it emphasises the remoteness of the destination, the narration implicitly recognises the possibility of physical access to it. Maoriland is separated from the rest of the world, but it exists as a potential object of the most intrepid travellers' appropriating gaze. In this sense, distance is just a corollary of the exotic character of the location and a function of the opposition between metropolitan centres and 'natural' peripheries. Seventy years later, the remoteness of the New Zealand location from the major hubs of the First World played an essential role in the branding of the country as the mythical, timeless land of Middle Earth.


**New Zealanders: "eternal tourists and proud pioneers"**

If 'the whole world is within reach' and New Zealand is 'the world in a nutshell', the process of visual commodification characteristic of the modernist age finds its fullest expression in an antipodean country. In this sense, New Zealand is devoid of any identity as it is destined to produce raw visual material; exotic views for the centre of the empire. Traces of the country's colonial legacy are found in contemporary marketing products. For example, the versatility of the New Zealand landscape has been recently promoted by a booklet titled *The Production Guide to the World in One Country*, published by Film New Zealand in 1999. The booklet claims that producers working in New Zealand have been able to reproduce: "Italian lake district, American North west, Scottish highlands and lakes, Norwegian fjords, [...] Korea, Ireland and Greece" (Film New Zealand, 1999: 21). This indetermination of the landscape has made possible, according to Wright, the utilisation of the New Zealand landscape to create a 'Tolkienesque' aesthetic characteristic of fantasy movies such as *Willow* (dir. Ron Howard, 1988), *LOTR* and *The Chronicles of Narnia* (dir. Andrew Adamson, 2005). Wright argues that

> New Zealand, a country that can be seen as remote and at the very edge of the earth, has an affinity with the realms of imagination, an affinity that aligns it particularly with the fantasy vision of J. R. R. Tolkien. (Wright, 2000: 52)[2]

In *Romantic New Zealand* the country is also described as "a fully established outpost of the great British Empire". The film takes spectators on a tour of New Zealand's major cities and popular tourist spots, such as the Southern Alps and the fjords. The travelogue includes re-enactments of settlement activities, such as early road construction, clearing of bush and surveying, but also the depiction of native flora and fauna from the tuatara to the iconic kiwi. Two sections of the film also include the use of the, then new, colour process named Truecolour, a two-colour technology developed simultaneously in different areas of the world such as the US, France and New Zealand (Martin and Edwards, 1997: 44).

From the very outset the film makes clear the connection between travel and appropriation, as it opens with the discovery of Aotearoa/New Zealand. A group of Māori on a *waka* (a traditional canoe) rejoice as they see the distant silhouette of land appearing on the horizon. The male voice-over provides a historical context for the film:

> Though one of the parts of the earth best fitted for man, it was about the last of such lands occupied by human beings, the Māori people. The first European to find it was a Dutch sea captain, who was looking for something else [...]. Indeed, it might never have been part of the British Empire, as England did not want it, and annexed it only to keep it from the French, who did.

As the film purports to traverse the nation, and 'discover' sites and sights, it places the spectator in the position of a voy(ag)eur or a modern-day explorer. The cinema-going activity is a logical extension of the act of exploring as discoveries, including that of New Zealand, were validated at a distance and took form through language and travel books in particular. As Mary Louise Pratt puts it: "In the end, the act of discovery itself, for which all the untold lives were sacrificed and miseries endured, consisted of what, in European culture, counts as a purely passive experience—that of seeing" (Pratt, 1992: 203–04).

According to Hillyer (1997), though, while the act of seeing may be a passive one, the act of viewing, also intended as spectatorship, offers varied 'discoveries'. The gregarious conditions of movie-going activity and the mobilisation of sociability that it engenders account for the ability of cinema to create and mobilise public spaces. The local reception of government travelogues such as *Romantic New Zealand* or its predecessor, *Glorious New Zealand* (dir. Arthur H. Messenger, 1925),[3] served to stimulate a sense of community. A review of *Glorious New Zealand* in the Wellington newspaper *The Post* describes the film as "the best moving picture yet produced illustrative of the Dominion, and may well be described as our first National picture. Being so, it is a duty as well as a privilege for all New Zealanders to see it" (cited in Hillyer, 1997: 22). In a similar press release, the Tourist and Publicity Department, the commissioner of both films, claims that

> [t]he big scenic film which has just been released under the title "Glorious New Zealand" is the forerunner of a campaign calculated to stimulate tourist traffic within the Dominion, thus fulfilling dual objects of creating a national New Zealand spirit and a keener appreciation of the beauties contained in the Dominion. The Publicity Office wishes it to be known that a large number of booklets illustrative of Dominion scenic, sporting, attractions and other information are available at all times for those who wish to help the advertising of the Dominion abroad. (cited in Hillyer, 1997: 22)

The release of *Romantic New Zealand* was accompanied by a very similar campaign that could be summarised as 'Know New Zealand First and Advertise to your Friends abroad'.

Both *Romantic New Zealand* and *Glorious New Zealand* provided local and international audiences with a double 'discovery'. On the one hand, due to their ability to mobilise the spectator gaze, they brought a series of New Zealand's 'scenic gems' closer. On the other hand, they allowed for the discovery of a spirit of nationhood. The national New Zealand spirit was meant to be shaped, according to the Tourist and Publicity Department, through the very consumption of the country's scenic views. The creation of a national community is strictly intermingled with its promotion as a tourist destination, at home and overseas. That the government chose to use cinema as a forum for advertising is particularly significant for two reasons. First, film enables the creation of a national public sphere through the production of images of national 'communion'. The communal experience of the consumption of scenic views of the Southern Alps or the fjords contributed to the creation of New Zealand's imagined community. In this sense, films such as *Glorious New Zealand* or *Romantic New Zealand* are not to be read as merely historical documents but also as crucial players in the construction of the New Zealand national imaginary.

Second, film technology is a spectatorial means of transportation, the inscription of motion in the language of film leads the (im)mobile spectator across an imaginary path that connects sites and moments distant in space and time. Eventually, the film spectator embraces the persona of the explorer/traveller. The mobilised virtual gaze of cinema spectatorship is, in its turn, the result of the conflation of social behaviours typical of the consumer culture that arose during the mid-nineteenth century. The coincident development of department store shopping, the experience of foreign spaces characteristic of tourist activity, the development of transportation technology, all contributed to the emergence of the mobilised virtual gaze. The premises of this new aesthetic of reception are strictly interconnected with its commodification. The mobilised virtual gaze is, therefore, a commodity sold to a consumer-spectator (Friedberg, 1993).

Government films, such as *Glorious New Zealand* and *Romantic New Zealand*, therefore produced, simultaneously, New Zealanders, tourists and consumers or rather the 'New Zealander-tourist-consumer'. Referring to the role played by the above-mentioned movies in shaping the New Zealand national identity, Minette Hillyer points out that "our institutional memory is created through a series of dehistoricised present moments—a view, a product, a holiday 'snapshot'" (Hillyer, 1997: 20). The few white New Zealanders depicted in *Romantic New Zealand* are presented as either responsible for the civilising improvements made to the land, or at play on ski slopes and rivers. They first tamed the land, making it a safe and pleasurable tourist playground that they can now finally enjoy. Again, in the words of Hillyer: "the Pākehā of *Romantic New Zealand* are both eternal tourists and themselves proud pioneers" (Hillyer, 1997: 18).

## The Māori: between ethnographic and tourist romance

The deep interconnection between tourism, cinema and consumer culture could explain the early prominence of travel films that flourished in the period preceding the emergence of classical cinema. Tom Gunning describes the travel genre as an important component of a 'cinema of attractions', characterised by an emphasis on the visual pleasure of the moment of viewing rather than the narrative presentation of its subject (Gunning, 1990: 56). Extreme forms of cinema of attractions connected to the travelogue, such as Hale's Tours travel rides that simulated the experience of gazing at the landscape from a train's window, benefited from a wide distribution and success until 1910, when the narrativisation of cinema and the consolidation of the movie industry eventually took over.

In New Zealand the production of travelogues and ethnographic films was relatively prolific, as these genres gained the support of governmental authorities from the outset. In 1916, *The Southern Alps of New Zealand* was shot by S. B. Taylor for the Agriculture Department and later distributed by the Tourism Department in

Australia (Dennis, 1981: 7). By 1907, even before Taylor, James McDonald was already shooting travel films for the Tourist Department (Blythe, 1990: 94). The highlights of MacDonald's career are considered to be the scenes of Māori life that he filmed for the Dominion Museum between 1919 and 1923. The films that record informal demonstrations of traditional Māori activities are shaped by ethnographic style and tourist advertisements. This is consistent with the fact that the government of the day was more interested in the potential tourist publicity generated by the films rather than preserving records of the Māori race, despite the fact that this race was supposedly disappearing and abandoning old ways. At the beginning of the last century the differences between the tourism of the upper-middle class and the activity of early ethnographers were quite subtle. The remote position of New Zealand (two months by boat from Britain) implied that its appeal was realisable only by an international elite that could afford time and money to sightsee. Often tourists published accounts of their journey that focused on Māori life and 'thermal wonders' while ethnographers were motivated by a kind of 'tourist' fascination and curiosity for native culture. Early films likewise criss-crossed these two practices and their respective cinematic genres: the ethnographic romance and the tourist romance.

Māori and Maoriland were, from the origins of New Zealand tourism, an essential part of the package, as Thomas Cook had used them in advertising the country since the beginning of the twentieth century: "The Māoris, whose presence, together with their strange habits, customs and legendary lore, adds greatly to the interest of a visit to New Zealand" (Cook Tours, 1902, cited in Blythe, 1990: 90). Maoriland was on display in the very popular thermal resort of Rotorua, on riverboat tours and in museums. The Māori village of Whakarewarewa near Rotorua was the most filmed location in New Zealand (Blythe, 1990: 91). Travelogues and tourist romances juxtaposed side by side two separate and spatially defined worlds: Maoriland and the modern Pākehā (European) New Zealand. As Martin Blythe points out: "Maoriland is a world outside time, a lost world even, into which the tourist may step briefly and tantalisingly before returning to the luxury and comfort of the nearby hotel, and the hotel is of course in real historical time (the present)" (Blythe, 1990: 93). Māori are represented firmly alongside the scenic environment existing unchanging in a timeless, natural world. In early tourism romances such as *Whakarewarewa* (dir. C. J. Morton, 1927), the narrative structure juxtaposes the primitive past of the Māori world with modern New Zealand. In the film, a group of tourists, led by a Māori guide dressed in traditional costume, can jump into Maoriland to see how 'primitive' men live in this eternal past. The tourists leave history entering the traditional Māori world, which comprised steam cooking, geysers and canoe travel, only to return to the present a few minutes later in the hotel or the golf course nearby. Rotorua, with its mix of thermal resorts, Māori model villages, scenic attractions and modern accommodations, embodied the ideal New Zealand film location and tourist destination. The specificity of Rotorua, border zone between Maoriland and modern

New Zealand, played an important role in mythologising the country. As a consequence the town attracted substantial government investment in infrastructure and tourism facilities which made Rotorua the only state-owned and managed town in New Zealand at that time (Cowan cited in Ateljevic and Doorne, 2002: 656).

Among the Publicity Office films that focus on Rotorua's tourist attractions are *Scenes in Māori Camp* (dir. James MacDonald, 1920) that features the welcome to the tribes arriving for the visit by the Prince of Wales; *The Prince of Wales at Rotorua* (dir. James MacDonald, 1920); *Scenes at the Rotorua Hui* (dir. James MacDonald, 1920). The Publicity Office also commissioned *Amokura* (dir. J. C. Morton, 1928), a romantic legend entirely set in Rotorua, and *Holiday Haunts* (dir. New Zealand Film, 1935), which showcases tourists visiting the usual local attractions: Whakarewarewa, penny diving, geysers and mud pools. Even overseas producers, such as the American film-makers of Fox Movietone newsreels, were attracted by the fame of the thermal town where they shot *The Māori: Everyone Bathes on Washing Day at Rotorua* (dir. Movietone News, 1937).

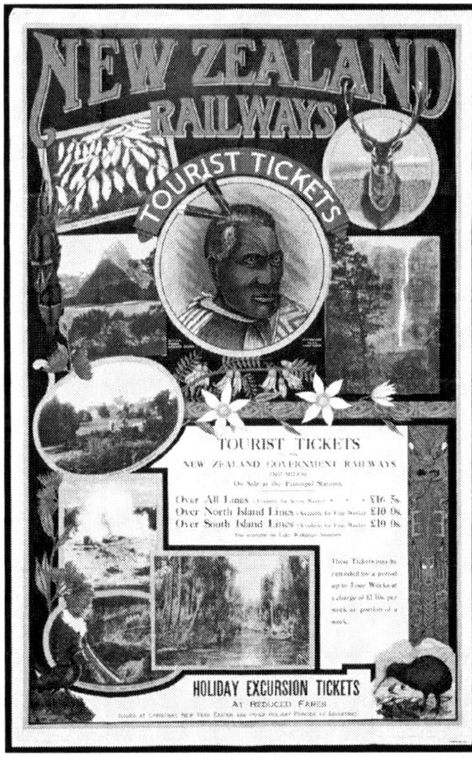


Figure 1.1. New Zealand Railways, 1923.

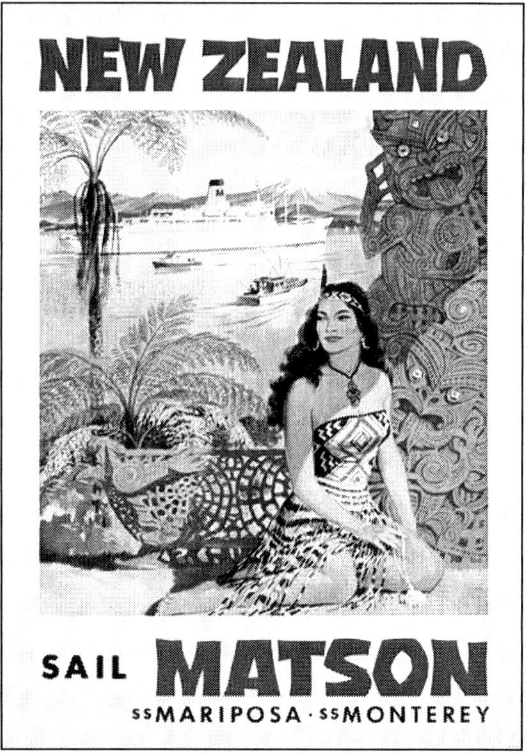


Figure 1.2. Matson Navigation Company, circa 1935.

In all these cases the narrative structure of the films is constructed around the stereotype of the 'happy Māoris', who live in a timeless land spatially separated from the actual New Zealand. This representation of Maoriland, as implicitly opposed to the time-bound world of the modern Pākehā, is perfectly exemplified by a 1923 promotional poster released by New Zealand Railways in which the image of a Māori elder is positioned alongside other scenic attractions as a mere object of the tourist gaze (Figure 1.1). Another travel advertisement of the time juxtaposes the image of motorboats with a Māori maiden in traditional costume standing against a background of Māori carvings (Figure 1.2). On the one hand, the motorboats and the cruise line epitomise the industrial progress of the country that grants the tourists mobility, security and high levels of comfort. On the other hand, the erotic/exotic Māori maiden represents the timeless oases of Maoriland preserved for the middle class, male gaze of Western tourists.

Contemporary New Zealand film-making still celebrates Māori as the repository of traditional and spiritual values. The narrative of recent movies such as *The Piano* or *Whale Rider* centres on an equation between Nature and Māori. In this sense, it is particularly interesting how both these movies induced a remarkable flow of international tourists to the film locations. For example, *Whale Rider*'s sentimental depiction of an isolated Māori community separated from the present-day modern nation evokes many of the tropes of legendary Maoriland, as represented in tourism romances of the beginning of the last century. The locations of the film (shot around Gisborne) have replaced Rotorua in the imaginary of today's international tourist seeking the authentic, pure New Zealand.

## Empty landscapes and (post)colonial enterprises

Like many other films of the time, *Romantic New Zealand* showcases images of Maoriland. The film features a six-minute colour sequence in which the famous Guide Rangi conducts a cinematic tour of Whakarewarewa and Rotorua, showing aspects of Māori life such as steam cooking and traditional dances. As in all the other tourist romances, the Māori are assimilated into nature and represented as a dying race destined to integrate with modern New Zealanders.

The establishment of the Publicity Office in 1921 corresponded with the commencement of regular government film production, mainly scenic short documentary pieces and travelogues. During the mid-1920s the government approach to cinema began to be marked by the creation of national propaganda. The transfer in June 1930 of the Publicity Office from the Department of Internal Affairs to the Department of Tourism and Health Resorts clearly indicated the establishment of a stricter relationship between national propaganda and the country's tourist promotion.

The production of both *Glorious New Zealand* and *Romantic New Zealand* has to be placed in this context of governmental control over the representation of the nation. In his history of New Zealand cinema in the silent period, Jonathan Dennis points out how, during the 1920s, the directive to the Publicity Office was to empty the films of people in order to prevent "them from being dated by changes in fashion" (Dennis, 1993: 9). The depopulated narratives of the travelogues produced by the Publicity Office allowed only the representation of empty landscapes, occasional tourists or timeless Maoriland. From the analysis of *Romantic New Zealand* emerges another important element. The film opens with the re-enactment of Abel Tasman's discovery of New Zealand and the representation of his vessels. In the rest of the film virtually every shot is characterised by the presence of a means of transport. The scenic views of the country are punctuated by stagecoaches, steamships, planes, trains, ferries, kayaks, sailboats, cars or motorboats.

The omnipresence of mobility technologies in the travelogue is emblematic of the strict connection between tourism and the modern experience of rapid mobility across long distances. Lash and Urry claim that "modernity is a society on the move" (1994: 252). Motorised mobility has changed the nature of vision as trains, cars or steamboats are not only vehicles for transporting visitors to a given destination but are also technologies for visually experiencing and consuming those places through sightseeing. *Romantic New Zealand* reinforces the modern relationship between tourism and mobility, collapsing the representation of transport technologies into a 'travel glance'. In the travelogue the representation of moving vehicles is often accompanied by the representation of the landscape from a mobile point of view. The spectator is offered the vision in motion of the Fox Glacier from an airplane or mobile views of Milford Sound from a modern cruise line. John Urry argues that the gaze dominates tourism, which, in its turn, is primarily concerned with commodification of images and visual consumption. According to this British scholar: "travel is a strategy for the accumulation of photographs" (2002: 128). Urry's notion of the tourist gaze, inspired by the work of Foucault, is bound up with the representational practice of photographing. The tourist gaze prefers immobility as, in the decisive moment, the tourist consumes the attraction without moving, in a 'photographic way'. This is why the notion of the tourist gaze resists theorising practices of mobile seeing. The travel glance, as theorised by Larsen, on the contrary, is able to capture practices of mediated mobile vision. According to Larsen, the notion of travel glance explores mobile vision:

> As a product of a machine-generated movement of the spectator's 'immobile' body, which subjugates all tourists, willy-nilly, to a spectacle of ephemeral landscape scenes that are only perceptible to the fleeting look of the glance. (Larsen, 2001: 93)

*Romantic New Zealand* offers a 'travel glance' of the country and in doing so the film hyperbolises the affinity between modern tourism and cinematic experience: speed, mobile visual perception, bodily immobility and the promise of a pleasurable journey.

Furthermore, the proliferation of mobile technologies alongside empty tourist landscapes in the film epitomises the government authorities' aspirations to modernity. The message is clear: the penetration of industrial progress has tamed the land, making it a safe place for prospective tourists/settlers. Modern technology allows for the colonial exploitation of New Zealand's huge reservoir of natural resources. This is absolutely consistent with the threefold strategy of the Publicity Office that aimed to increase tourist traffic value, attract the potential settlement of 'good-type Europeans' and boost national goodwill in general.

The cinematic representation of New Zealand as a natural, though domesticated, paradise is analogous to the picturing of the American West by early Hollywood producers. As Peterson points out, "silent travel films do indeed represent the West as an Edenic Garden, then, they also upset the myth of the West as an uncivilised wilderness by depicting a region traversed by trains and peopled with tourists" (Peterson, 2006: 80). One of the earliest Edison productions, *Tourist Train Leaving Livingston, Mont.* (dir. Edison Manufacturing Co., 1897), shows a train heading to Yellowstone crowded with tourists waving goodbye (Musser cited in Peterson, 2006: 80). The major railroad companies played an important role in promoting the idea of a scenic West, using modern marketing tools such as newspaper advertisements or films. In fact, the film industry often collaborated with the railroad companies to promote both the use of the train and visits to national parks. In 1911, for example, The Great Northern Railroad contracted a series of scenic films to be made in the cities along its line (Peterson, 2006: 92). The Atchinson, Topeka and Santa Fe Railroad offered travellers the opportunity to witness the Western landscapes from the comfort of luxury railway cars or hotel rooms dotted along the Santa Fe route (Bregent-Heald, 2007: 55). The American tourism industry thus capitalised upon the interplay between civilisation and wilderness by offering travellers a domesticated nature. While they marketed the West as the antithesis of industrial and modern society, they also promoted comfort and a sense of familiarity that was attractive to American tourists. The West was characterised as the American landscape *par excellence*, the embodiment of national identity as opposed to the urban character of Europe and the East Coast of the United States.

This representation of the West as an iconic primeval, but at the same time, tamed wilderness, echoes the New Zealand myth of the bush as the core of national identity. The celebration of the West as *the* tourist destination was accompanied by 'See America First', a campaign advocating domestic tourism to the mythical Western frontier zone. Once again, the slogan and the contents of 'See America First' evoke the tones of the 'Know New Zealand First and Advertise to your Friends Abroad', the campaign launched by the Tourist and Publicity Department during the 1930s. In both New Zealand and the United States domestic tourism and travel films played a critical role in shaping the countries' respective national identities. In both cases, films emphasise the magnificent scenes of the local wilderness, but also the process of getting to that scenery. As in New Zealand, American travelogues depict travellers using cars, motorboats and railroads to reach their destination. They also provide the spectators with "mediating tourist figures within the landscape, essentially holding the audience's hand while leading it into the spectacular places on-screen" (Peterson, 2006: 87). The tourist gaze and the travel glance characteristic of the travelogue appropriate the land and offer it to the movie audience; "a provisional 'nation' forged by spectatorship" (Shohat and Stam, 1994: 103).

Another crucial analogy between New Zealand and American tourist romances is the common trope of the 'primitive native'. Like the Māori, Native Americans are frozen in their wilderness context and assimilated with the natural space. The timeless primitive 'Indian' is just a component of the scenery, in the same way that the Māori is represented as symbiotically bound to nature. The similarities are also evident in the separation of the timeless oases inhabited by Māori/Native American from the present modern world of the white New Zealander/American. The only human beings to populate American or New Zealand travel films are either simulacra of the tourist/spectator or dehumanised Natives equated with the scenery or the natural backdrop. New Zealand landscape in particular is represented as raw material that can be imaginatively and materially processed and consumed by the tourist/spectator or the settler. The mobile vehicles that cross the filmic landscapes of *Romantic New Zealand* simply reinforce the fact that the land is subject to the process of visual and physical appropriation typical of Western culture. In this sense, scenic views of the fjords or the Southern Alps are timeless and literally interchangeable. The very same footage of alpine landscape is used in *Romantic New Zealand, Happy Altitudes in New Zealand Southern Alps* (dir. Filmcraft Ltd, 1933) and *New Zealand Charm: A Romantic Outpost of the Empire* (dir. Filmcraft Ltd, 1935). *Aorangi: In New Zealand's Alpine Playground* (dir. New Zealand Publicity Office, 1929) features very similar scenes and ways of framing the landscape.

The representation of empty landscapes implies that the natural and social environment is subject to the colonial enterprise. Following the creation of the Publicity Office in 1921, New Zealand Governments encouraged the diffusion of their films to Australia, India and other British colonies. In 1939 New Zealand Trade commissioners made a deal with Twentieth Century Fox for the distribution of New Zealand films to Indian, Burmese and Ceylon theatres which catered for colonists of British extraction. In June 1939 The Tourist and Publicity Department sent the distributors *Deep Sea Thrills* (dir. Government Motion Picture, 1934), *Holiday Sounds* (dir. Government Motion Picture, 1937) and *Glacier* (dir. Filmcraft Ltd, 1938), films which targeted colonial clubs and wealthy planters longing for more temperate climates (Hillyer, 1997). According to Hillyer, "this communication between colonials was then based on an understanding as to the use-value of the lands in which they found themselves" (Hillyer, 1997: 16).

The denudation of New Zealand landscapes provoked the reaction of the popular English documentary-maker John Grierson, who visited the country in 1940. In his famous talk titled "The Face of a New Zealander" he claimed:

> Over in England we seem to hear a lot about New Zealand but never anything about the human beings that live in it [...]. I knew that you had a lot of Māoris that staged shows for rich tourists and that you had mud that bubbled, and hot water on tap from out the earth. [...]. You may make very pleasant scenic pictures but it just is not enough to appear before the world as a mere tourist resort plus a butter factory. I have no doubt you want to sell your butter and your tourist attractions and that is why you send these films. (Grierson, 1981: 21)

In his talk, Grierson deconstructs the structural environment and the social relations of production that characterised New Zealand settler culture during the 1940s. According to Grierson, the human factor is essential for the construction of a truly national spirit detached from colonial allegiances. Thus, he suggests that "when you send us your films never send merely the scenic ones. Put in something about the real things you do" (Grierson 1981: 22). Sixty years after Grierson's talk, thanks to *The Lords of the Rings*, New Zealand and New Zealanders became famous around the world for the 'hyper-real' things they do. As in the scenic films of the 1920s and 1930s, in *LOTR* the New Zealand landscape has been emptied of its culture and its people to accommodate the colossal production of Middle Earth. In this sense the marketing strategy that branded New Zealand as Middle Earth creating a 'hyper-real tourist' destination, was totally consistent with the use Peter Jackson made of the actual landscape.

The parallel processes of the emplacement of Middle Earth and the emptying of New Zealand carries residues of the country's own history. According to Kavka and Turner, the *LOTR* production might be taken as a cinematic synonym for the political logic of settler societies (Kavka and Turner, 2009). The physical and imaginary projection of Middle Earth onto New Zealand is the result of a settler idea of place: "for the enterprise of settler New Zealand to succeed it has had to remove the place from its peoples and history" (Kavka and Turner, 2009: 231)—not unlike the production of the film itself. The history of New Zealand has been marked by its political, economical and cultural dependence on the British Empire. Britain's entry into the European Community during the 1970s meant that it no longer needed the supply of cheap lamb and wool produced in New Zealand. From that time on, the franchise economy typical of a settler *modus operandi* has been shaken by the decline of the colonial hold. Nevertheless, the production of *LOTR* replicates the logic of the settler enterprise:

> *LOTR* uses the place as raw material for an export initiative, so that the local place and people may be fully de-linked from the screen image. New Zealand history is evident in the logic of settler franchise rather than in the content of representation. (Kavka and Turner, 2009: 236)

*LOTR* is not the only example of the 'cine-colonial' franchise economy that characterises contemporary New Zealand. Along with other countries, such as Canada and Australia, New Zealand has been a favourite destination of so-called American runaway productions searching for cheaper locations and labour. The result has been an increasing number of film features shot and set in New Zealand. In ways not much different from the 1930s definition of the country as a 'world in a nutshell', New Zealand still promotes the cinematic lease of its landscape.

Analysing some of the most recent blockbusters filmed in New Zealand, such as the *Hercules* saga (1995–99) and *LOTR*, Perry inverts the commonplace of a 'unique New Zealand landscape', arguing that New Zealand is the perfect location for such productions as "a low wage country that otherwise exists only as just such a scenically diverse, but temporally and spatially indeterminate, fiction" (Perry, 2001: 106). For Perry:

> *Hercules, Xena, The Lord of the Rings* and other such fantasies, and with them an explicitly willed and actively motivated indifference to their geographical specificity, are thus designed and destined to circulate and flourish in 'actual existing knowledge societies' where their efficacy as fictions is enhanced by the knowing orchestration of such ignorance. (Perry, 2001: 106)

In another Hollywood production, *The Last Samurai*, New Zealand and Taranaki in particular stand-in for another 'real' country, a nineteenth-century Japan accurately reconstructed by the American film-makers. The subsequent tourist (re)branding of Taranaki as 'Land of *The Last Samurai*' and the celebration of the interchangeability of Mt. Fuji/Taranaki are consequences of the same cultural and economic processes that characterised the *LOTR* production.

The deconstruction of tourist imagery reveals the ideological conditions in which the former was produced. In the case of New Zealand, the logic of production inherent to a settler culture strongly influenced the local tourist representations. At the beginning of the twentieth century tourism served as a political agent for the reproduction of colonial ideology. The travelogues produced by the government Publicity Office mainly targeted three, occasionally overlapping, social groups: a tourist elite coming from the most privileged sectors of Anglo-Saxon society; potential British settlers; actual settlers from other British colonies such as Burma or India. Furthermore, the local reception of New Zealand-made travel films contributed to forging a spirit of nationhood. Tourist promotion played a crucial role in shaping the myth of New Zealand as a scenic wonderland and constructing New Zealanders as eternal tourist-pioneers. The history of the relationship between early New Zealand films and tourism elucidates the contemporary emphasis of local authorities on film-induced tourism. The natural interconnection between cinematic and tourist experience seems to be particularly prominent in an antipodean country, such as New Zealand. This prominence is a function of the most negative power of vision: aggressive appropriation, control and hegemony of the gazer over the object of the gaze. After all, early travel-films were the instrument of a colonial system, the legacy of which is still active, in different forms, in contemporary New Zealand society.

Nevertheless, if we refer to Benjamin's utopian conception of cinema, films also have a liberating power, as the cinematic image "burst[s] this prison-world asunder by the tenth of the second" (Benjamin, 1979: 238). Cinema liberates subjectivity, as a person does not end with the limits of his/her physical body. The spectator follows the line of escape traced by the emotional cartography of cinema, enjoying the pleasure of 'dwelling-travelling'. Cinema is *transito*. Giuliana Bruno draws this notion from Italian philosopher Mario Perniola. In her words, *transito* is a wide-ranging notion of circulation "which includes migrations, passages, traversals, transitions, transitory states, spatial erotics and (e)motion" (Bruno, 1997a: 22). The daily consumption of the media encourages an (e)motional and cognitive disposition, one which could potentially be transformed into tourist activity. In their turn, tourist practices must be understood as essentially imaginative and emotional processes (Crouch et al., 2005). There is no research on the influence of *Romantic New Zealand* on actual tourist travel to Aotearoa, but it certainly provided Western audiences the time with an extraordinary vehicle for a psycho-spatial journey to the country. Seventy years later, in movies such as *The Piano*, *Whale Rider* and *LOTR*, New Zealand has become an even more powerful tool of imaginative liberation for contemporary voy(ag)eurs.

**Notes**

1.  The film was realised thanks to a great deal of unpaid labour from the Māori who participated in the movie. After the shooting, Markey left New Zealand with a great number of unpaid bills and took with him many stolen Māori artefacts (Martin and Edwards, 1997: 46).

2.  The connections between the *LOTR* production and New Zealand settler culture are extensively discussed in Chapter 6.

3.  Directed and produced under the supervision of Tourist Department officer Arthur Messenger, *Glorious New Zealand* was one of the first enterprises of the Publicity Office. The ten minutes of the surviving film show images of lakes, fjords and alpine landscapes. Realised with the explicit aim of attracting both tourists and new settlers, *Glorious New Zealand* "confirms the myths of empty landscapes ripe for the plough" (Martin and Edwards, 1997: 36).

# 2

# 1940–1990: New Zealand Film Landscapes for Prospective 'Cinenauts'

## Introduction

> In the beginning it was only to escape...
> but he was a young man in a hungry hurry
>   ... his blood on fire
>   ... from the warm beaches of Northland
> to the ice-bound wilderness of Westland glaciers
> the New Zealand you know...
> for the first time in a film that is
> compelling, intimate and brilliant entertainment!

The poster for New Zealand's first road movie, *Runaway* (dir. John O'Shea, 1964), presented the film in this fashion. For the first time, local spectators were able to vicariously travel all around the country through the eyes of a New Zealander, David Manning, the protagonist of the film. From the beginning of the 1940s New Zealand film-makers started to fill the empty landscapes of the tourist travelogues with New Zealanders and their stories. This is not to say that no one had tried to tell New Zealand stories before 1940. During the 1920s and 1930s Rudall Hayward directed many 'community comedies': popular short films, such as *Daughter of Dunedin* (1928) and *Natalie of Napier* (1929), that employed local people in the cast. Hayward also resourcefully made six more features, among his most important films are *Rewi's Last Stand* (1925, remade with sound in 1940) and *The Te Kooti Trail* (1927), both of which tried to popularise New Zealand history by putting it on the big screen. The few fictional films directed by Hayward were, however, outnumbered by the production of travel films commissioned by the Tourist Department. The scenic shots of natural beauty devoid of people encouraged a voyeurism that sought to impose its power over the object of the gaze—the land. In this way, New Zealand landscapes were just a framed 'Other', ready to be appropriated by the gaze of early voy(ag)eurs. From 1940, however, as a consequence of John Grierson's famous intervention on New Zealand cinema, the representation of the landscape started to be combined with that of actual people (Grierson, 1981). The end of World War II was characterised by the appearance of a 'local' subject whose identity was defined by his or her relation to the land: New Zealanders started putting their faces on their films.

This was accompanied by the progressive emergence of a more complex relation between narration and landscape, that was the function of a nationalist discourse. In the post-war period landscape was no longer just blank, raw material ready to be filled with meaning imported from the centre of the empire. In most of the films analysed in this chapter, landscape is also an *actant* that plays a crucial role in the narrative economy as well as in the construction of a national identity. The great majority of the films of this period deal with travel and mobility: *in the beginning it was only to escape....* The constant mobility of the protagonists is determined by their problematic relation to a land which is at once supposed to be home, but is also still largely unfamiliar. The narratives of these texts revolve around the quest of the Pākehā protagonists for the 'authentic' New Zealand and the encounter with the 'real' land which has revolutionary effects on their destiny.

During the 1920s and 1930s, travelogue voy(ag)eurs identified with the camera that took them around from the fjords to Northland. The only human figures occasionally represented in these films are anonymous tourists shown gazing at the landscape. The narrative possibilities in these films are limited by the fact that the land is a passive object of the gaze. By contrast, the spectators of fictional films such as *Runaway* had to rely on the mediation of the protagonist's gaze, which in turn engaged in an active relation with the landscape. These films interpellate a new category of textual spectators that I will define as 'cinenauts'. As voy(ag)eurs, the cinenauts still travel in and through the films, but in a different way to their predecessors: the double identification of the cinenauts with *both* the gaze of the camera *and* the gaze of the (travelling) protagonists allows them to experience enhanced mobility within the cinematic landscapes. The inner structure of the fictional narration itself is deeply connected with the notion of mobility. The development of the narrative is in fact determined by the sense of something lacking, which in turn installs the desire to explore, to find out what is missing, to move into a new scene.


**From the National Film Unit to the Film Commission**

During the 1940s film production in New Zealand suffered a steady decline. The New Zealand film industry had already stumbled during the 1930s, with the passage from silent to sound films. This transition necessitated the use of more expensive sound-recording equipment, often unaffordable for local film-makers. After the war this structural weakness of the film industry contributed to a significant drop in production. All the national films had to compete fiercely with foreign movies, mainly British and American, in order to conquer a share of the New Zealand market. The virtual lack of film features made in New Zealand from 1940 to 1970 is at odds with the crucial role played by cinema, particularly Hollywood, in the formation of a 'New Zealand culture'. In 1945 Gordon Mirams defined New Zealanders as "a nation of film fans" (Mirams, 1945: 5). He calculated that during the 1940s there was one movie theatre for every 3000 New Zealanders, compared with one for every 8700 in the USA (Mirams, 1945: 6). The paradoxical absence of local production is partly attributable to the absence of any form of protection for the national film industry. New Zealand was, in fact, one of the few countries in the world that had free trade in films. The 1928 Cinematographic Films Act had only partially limited the power of American distributors who effectively controlled what was screened in New Zealand cinemas (Churchman, 1997: 16).

During the 1940s and the 1950s the only two active production centres in the country were the National Film Unit and Pacific Films. Established in 1941 after the visit to New Zealand by famous British documentary maker John Grierson, the National Film Unit (NFU) started producing a short weekly news film entitled *Weekly Review*. Film-making during the war was confined to producing information-films showing New Zealand's contribution to the war effort. The *Weekly Review*, which began on 3 July 1941, ended with the 459th issue on 8 August 1950 and, from this point on, New Zealand was to be without any regular representation of its current events until the arrival of television in the 1960s. After the war the Information Services, the National Publicity Studios, the National Film Unit and other information and publicity components under the control of the Prime Minister's department were incorporated within the department and formed its Publicity Division. The designation of the department was changed from 'Tourist and Health Resorts' to 'Tourist and Publicity'. The reorganisation followed a review of government publicity objectives within New Zealand and overseas. The National Film Unit continued the work begun by the department during the 1920s and 1930s, producing tourist and general publicity films for use overseas and within New Zealand. Several of the unit's films were bought by American distributors and released in various languages for worldwide distribution, each film having an estimated audience of 80 to 100 million (NZOYB, 1976). Among the most famous travelogues produced by the NFU and award winning at several international tourist festivals are *Snows of Aorangi* (dir. Brian Brake, 1955), *Somebody Else's Horizon* (dir. Hugh MacDonald, 1976) and, particularly, *This is New Zealand* (dir. Hugh MacDonald, 1970), a vastly entertaining three-screen film first shown at Expo '70 in Japan and seen by approximately half of the country's population when it was screened in New Zealand.

In 1948, disappointed by the political agenda of the *Weekly Review*, ex-NFU staff Alun Falconer (writer-director) and Roger Mirams (cameraman) established Pacific Films. In 1950 John O'Shea joined the company while Falconer left to pursue a career in China. In 1957 Mirams left as well, and from that time on O'Shea became synonymous with Pacific Films (that had meanwhile changed its name to Pacific Film Productions Ltd). O'Shea was responsible for the production and direction of three of the only five feature films made in New Zealand between 1939 and 1972: *Broken Barrier* (1952), *Runaway* and *Don't Let It Get You* (1966). Although none of these films managed to succeed at the box office, either locally or overseas, they are considered essential milestones in the history of New Zealand cinema. Apart from the fact that they exist at all, they are important because they offered local film-makers inspiration and the opportunity to gain significant experience in the film industry.

Until 1977, the year when both *Off the Edge* (dir. Mike Firth) and *Sleeping Dogs* (dir. Roger Donaldson) were produced, seeing local landscapes at the cinema was an extremely rare experience for many New Zealanders. These two productions and particularly *Sleeping Dogs*, as the first 35mm colour, feature-length, fictional New Zealand film, set the basis for the establishment of a professional film industry. Both films were released in America[1] and played a crucial role in influencing the government decision to establish the New Zealand Film Commission the following year. The idea of a national film commission was first proposed in 1970 at an Arts Council conference in Wellington. The New Zealand Arts Council chairman, Bill Sheat, supported by local film-makers such as O'Shea, campaigned for a national screen organisation. The conference made two recommendations: "To foster creative activity in films for cinema and television; and create an archive for film" (O'Shea, 1999: 88).

The 1970s were characterised by a revival of the local film industry. Critics and intellectuals started to consider cinema as something worthy of serious consideration and a few New Zealand universities began to offer film courses. It took seven years of campaigning and recommendations until New Zealand film-makers, reunited at an arts conference, signed a petition arguing that the only way New Zealand could develop a film industry would be with the support of the state. In 1977, with Bill Sheat in the chair, the interim Film Commission held a meeting where it sought "to advise the Government on legislation, to establish a permanent commission, and to establish policy guidelines for developing a sound motion picture industry" (Martin and Edwards, 1997: 13). Convinced by the local and international success of *Sleeping Dogs* and *Off the Edge* the National Government minister for Arts, Recreation and Sport, Alan Highet, introduced a law that established the Commission, claiming that "we need our own stories and our own heroes. We need to hear our own voices" (Shelton, 2005: 24). In November 1978 the New Zealand Film Commission board met for the first time in Wellington, with the task of funding and supporting local productions having 'significant New Zealand content'. Under the Film Commission Act (1978) a 'significant New Zealand content' was defined as having regard to the films' subject matter and the nationality of both film-makers and investors.

Some of the films produced between 1940 and 1990 do not fit all these categories but nevertheless have significant New Zealand association. This is the case, for example, with respect to *Green Dolphin Street* (dir. Victor Saville, 1947), set in New Zealand but shot in California by American film-makers, or *The Seekers* (dir. Ken Annakin, 1954) set and shot in New Zealand but produced by a British company. As Laurence Simmons points out:

> These 'international films', I believe, are also interesting and thus of contemporary relevance, for what they reveal about the constraints on a subsequent local film industry if it is to successfully market its films internationally, since they were to provide us with valuable models and indications of how we might best be perceived from afar. (Simmons, 1999b: 42)

The 1980s are considered a coming of age for New Zealand cinema, as the first half of this decade was characterised by a burgeoning of film production: from two films in 1980 to six in 1982 and fourteen in 1984. The main reasons for this rapid increase in the production of features are, on the one hand, the establishment of the Film Commission which took New Zealand films to the Cannes festival for the first time and, on the other hand, the loopholes in the New Zealand tax laws which allowed movie production to become a means of obtaining tax relief. The first executive director of the New Zealand Film Commission, Don Blakeney, was an accountant and his economic focus played a decisive role in the establishment of the tax shelter.[2] The tax shelter engendered mixed reactions, as some in the industry saw it as a unique opportunity to develop film-making activity in New Zealand, while others feared an 'Americanisation' of the industry (Jesson, 1984: 19) that would attract ruthless foreign investors who would exploit the system to make poor quality productions. The tax loopholes were gradually closed in 1984, causing a temporary decline in the number of features produced, but the basis for a stable film industry had been set, thereby preparing for the international successes of the 1990s. From 1940 to 1990 the travelogues of the NFU and the fictional film features of local and international film-makers (whether or not sponsored by the Film Commission) all helped to forge the complex filmic image of New Zealand.


**Mapping New Zealand landscapes**

In recent decades geographers have engaged more and more with film because of its impact on their traditional objects of inquiry: landscape, space and identity. Contemporary geographers in fact claim that landscape is a way of seeing that is embedded in a tradition of communication and signifiers, which can be invoked or reshaped to express meanings and values (Mitchell, 1994). The physical medium of landscape exists, but is in many respects socially constructed. Films are temporary embodiments of social processes that constantly construct and deconstruct reality as we know it. They are a constitutive element in the production of geographies (spaces, places, landscapes and mobilities) while geographies themselves become implicit tools in the production of film (Cresswell and Dixon, 2007). As Hopkins notes, "the cinematic place is not […] limited to the world represented on the screen (a geography in film), but the meanings constructed through the experience of film (a geography of film)" (Hopkins, 1994: 50). The pleasure and power of film lies, therefore, in its ability to create its own cinematic geography. As Aitken and Zonn point out, the camera does not mirror reality but creates it, endowing it with meaning, discourse and ideology. The cinematic landscape is, therefore, a cultural creation, a 'sign of reality' that speaks a history, a memory, a meaning (Aitken and Zonn, 1994: 20).

In this section I will dissect the elementary structure of signification, the system of oppositions which determines the meaning of the meta-text 'New Zealand' as forged by the films of the period considered. In particular, this study will focus on the analysis of different *topoi* of the New Zealand landscape, arguing that the deep paradigmatic axis of opposition between these *topoi* will influence, on the one hand, the representation of the landscape by successive film-makers and on the other hand, the construction of an ideal spectator and potential film tourist. The methodology of this section will draw on the Greimasian generative textual semiotic, in order to detect the primary structure of signification in the text 'New Zealand'. For this purpose I will consider a range of films that illustrate the diversity of New Zealand feature films during a fifty year period: 1940–90.

The films analysed are:[3]

| **Title** | **Year of Production** | **Director** |
| --- | --- | --- |
| *The Seekers* (aka *Land of Fury*) | 1954 | Ken Annakin |
| *Runaway* | 1964 | John O'Shea |
| *This is New Zealand* | 1970 | Hugh Mac Donald |
| *Off the Edge* | 1977 | Mike Firth |
| *Sleeping Dogs* | 1977 | Roger Donaldson |
| *Goodbye Pork Pie* | 1980 | Geoff Murphy |
| *Smash Palace* | 1981 | Roger Donaldson |
| *Utu* | 1983 | Geoff Murphy |
| *The Quiet Earth* | 1985 | Geoff Murphy |
| *The Leading Edge* | 1987 | Mike Firth |

Even though the corpus of films considered is quite diverse, it is nevertheless possible to identify some semantic categories founded on the isotopy of distinctive features. An isotopy is the recurrence within a text of semes[4] or semic categories that assign it homogeneity. In the case of the films considered, the isotopy is represented by the dialectic between corrupted civilisation and an idyllic rural environment. The simple, almost banal, opposition Nature-Culture, that characterises the filmic representation of New Zealand, could be further articulated through the use of the semiotic square. According to Fredric Jameson, the semiotic square is an essential tool which enables the spectator or reader to open up the 'black box' through which narrative is somehow converted into cognition and vice versa: "its capacity to be indifferently static or dynamic (is) what accounts for its powerful mediatory capacity: it can, in other words, 'reduce' a narrative movement into a series of 'cognitive' or ideological, combinatory positions" (Jameson, Foreword to Greimas, 1987: xvii).

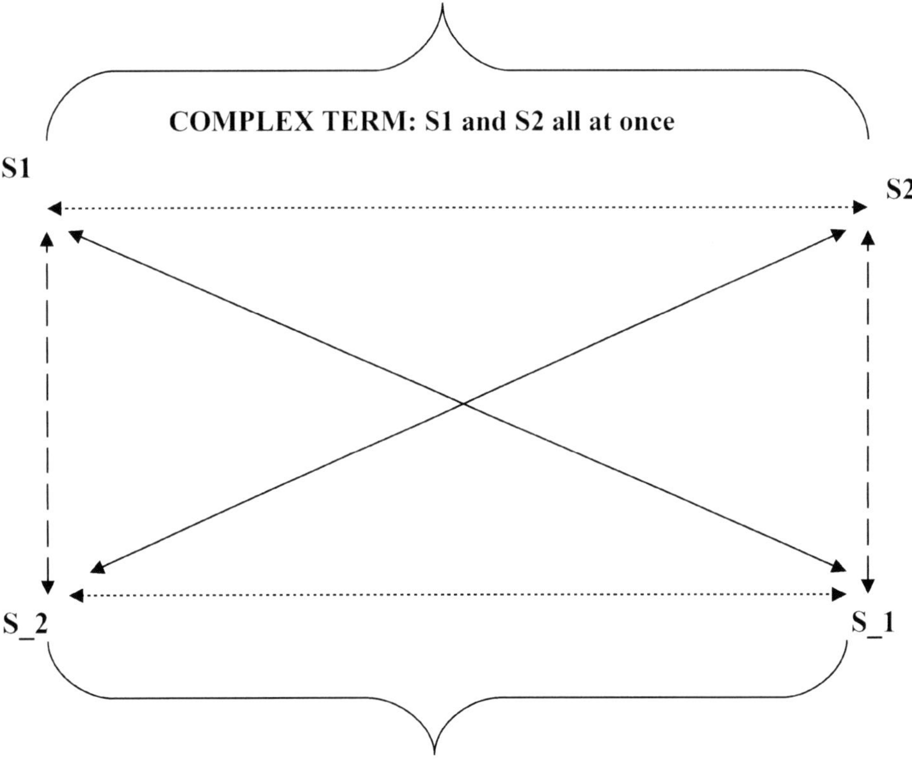


Figure 2.1. Model of semiotic square

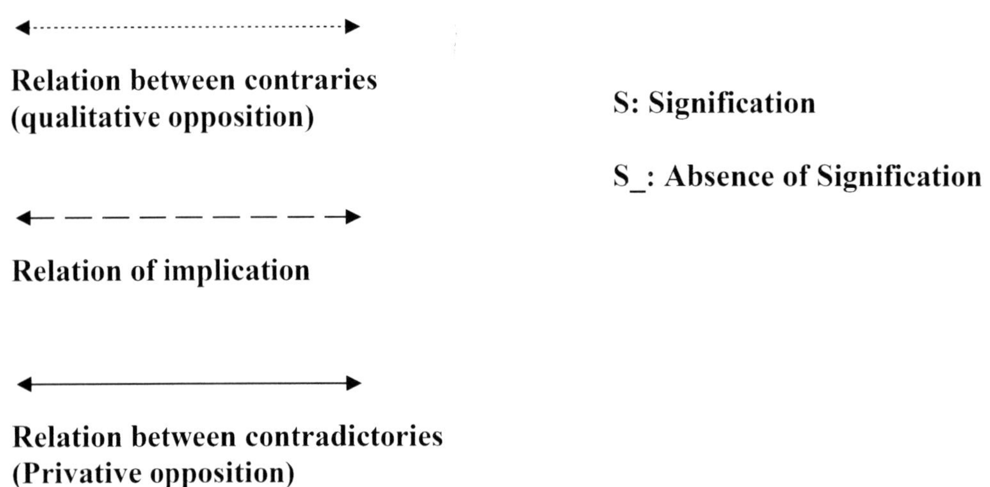


Figure 2.2.  Connections, contradictions, oppositions and implications.

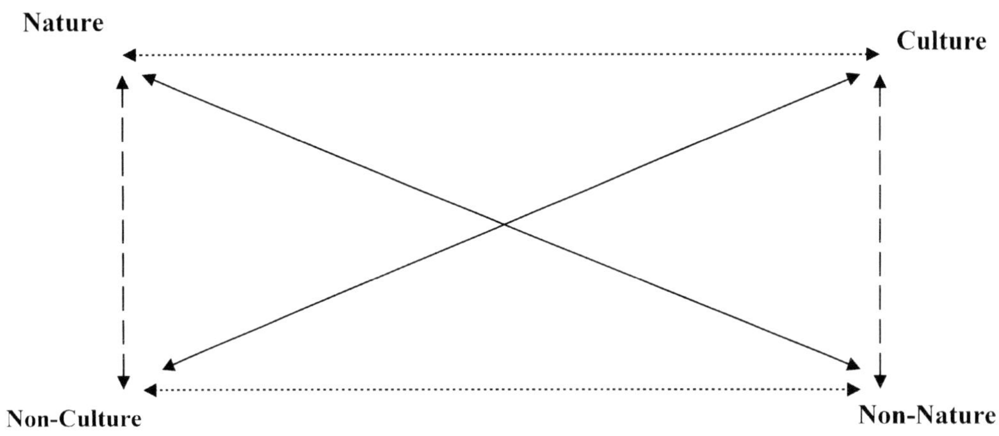


Figure 2.3.  Semiotic square Nature-Culture.

The semiotic square is a graphic representation of elementary semantic categories that constitute a micro-universe of signification (Figure 2.1). The square is based on the assumption that every semantic category can be identified through the relation this latter entertains with the other semantic categories. The different terms of the square are, therefore, determined by a system of connections, contradictions, oppositions and implications that are logically organised (Figure 2.2). The semiotic square is an extremely useful tool as it uncovers the process of the generation of meaning that determines the consistency of a discourse.

The square is the logical development of a binary semic category, the starting point being a couple of opposed categories defined as an axis of contraries, I will show a practical application of the semiotic square developing the oppositional couplet Nature – Culture. These categories imply two supplementary slots called contradictories, the simple negatives of the two dominant terms, namely Non-Nature and Non-Culture (Figure 2.3).

The first binary opposition that forms the superior line of the square (Nature – Culture) is defined in the language of philosophical logic as a 'contrary', the two terms connected by the diagonals (Nature – Non-Nature / Culture – Non-Culture) are defined as contradictories while the two terms that form the lower line of the square (Non-Culture – Non-Nature) are defined as subcontraries. The subcontraries are not strongly opposed and it is possible to find a neutral term in which all the privations and negations are assembled. In the same way, it constructs a synthetic position that transcends the opposition Nature—Culture. The vertical sides of the square are called deixes and they are characterised by a relationship of complementarity. Non-Culture implicates Nature, while Non-Nature implicates Culture.

At least 10 *topoi*[5] emerge from the analysis of space in New Zealand films produced between 1940 and 1990. They can be summarised as follows:

Centre of the Empire (Britain, America)
City
Mountain
Bush
Beach
River
Road
Maoriland
Volcanoes or geological instability
Ocean

It is possible to position every *topos* on each corner of the square as shown in Figure 2.4.

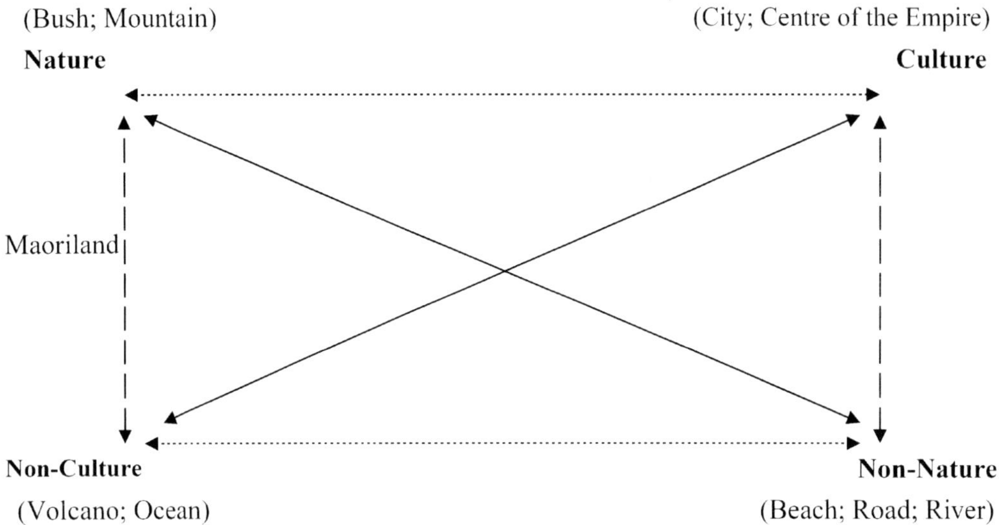


Figure 2.4. Semiotic square and New Zealand topoi.

In all the films analysed the opposition city (or centre of the empire) versus nature (mountain or bush) is always central. In *The Seekers*, for example, the protagonist Philip leaves the corrupted mother country, where he has been wrongly accused of smuggling Māori shrunken heads, looking for a new start with his wife in New Zealand. New Zealand is metonymically identified by the first sequence of the film showing scenic shots of the Alps and the bush. The bush is perceived as an ambivalent element. On the one hand, it is defined as an 'Opponent', for the settlers have to fight against it to clear the land surrounding the settlement; on the other hand these settlers, Philip in particular, establish a relation of complicity with the bush as they become progressively more familiar with it. The beach is a liminal space between Culture, represented by the centre of the empire and its emissaries (British ships), and Nature, represented by the bush and the Māori. Māori and geological instability in this film are the most subversive elements, as they are unpredictable and represent the biggest threat to the settler enterprise. In *The Seekers*, earthquakes, spouting geysers and bubbling mud pools translate, metonymically, the infancy of the nation into the geological youthfulness of the land. In Simmons' words: "Geological evolution is collapsed into the history of colonisation and it seems that nation, history, rock and soil are all products of a single, fantastic, volcanic eruption" (Simmons, 1999b: 42). The dangers of the amorphous New Zealand identity, literally a 'non-culture', are represented during the fight between the English settler and the crazed Māori warrior against the background of the bubbly mud pools. The settler community temporarily overcomes these dangers but it is eventually swept away by the irrational and lethal attack of a Māori tribe that has the destructive power of an earthquake.

The *topos* 'Māori-Maoriland' is the most problematic one as it is difficult to attribute a consistent position to it within the semiotic square. In *Runaway*, for example, Māori and Maoriland belong to the semantic category of 'Nature'. In O'Shea's film the protagonist escapes the city, seeking a sort of existential rebirth first in a Māori community, then in the bush and eventually in the mountains of the West Coast. The dialectic Culture-Nature is once again very apparent. The space of transition, which is allocated a prominent role this time, is represented by the road. The road is an intermediate element that hides the dangers of civilisation, such as police or racist motorists, as well as promising spaces of escape and liberation. However, the road never completely fulfils the promise of 'going far', as the protagonist David Manning never succeeds in going far enough. The semiotic square of *Runaway*'s filmic places is completed by the representation of a volcano. In *Runaway* the presence of the volcano, as a symbol of a primal instability, is metaphorical rather than literal. Nevertheless, the opening sequence of the film explicitly connects the silhouette of Rangitoto[6] with the troubled protagonist. In Simmons' words,

> the superscription of title and credits above David's supine body, together with the previous image of Rangitoto—itself a reclining body rising out of the Waitemata—inaugurates potent and recurrent associations between landscape and the male body in this film, the potentiality of the male psyche to lose itself in the landscape. (Simmons, 1995a: 58)

While in *The Seekers* the geological instability represented the youthfulness of the nation in order to unproblematically justify the settler enterprise, in *Runaway* the unpredictable David-Rangitoto, and its anti-materialist angst, symbolises the crisis of identity of New Zealand itself, abandoned by Britain during the 1960s and now seeking new economic, social and cultural references.

Unlike other *topoi*, the ocean is often not directly represented in the films considered, and yet its presence is always strongly felt. The ocean is a non-cultural element that (negatively) shapes the borders of the country. Both volcanoes and the ocean share the notions of liquidity and instability that relate to the (ongoing) construction of a national cultural identity.[7]

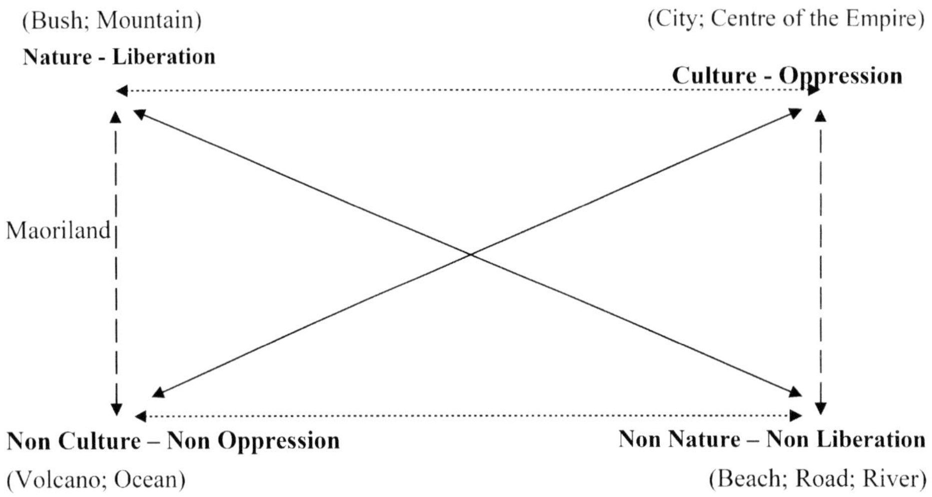


Figure 2.5. Semiotic square Liberation-Oppression.

What emerges from a number of films of this period, parallel to the opposition Nature-Culture, is the dialectic Oppression-Liberation. It is easy to superimpose these new semantic categories on the four corners of our semantic square (Figure 2.5).

The most obvious example that encompasses this semiotic relation, apart from the above-mentioned films, is *Sleeping Dogs*. In *Sleeping Dogs*, the protagonist Smith, like David in *Runaway* and Philip in *The Seekers*, leaves the city, space of oppression, to seek refuge in the authenticity of the bush, or more precisely, an island in Coromandel. The bush is configured as a *topos* of liberation as it helps Smith and Bullen to escape from the pursuing army. The recurrence of the literary trope of the Man Alone, who fights against both the cultural and geographical background of the country, is quite apparent in all these films. Both roads and beaches have an ambiguous status, for they offer the promise of escape while remaining open to the arrival of external threats (police or villains). It is through the beach that the army special force eventually access

Smith's sanctuary and arrest him. As in *Runaway*, the road is not a space of complete liberation, as New Zealand is an island nation and there are no neighbouring states with more lenient laws (like Mexico or Canada) to which the protagonists may escape. The road is always destined to end in Invercargill, as in *Goodbye Pork Pie*, or at the feet of the Southern Alps, as in *Runaway*.

The semi-fictional feature films *Off the Edge* and its sequel *The Leading Edge*, by Michael Firth, replicate the usual formula of escape from oppression (or in this case boredom) at the centre of the Empire (America) and the pursuit of liberation in the New Zealand Alps. In both cases, the road does not offer complete liberation, as the protagonists are frustrated in their attempts to go 'off the beaten tracks' using the conventional roads. In both cases, there are extensive references to the geological instability of the land. Skiing on an active volcano like Tongariro or bathing and smoking a joint in a hot pool at the base of the Southern Alps adds an extra thrill to the 'New Zealand experience'. The notion of 'geological instability' can eventually be extended to the atmospheric conditions that challenge the protagonists. During the hang-gliding sequences in *Off the Edge*, the protagonists, Jeff and Blair, dangerously lose height flying over the Tasman Glacier, and the narrator points out that there is "no place as unforgiving as the air". In another scene, a blizzard has them confined to their hut for a week. In a surprisingly similar scene, the protagonists of *Snows of Aorangi*, a travelogue shot by the National Film Unit twenty years earlier, three international skiers face the sublime power of nature when a storm traps them inside their hut. The unpredictability of the land, the 'non-cultural' elements such as the storm, the wind and the hot pools, have a subversive function in relation to the norm represented by 'Culture'. As is shown by the semiotic square they are, in fact, in a relation of contradiction with the semiotic category of 'Culture', an opposition actually stronger than the relation of contrariety implied by the couplet 'Culture – Nature'.

The analysis of the elementary grammar of oppositions that forge the text 'New Zealand', as represented in the film features produced between the 1940s and the 1990s, discloses certain points for consideration. Carrying out two operations of negation (by adding the prefix 'non' to the primitive terms) enables, simultaneously, the generation of two contradictory terms and two implications, which are characterised by a relation of complementarity. While it is obvious that all the films considered are articulated along the line of opposition between Culture (Oppression) and Nature (Liberation), it is less apparent how these semiotic categories are related to 'Non-Culture' (Non-Oppression) and 'Non-Nature' (Non-Liberation). The semiotic square helps to clarify these relations, revealing that Non-Nature (Non-Liberation) is in a relation of presupposition with Culture. The beach and the road, typical 'non-natural' spaces while promising liberation, are constantly infiltrated by the dangers of 'Culture'. If we translate this into a more tourist-oriented discourse it becomes apparent that both roads and beaches fail to fully liberate the tourist from the oppression of 'Culture'. Both the beach and the road are, by definition, liminal places at the margins of geographic, social and psychological experiences. From the tourist perspective, both the beach and the road are significant pleasure spaces, which are nevertheless associated with standardised forms of mass tourism, such as the seaside resort or bus sightseeing. In this way, they both fail to offer access to the liberating power of 'Nature'.[8]

It is interesting, from this perspective, to note that in the history of spatial imagination, the notion of elevation has always had a positive connotation. From the symbolic point of view, the mountain represents the link between the heavens and earth. The pilgrim who reaches the top of the mountain transcends the secular space (low being equated with chaos) to attain a more pure state. The mountain is usually associated with values of physical, spiritual and moral elevation. That is why the mountain is considered to have more dignity and to be more 'natural', as a tourist destination, than the beach. *This is New Zealand*, the most popular travelogue produced by the NFU, ends with a glorious aerial view of the southern Alps, while the last sequence of *Runaway* shows the protagonist David Manning progressively disappearing up a mountain. The mountain and the bush are the most 'natural' film landscapes. They are in a relation of contradiction with the Non-Natural elements, the beach and the road, as they can potentially contaminate their natural purity. They are also in a relation of complementarity with the Non-Cultural elements, such as geological instability, as they are 'Pre-Natural', primeval powers that shape nature. The semiotic square reveals how the geological instability is positioned in a relation of contradiction with Culture. Both terms are defined by the impossibility of being present together. Earthquakes, volcanoes, storms negate, both literally and metaphorically, the establishment of culture while at the same time reinforcing the purity of Nature.

It is now possible to conclude the mapping of the square with the second generation of categorical terms: the so called contradictory meta-terms and the contrary meta-terms, these latter representing the lateral or deictic syntheses (Figure 2.6).

The four synthetic positions are:

> **Nation (or identity)**: this complex, or (in Greimas' words) 'utopic', term synthesises the couplet of contraries Nature-Culture. They are the foundation of the 'national' element as New Zealand identity is defined simultaneously by the myth of nature and by its British heritage. The piano on the beach in *The Piano* is, for example, a powerful icon of this synthesis.[9]

> **Regeneration**: volcanoes (or geological instability in general) and beach (or road) are spaces of openness, as they both contribute to define identity. Volcanoes shape nature while the beach shapes culture.[10] In *Runaway* volcano and beach coexist, the former being

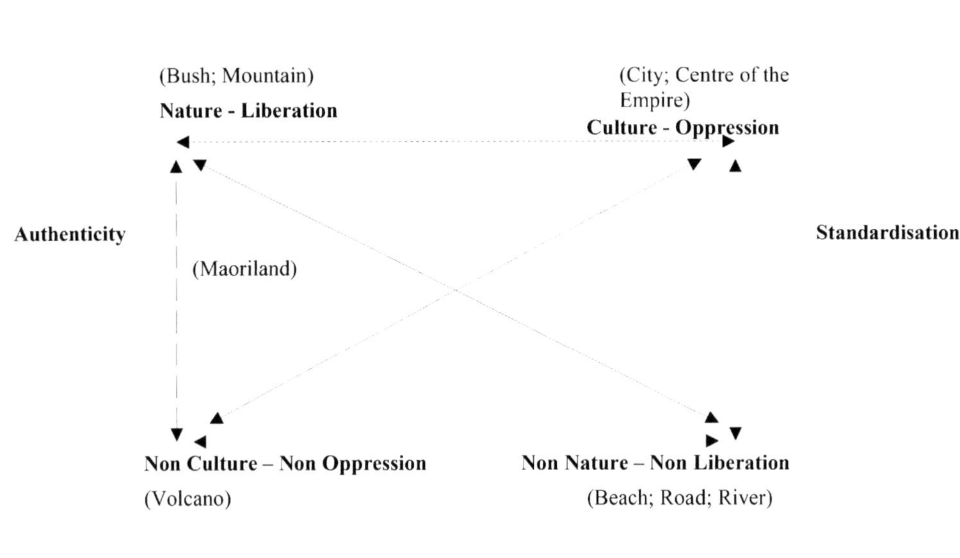


Figure 2.6.  Semiotic square and meta-terms.

a metaphor for the character's instability while the latter symbolises the influence of external elements (*dolce vita*, European lifestyle) on local culture. In a similar way, *The Seekers* deploys both mudpools and beach as symbols of the youthfulness of a nation whose identity is being progressively defined.

**Authenticity:** the sum of Nature and Non-Culture produces authenticity or purity. Skiing on an active volcano (*Off the Edge*, *The Leading Edge*, *Snows of Aorangi*) is the most authentic experience possible.

**Standardisation:** when cities and roads (or beaches) coexist they are depicted as negative symbols of materialism and conformism. For example, in Auckland David Manning drives an expensive European car that is the source of his financial troubles and will cause him to leave the city. Similarly, in *Sleeping Dogs* Smith is brought back to Auckland in a police van.

Building on the process of generation of signification, the following sections shift my analysis from the elementary to the superficial structures of signification, also defined as superficial narrative grammar. I will focus on the close reading of the sub-texts (the films) to identify how their enunciative strategies practically develop the logical oppositions that characterise the semiotic square. The analysis of selected New Zealand film *topoi* (the road, the city, the bush, the mountain, volcanoes) will be preceded by the definition of cinematic place and cinematic space.


**Place versus space**

Cinema establishes an isomorphism between all the spatial forms and the flat surface of the screen. As cinema theoretician Juri Lotman points out, the stability of the screen boundaries and the physical reality of screen flatness are necessary conditions for generating cinematic space. In cinematography, space is delimited and confined within a certain framework, while it also attempts to actively break up and surge beyond the boundaries of the frame (Lotman, 1976). This persistent conflict is a basic component of the illusion of cinema space reality. For Soviet film-maker Sergej Eisenstein, film landscape operates like music, conveying moods, emotions and spiritual experiences. In fact, in Eisenstein's words: "landscape is a complex bearer of the possibilities of a plastic interpretation of emotions" (Eisenstein, 1987: 355). In his seminal work about film landscape, Martin Lefebvre traces back the origin of the latter term to the German *Landschaft* (Lefebvre, 2006: xv). The German suffix *–schaft* is linked to the notion of 'form' and 'shape'. Therefore, for Lefebvre "the term itself betrays the process involved: that of finding a view by creating or shaping it through framing" (Lefebvre, 2006: xv). Landscape and space play an essential role within the cinematic medium, not only because of their capacity to express the inexpressible but also because they reproduce the cultural interaction with nature and the environment. For Maurizia Natali film landscapes "bear the traces of political projects and ideological messages" (Natali cited in Lefebvre, 2006: xx) as they are constructs of the imagination that can serve different social and cultural functions. The study of cinematic space and landscape implicitly provides a deeper insight into a certain culture. Every landscape is a symbolic form *and* a cultural product and, therefore, aesthetic research is strictly interconnected with cultural anthropology and philosophy.

Italian film scholar Sandro Bernardi distinguishes between narrative and pictorial landscapes.[11] The former is a function of the narration: in this case the film controls and integrates the space whose sense is closed and defined. Rather than being a function of the diegesis, the pictorial landscape preserves its plastic characteristics. Its sense is not univocally determined by the narration, rather, this landscape on the one hand, produces a visual pleasure that is not strictly a function of the narrative, on the other hand, can activate other potential stories that lead off from the main one (Bernardi, 2002). Similarly, Bernardi distinguishes between cinematic place and space. The pictorial landscape depicts places which are not connected to the narration and which can potentially generate other stories. On the contrary, the narrative landscape transforms a place into a diegetic space whose meaning is a function of the narration. These two categories are not considered mutually exclusive or incompatible, rather they always coexist in different degrees and forms in the same film. Drawing from this basic distinction between cinematic place and space, Bernardi formulates a typology of relations between landscape and story. Even though these different typologies emerge in different moments in the history of cinema, they coexist in contemporary movies and, in many cases, within the same film. The main types of relation between landscape and narration are defined as:

Panorama (*Vedutismo*)
Time of Myths (*Tempo dei Miti*)
Time of Reflection (*Tempo della Riflessione*)

The first type, the 'Panorama', is typical, although not exclusively so, of early non-narrative cinema where the landscape had mainly a pictorial value and was not connected to any story. In this case, figure and backdrop overlap and the landscape is characterised by the prominence of the place over the space. The images are extremely rich and complex as every fragment is the centre of a potential story. The Panorama attempts to enlarge the scope of the visible, creating the opportunity for countless potential narrations which are nevertheless never fully explored. This type of cinema presupposes a gaze which cannot actually 'see': as the spectator is confronted by an overwhelming quantity of visual information, s/he has to deal with the opacity of reality. The spectator knows what s/he is watching only because of the opening title sequence, as the film proposes images which are either too obvious or too obscure. The spectator knows for example that s/he is watching a mountain, but the film does not provide the object of the gaze with any established meaning. The Panorama cinema is therefore a celebration of place and the act of gazing.

The work of subsequent cinema depends upon the reduction of the narrative potential of filmic images. In the 'Time of Myths', which emerges in correspondence with the development of classic cinema, landscape is perfectly integrated and controlled by the narration. The camera and the spectator are omniscient, as everything is constructed and ordained around them. In this kind of cinema the plurality of the world is tamed. In exchange for the reduction of the potential of images the landscape now provides the spectator with meaning. Different places, such as studios or physical landscapes are used to construct a single narrative space. The classic Western movie, for example, which is a typical expression of the 'Time of Myths', tames and controls nature, assigning the landscape a specific role in the narrative economy. The Western genre creates a powerful myth of nature, assimilating within a single entity defined as 'otherness' everything (Native Americans, horses, nature, women) different from the American WASP (White Anglo-Saxon Protestant). Narrative cinema stages the otherness and creates myths for a spectator who is always in a central position in relation to the story.

If a story is made up of several images, a single narrative contains, potentially, several stories. The 'Time of Reflection' is based on this principle. In this kind of cinema, place is not always subjugated to the main narration and does not always become diegetic space. Rather, place often provides a narrative pause, opening to other potential stories inscribed in the pictorial landscape. The spectator, who had a central omniscient position in the 'Time of Myths', as everything revolved around him or her, is now overwhelmed by the density of the filmic image. Bernardi suggests that modernist cinema, and the films of Antonioni in particular, are an extreme example of the 'Time of Reflection', where the landscape is never entirely subordinated to the narration and frequently offers occasions for narrative digressions (Bernardi, 2002: 81). The cinema of the 'Time of Reflection' emphasises the plurality of potential point of views, as the gazes of the film character, the camera and the spectator do not overlap anymore. As a consequence, the character is often able to see what the spectator cannot and vice versa.[12]


**Escape from the narrative space**

Several film critics have pointed out the centrality of landscape in New Zealand cinema (Horrocks, 1989; Neill and Rymer, 1995; Harvey and Bridge, 2005). How is the landscape central in all these films? What is the relation between the landscape and the story? How are different *topoi*, such as the beach or the mountain, treated and represented? Is it possible to apply Bernardi's typology to New Zealand cinematic landscape between 1940 and 1990? Of course, such a lengthy period of time, which includes directors, genres, films very different from each other, makes any kind of generalisation difficult. Nevertheless, it is possible to find some common features. In most of the films considered the landscape tends to escape the control of the narration; the diegetic space often comes back to its original status of plastic place. The beauty of the pictorial landscape is emphasised, on the one hand, by its opposition with the narration, and on the other hand, by the discovery of the landscape's multiple narrative potential. Of course, this narrative potential is present in different films to different degrees.

In *The Seekers*, the resistance of the landscape to being controlled and integrated within the story is most apparent. In this film, the spectator is constantly confronted by a surplus of pictorial landscape. The movie opens with a sequence of scenic views of New Zealand: from the mountains and lakes of South Island to Cape Kidnappers on the East Coast of the North Island and back to the Fiordland again. While a male voice-over tells the Māori legend of the earth, sky and man, establishing a loose narrative path that connects nature, the land and the Māori, the spectator is actually left free to gaze. For a moment, the relation between figure and backdrop is blurred and the landscape seems to gradually emerge from the background to become the foreground/actor of the story. The opening sequence ends with an extreme long shot of a bay and an anchored vessel. The composition of the shot is reminiscent of the romantic tradition of the picturesque, as the scene is represented from a commanding vantage point and framed by the branches of a tree. The extreme long shot of the beach and the vessel is punctuated by the voice-over which proclaims: "this was New Zealand". This shot is particularly significant for several reasons. First, the spectator is introduced to the 'beach'. As was apparent from our semiotic analysis of the New Zealand filmic *topoi*, the beach is a place of transition between Nature and Culture, or more precisely, it is a 'non-natural' place. The beach connects Nature to the centre of the empire and other external threats that will eventually contaminate the purity of the land and justify the narrator's nostalgic remark. Second, this shot is important because it represents the passage within the film from the centrality of the *place* to the narrative *space*. The opening sequence does not explicitly connect the views of the natural wonders to any specific point of view, providing the illusion of a sort of autonomy of the landscape. The shot of the beach and the consequent introduction of the protagonist, prospective settler Philip, imply the re-interpretation of the first sequence. The spectator is now able to connect the images shown on screen with the point of view of the protagonist. This is confirmed by the scene that immediately follows: a long shot of a huge kauri tree, the very same shot shown during the first panoramic sequence. The only difference is that this time Philip and his mate Paddy enter the scene, making clear the relation between figure and backdrop. The compositional mode has not changed and this reveals and confirms the identity of what can be defined as the 'enunciator'.[13] The spectator has been seeing through the eyes of the same enunciator since the outset. In the first case, though, the absence of an explicit guide through the enunciation, the protagonist Philip, created the illusion of a 'liberation' of the landscape from the boundaries of the diegesis. It is now clear how the place has been transformed into a controlled and integrated narrative space. In its second appearance, the kauri is a mere backdrop to the action. Similarly, in the following scene, Philip's entrance into the Māori burial ground, shot in a studio, focuses entirely on the protagonist.

As soon as Philip enters the scene the spectator enters the 'Time of Myths'. Michelangelo Antonioni defines the endless narrative possibilities contained within an image as "the mystery of images" (Antonioni cited in Bernardi, 2002: 11). The mystery of the image is somehow related to the mystery of nature. Antonioni's cinema acknowledges the impossibility of reducing nature to a single, central point of view. In his films nature is never a function of the characters or the spectators. Instead, it is constantly escaping the control of the enunciator and straying from the narrative path. The mystery of Nature is preserved by the refusal to construct the film places as a cosmos. On the contrary, in *The Seekers* the space is ordered and organised around the film characters. The mystery of nature is revealed and replaced by a more nostalgic myth of nature; "This was New Zealand". As in the American Western film tradition, *The Seekers* celebrates the accomplishment of the early settlers who tamed Nature. In the film the protagonists are constantly confronted by the dangers of Nature: the bush, the mud pools, the Māori. Nevertheless, these dangers are relegated to the dimension of myth. At the enunciative level the wilderness seems to be tamed: nature is the result of real and artificial locations entirely controlled by the film-makers. The enunciator has almost total power over the filmic places. 'Almost' because the spectator seems at times to be confronted by a surplus of visual information, a sort of narrative break, where s/he finds a hole in the narrative space.

One of the most popular activities of the characters of *The Seekers* seems to be gazing or inviting the others to gaze. After Philip and his mate Paddy have been captured by the Māori they are conducted to the chief. During the journey to the village Paddy falls on a mud pool and screams "Look!" The film cuts to a long shot of a geyser blowing steam. The light and the quality of the shot make it different from the rest of the film. In fact, this footage is rather reminiscent of those New Zealand travelogues whose subjects were often geysers and hot pools. These kinds of sequences in the film reveal an unnecessary indulgence in the pictorial character of the landscape. Nature seems to escape for a moment from the control of the diegesis, the characters look out of the narrative space into the external world. As in the opening sequence, the relation between *place* and *space* is temporarily reversed and *place* triumphs. Once again, the comparison with avant-garde cinema proves useful. In Antonioni's films, for example, the protagonists are often busy gazing at nature. In these films though the spectator discovers, along with the protagonist of the story, that s/he is not anymore at the centre of the world. The spectator is overwhelmed by the multiplicity of perspectives and points of view. The most obvious example is *L'Avventura* (dir. Michelangelo Antonioni, 1960), a film that overtly deals with the problem of landscape. In *L'Avventura* the space ceases to be a cosmos organised around a principle of unity and becomes a confused chaos, within which there is no dominant point of view. The island where the protagonists disembark, after the mysterious disappearance of a woman, seems to be huge or extremely small depending on the perspective of the different characters. The landscape itself is not a function of the story and the narration itself is subjugated to the power of the place instead. The spectator is not able to 'see' nature anymore. On the contrary, in *The Seekers*, even during the narrative breaks that indulge in the representation of natural wonders, the spectator is constantly reassured by the presence of a single dominant gaze. The illusory power of nature that often tries to break through the boundaries of the narration, as in the above-mentioned opening sequence or in the geyser shot, is frustrated by the constant control of the camera that imposes a tourist-settler-male gaze over the landscape. As Simmons points out: "the wet, steaming pools mark the film's landscape as a sexual terrain" (Simmons, 1999b: 46). The bubbling mud pools and the exploding geysers have a sexual connotation as they are associated with the character of the 'dusky maiden' Moana, the wife of the Māori chief, who eventually manages to seduce the settler Philip. The British settler will eventually manage to metaphorically fecundate the New Zealand soil, hiding his baby underground. When the Māori chief disinters the baby in the final scene, Pākehā settlement is symbolically enfranchised. It is not by chance that the subjects of these panoramic escapades are the mountain, the bush and the geysers (or geological instability in general). These three *topoi* are positioned on the left side of our semiotic square and represent the elements of authenticity which constitute the meta-text New Zealand. The enunciator seems, therefore, to claim that nature has been almost entirely tamed and subjugated under the control of the film narration. The elements that still escape the diegesis are controlled by the camera and are ready to be eventually consumed by the tourist gaze. The spectator of *The Seekers* participates in this virtual conquest of New Zealand, vicariously witnessing the integration of the places into narrative space and more actively imposing a tourist gaze over the most challenging elements of nature. The trope of geological instability is central to the narrative economy of *The Seekers*, which celebrates the period of early settlement and the infancy of the nation. As the country gradually acquires its own identity and maturity, cinematic volcanoes become the symbol of a silent but constant threat. This is the case in the afore-mentioned *Runaway*, where the volcanic island of Rangitoto stands for the dangerous instability of the protagonist David Manning. Similarly, the opening sequence of *Smash Palace* features a red dawn behind the black silhouette of what appears to be Mt. Ruapehu, the largest active volcano in New Zealand (Figure 2.7). As in *Runaway*, the representation of the volcano becomes a metaphor for the explosive rage of the protagonist Al Shaw, a former professional racer who operates a backcountry auto salvage with his unhappy French wife. When she leaves him, beginning an affair with his best friend, Al's frustration explodes in a series of shocking actions that threaten to destroy them all.

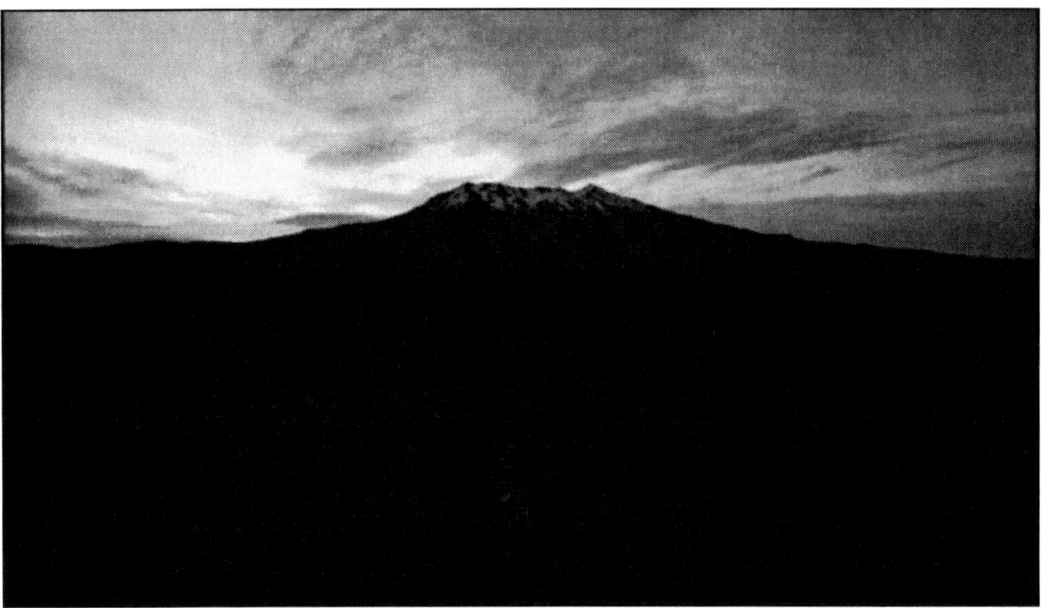

Figure 2.7. *Smash Palace*, Aardvark Films.

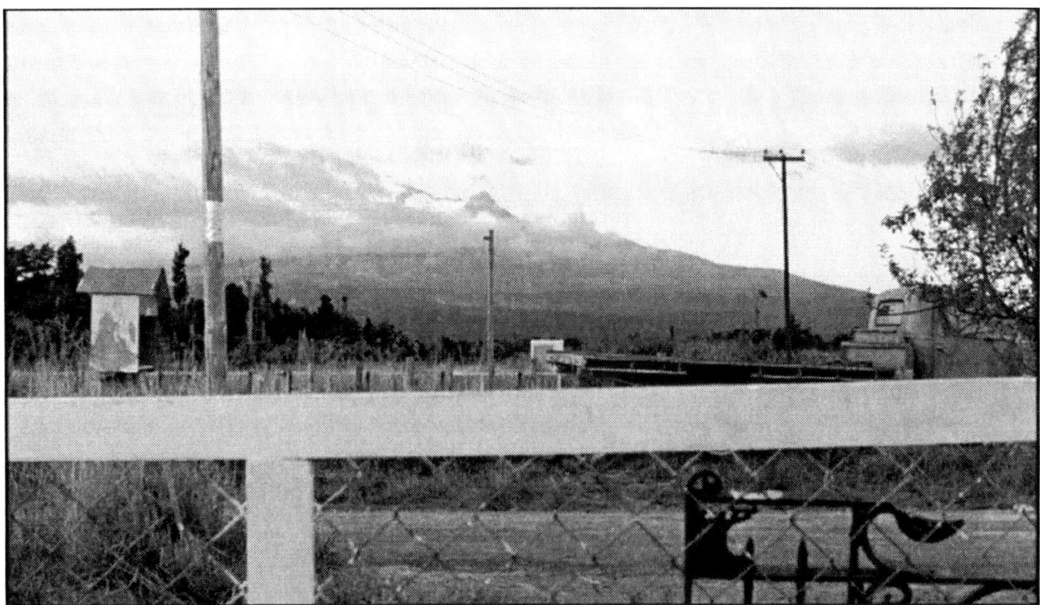

Figure 2.8. *Smash Palace*, Aardvark Films.

## Transitional space, porous space: the road

Like most New Zealand films, *Smash Palace* represents place as beyond the control of the narration. When Al's ex-wife Jacky says to her new lover—"look at that mountain"—the camera indulges in a brief glimpse of an awe-inspiring peak that contrasts starkly with the fast pace of the following scene, that features Al racing (Figure 2.8). Similarly, the film opposes the town and the bush where Al seeks refuge when he is escaping from the police. I have already mentioned how the narrative of many New Zealand films is based on the dialectic of 'city versus bush'. New Zealand directors have widely explored the notion of mobility, from *Runaway* to *Goodbye Pork Pie* or *Sleeping Dogs*, where the protagonists move from the city to the interior of the country. While in period films the narrative is often initiated by travel from metropolitan centre (Britain) to periphery, in films set in contemporary New Zealand the travel is internal. As Perry points out, the European settlement of New Zealand is a product of the extension of the distinction between country and city beyond the boundaries of the nation state: "New Zealand as a country derived from the expansion of British cities; geographically it may have been in the Pacific, but structurally it was a part of Britain's rural hinterland" (Perry, 1994: 46). In spite of the fact that New Zealand is one of the most urbanised countries in the world with 85% of the population being defined as urban, in popular mythology it is the rural which is considered the 'real' New Zealand. Unlike Britain, New Zealand's economy is mostly reliant on agriculture, tourism and the countryside. Therefore, the rural is not just a nostalgic place in which to escape the modes of control characteristic of metropolitan life, but rather stands for national culture.

The tropes of the car and the road have a crucial role in negotiating the relation between urban and rural. Furthermore, the low density of urban development in New Zealand and the consequent low level of available public transport implies a high reliance on the motor car as a means of transport. The relation between landscape and car is, therefore, particularly significant in the New Zealand context. First, the car is an essential visual medium as the tourists experience the country through the frames of the car's windscreen, which in turn replicate the boundaries of the cinematic image. Second, and most important for our present purpose, New Zealand film landscapes are dotted with cars. In most cases they are fancy, unusual cars like Laura Kossovich's American car in *Runaway* (and more recently in *Snakeskin*, directed in 2001 by Gillian Ashurts), the yellow mini in *Goodbye Pork Pie* or the race car and the tow truck in *Smash Palace*. In the latter film this logic is pushed to the extreme, as the cars contaminate the rural landscape creating a new hybrid space which curiously reconciles metropolitan centre and countryside. The aerial view of Al's auto salvage yard in *Smash Palace* integrates the expanse of wrecked cars within a traditional landscape of mountain and bush, as the brown colour of the rusty cars gradually slips into the green of the trees that surround the salvage. This particular shot could be interpreted as a modern variation on the theme of the 'landscape with ruins'. According to Walter Benjamin these romantic views of ruins, like Friedrich's paintings, are so fascinating and popular because they capture the borderline between nature and culture (Benjamin, 1977). It is not surprising that after the release of the film, the set of *Smash Palace* became a local tourist attraction (Bushline Lodge, 2008).

Nevertheless, within the local cultural context the auto salvage landscape could be interpreted as an expression of what Perry defines as Antipodean Camp (Perry, 1998). Perry has formulated the concept of Antipodean Camp to suggest that postmodern pastiche has acquired a specific form in cultures instituted by colonisation such as Australia and New Zealand where bricolage is a way of life and where "one of the consequences […] has been to induce a developed awareness of culture, including the very idea of a national culture, as artifice" (Perry, 1998: 14). Even though Perry uses *Heavenly Creatures* (dir. Peter Jackson, 1994) and Ward's *The Navigator* (dir. Vincent Ward, 1988) as his examples, it is possible to read the auto salvage in *Smash Palace* or in *Goodbye Pork Pie* (where the two protagonists hide the yellow mini in another wrecked car) as expressions of the Antipodean Camp. In these two examples the car, which is a foreign element *par excellence*, as New Zealand imports its motor vehicles particularly from Japan, is recomposed in a 'local' way. Furthermore, the merging of the auto salvage with the landscape somehow anticipates the 'aesthetic of superimposition' (Macassey, 2008) characteristic of other New Zealand films such as *The Piano*, in which sophisticated artefacts are picturesquely transposed onto empty and wild landscapes. To a certain extent, the juxtaposition between quirky, exotic cars and local landscapes is another symptom of the cultural dislocation characteristic of Antipodean Camp. The road is definitely a central theme in New Zealand films from the 1960s to the 1980s and *Runaway*, for example, adopted and adapted this genre mixing the influence of the French Nouvelle Vague and James Bond style films for promotional purposes.

Within the semiotic diagram of New Zealand filmic places, the road, like the beach, is a space of transition between nature and culture. As in *The Seekers*, where the shot of the beach corresponds with the commencement of the filmic narration, road movies such as *Runaway* or *Goodbye Pork Pie* position the road as the narrative engine that opens up the narrative. The road, particularly the New Zealand road, is a porous narrative space that, adopting Bernardi's terminology, points to filmic places which in turn provide the possibility to stray from the main narrative path. Upon its release many local commentators noted that *Runaway* exploited the New Zealand scenery in a way that closely resembled the standard tourist-oriented productions of the National Film Unit. In Catherine De la Roche's words: "There was some marvellous location-spotting too. Sequences were built up from aerial and ground shots all moving at continuous tempo—a bit deliberate, perhaps, but glorious to see" (De la Roche, 1988: 131). In *Runaway* the camera continually wanders towards what seems to be secondary. In this way, the place constantly tries to escape from the control of the narrative and seems reluctant to become an integrated cinematic space. Laurence Simmons notes that *Runaway* produces a tension between "narrative as a vehicle for meaning and detail of the image as a means of dissolution of the narrative—the way in which the narrative dissolves or stops on an image and details become no more than images" (Simmons, 1995a: 65). The numerous pictorial landscape shots are not causal or explicative, as they do not provide any meaning useful to the narration. Rather, they open up new narrative possibilities. *Runaway*'s landscape is a typical example of what Bernardi defines as 'Time of Reflection' landscape. Even in a film like *Goodbye Pork Pie*, which is characterised by very different stylistic features, the road still accomplishes the same task of opening onto new pictorial landscapes and new potential narratives. Even though most of the film is shot from the inside of the speeding mini as the scenery outside whizzes past, the spectator is still confronted by a surplus of pictorial landscape. This visual surplus could be justified by the intention of the producers to please the Film Commission in their support of a local film feature with 'New Zealand content'.

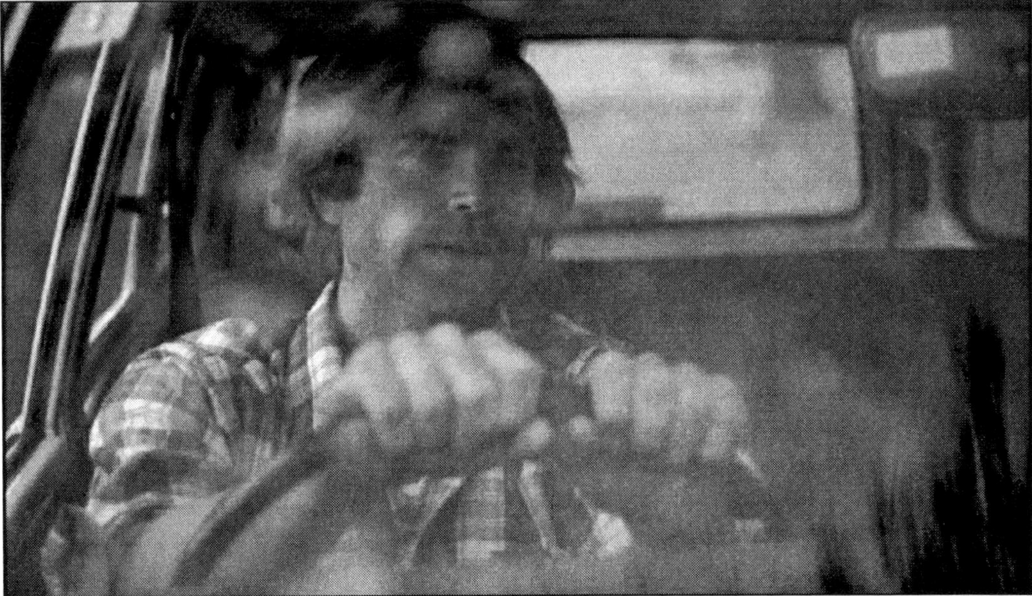

Figure 2.9. *Sleeping Dogs*, Aardvark Films.

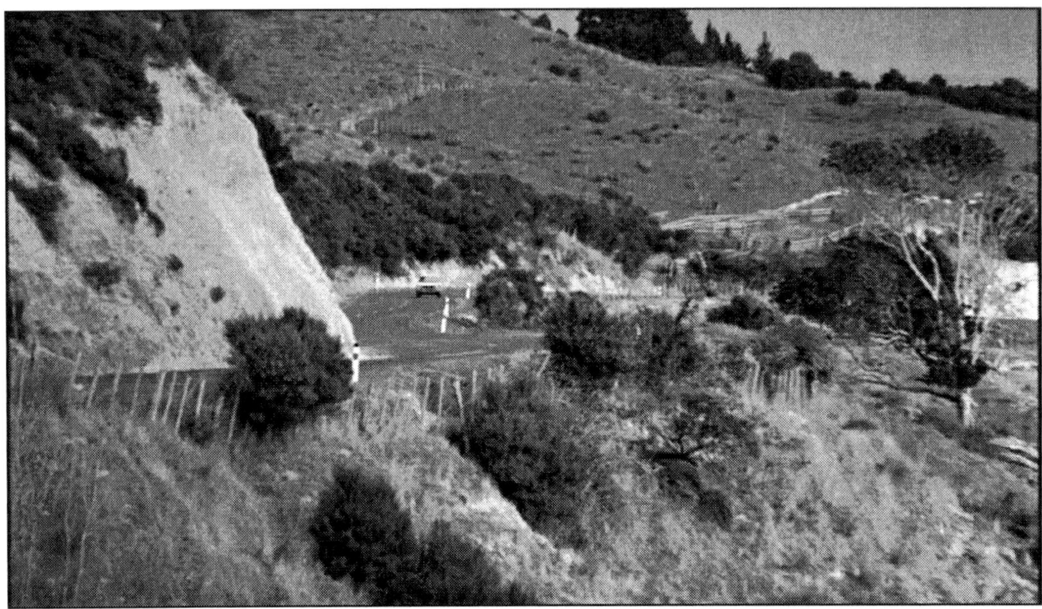

Figure 2.10. *Sleeping Dogs*, Aardvark Films.

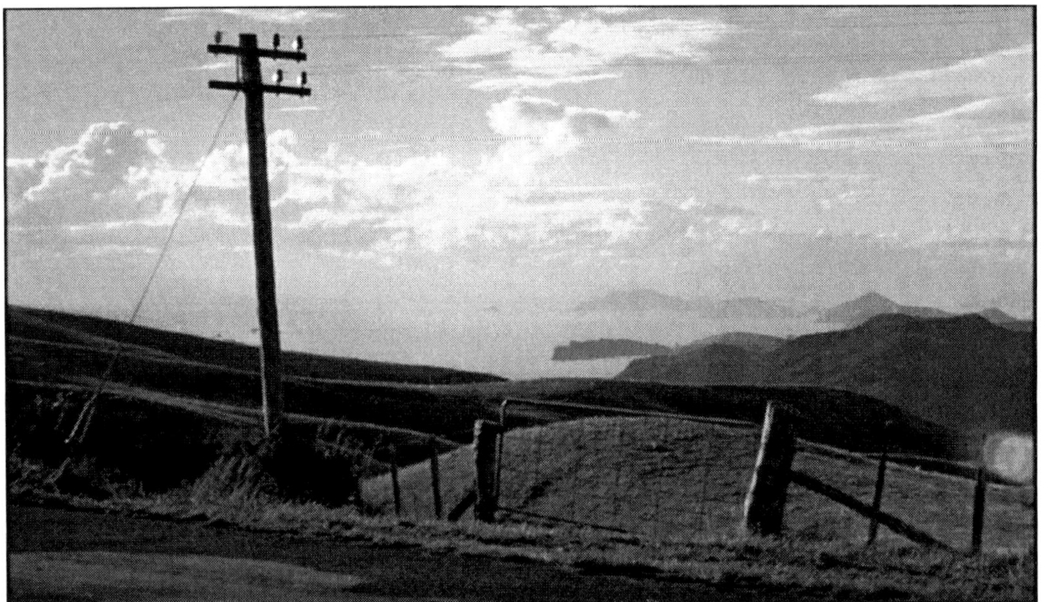

Figure 2.11. *Sleeping Dogs*, Aardvark Films.

In the case of *Sleeping Dogs* it was not necessary to please the Commission, as this institution was founded just two years after the movie's release. Nevertheless, in this film the camera focuses even more on the pictorial landscape. It is useful to analyse one of the sequences of the movie to show how the road accomplishes the role of narrative bridging. The sequence analysed begins when Smith (Sam Neill) leaves his family house after his wife has revealed that she has had an affair with Smith's friend Bullen (Ian Mune). It begins with a medium close-up of Smith driving, as seen through the windscreen from the front of the car (Figure 2.9). Through the rear windscreen the spectator sees the road whizzing past. The space seems completely integrated into the narration and the enunciator seems to encourage an identification between Smith and the viewer. The film spectator logically expects a subjective shot from Smith's perspective or a long shot of the car being tracked by the camera. Instead, the following shot is quite surprising: a static long shot of a couple of trees in a pasture field. As Smith's car enters the frame, the camera quickly pans left and zooms in trying to catch up with the protagonist's car. As the car progressively disappears the shot becomes an extreme long shot and the focus shifts onto the mountains that gradually move from the background to the centre of the frame. The following two aerial extreme long shots of the car, winding around a headland on the coast road, confirm the fact that even though the space still revolves around the main character, it is nevertheless progressively escaping the control of the narration (Figure 2.10). The following shot returns closer to the road and the car, as the camera tracks down trying to contain the car within the frame. However, when the car disappears beyond the boundaries of the screen, the camera does not follow, rather preferring to rest on a scenic shot of the Coromandel coastline (Figure 2.11). Then the camera comes back inside the car, focusing on a medium close-up of Smith, and this time the spectator is able to see the scenic wonders via a subjective shot. Smith eventually stops the car to gaze at Gut Island and the subsequent semi-subjective shot becomes a clear invitation for the spectator (Figure 2.12). Just like in *Runaway*, *Goodbye Pork Pie* or *Smash Palace*, the road in *Sleeping Dogs* is always a scenic road where the pictorial landscape breaks in, proposing alternative narrative detours that the protagonists may or may not follow. The sequence ends with an extreme long shot of Gut Island outlined against the setting sun. In this case Smith follows the narrative suggestion offered by the pictorial landscape, as he will eventually manage to live on the island. Thus, the cinematic place is transformed into narrative space. In the last shot of the sequence, the gaze of the camera, the spectator and the protagonist overlap with the tourist gaze. Upon the film's release commentators of the time obviously noted this confluence of film and tourist narratives. David Gunby, for example, referring to the above-mentioned sequence pointed out how "the constant temptation in New Zealand film-making has been to splice in a bit of landscape here and there" (Gunby, 1977: 135).

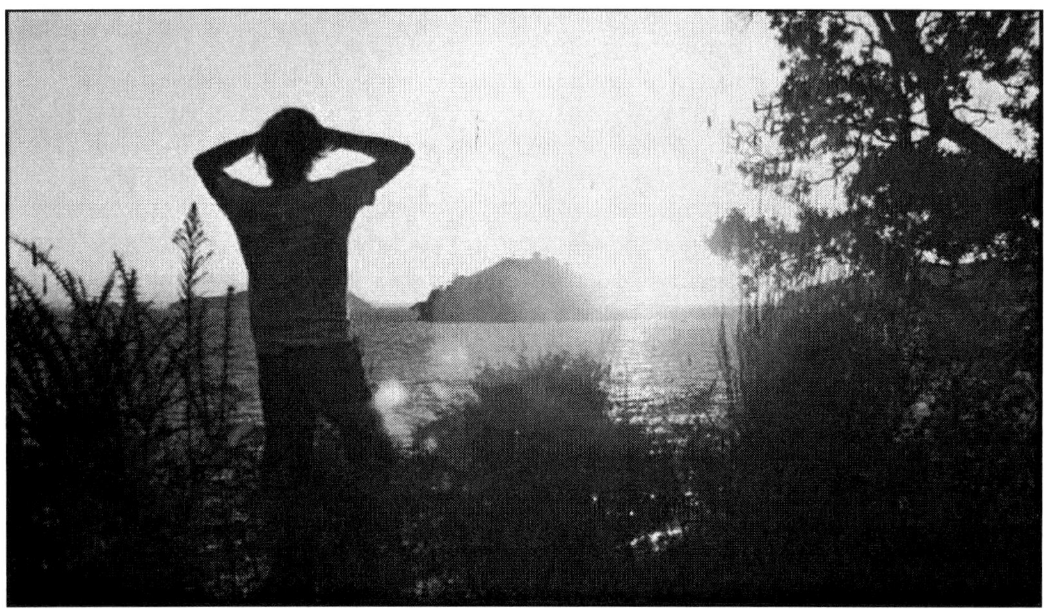

Figure 2.12. *Sleeping Dogs*, Aardvark Films.

As already suggested, the car plays an important role in the formation of this tourist gaze. Automobiles are not only machines for transporting drivers and passengers to particular destinations but also technologies for visually experiencing or consuming those very places through mobile sightseeing (Larsen, 2001). The extensive dependence of New Zealanders upon the car as a means of transport has played a crucial role in the formation of this mobile gaze. New Zealand cinema is the peculiar expression of a "mobilized virtual gaze" (Friedberg, 1993: 2) which finds its roots in the mobile gaze developed by the car.

Extending Bernardi's typology of the relation between landscape and narration it is possible to redefine spaces of transition such as the beach, the river and the road as 'porous spaces'. Porous because even if they are under the control of the narration they continuously break into the 'narrative other', as they show places that in turn could initiate new stories. Even though this section has focused on the road as the main example of a transitional space, the beach or the river often accomplish the same task. In *The Quiet Earth* the last shot of the protagonist Zac on the beach and a series of atomic explosions in the background imply the open ending of the story. Once again the landscape opens up to a new potential narrative. Similarly, rivers often represent narrative turning points. In *Smash Palace* Jacqui and Ray begin their affair near a river while Al 'goes bush' driving his truck onto the bed of a river. In *Illustrious Energy* (dir. Leon Narbey, 1988) the river becomes the turning point for the gold panners' lives as it marks their eventual success.


## The city, or New Zealand dystopia

The relation between cinema and urban space has had a defining influence on the ways in which history and the human body have been represented. The history of cinema has well documented the role played by the urban setting in so many films and has highlighted the cinematic qualities that cities seem to possess. The histories of cinema and the city are so imbricated that it is impossible to imagine the development of one without the other. Referring to the shift of perception caused by the development of cinema, Walter Benjamin claims that the emergence of "film corresponds to profound changes in the perceptive apparatus—changes that are experienced on an individual scale by the man in the street in big-city traffic" (Benjamin, 1979: 250). This structural similarity between city and film could perhaps account for the over-representation of the city in international cinema; the cityscape is the screenscape *par excellence*. Giuliana Bruno claims, nonetheless, that not all cities are cinematic. She suggests, in particular, that certain cities, by way of nature or architecture, translate better than others onto the filmic image. Harbour cities, like Naples or New York, absorbing the perpetual movement of the sea and conveying the energy of people's transit, are constantly depicted by the cinema. Referring to those cities Bruno claims that

> [t]heir very history is intertwined with tourism, colonization and voyage and their relative apparatuses of representation. In many ways, their filmic image partakes in a form of tourism: cinema's depiction is both an extension and an effect of the tourist's gaze. (Bruno, 1997b: 47)

Similarly, the ideological character of the cinematic city has been diversely mobilised within different social and cultural contexts.

New Zealand has been culturally constructed as a rural idyll and as an extension of the British countryside. The city, therefore, struggles to find a consistent identity within the collective imaginary of New Zealanders. Even when the existence of the cities is actually acknowledged, they are never understood as New Zealand cities: Dunedin is 'Scottish', Christchurch 'English' and Auckland 'American'. Even though it is necessary to distinguish between urban sub-spaces, such as the Central Business District, the Suburbia and the Small Town, it is possible to claim that all these subcategories are constructed as spaces of oppression or as cultural 'black holes'. In 1993 identity researcher Matthew Hirschberg revealed how New Zealanders are aware of the gap between the idealised identity imagery of the country and the daily experience of living in an urban setting. One of the students tested during Hirschberg's research claimed: "I tend to think of the whole country except Auckland as New Zealand. Auckland is too cosmopolitan to fit in" (Hirschberg cited in Bell, 1996: 10). The figuration of the city in New Zealand cinema between 1940 and 1990 is mostly dystopian. In most of the films of this period, from *Runaway* to *Sleeping Dogs*, from *Goodbye Pork Pie* to *The Quiet Earth* and *Smash Palace*, the protagonists escape the impersonal modes of control characteristic of the urban setting to find a physical or spiritual regeneration in the countryside. In *Sleeping Dogs*, the film restarts and the title credit reappears when the protagonist Smith leaves his suburban house headed for the Coromandel. In the city even the car loses its mobile and liberating power: in *Goodbye Pork Pie* Blondini is stopped by the cops in Auckland and escapes from Wellington by hiding the car in a train carriage. In *Sleeping Dogs*, the car becomes a means of oppression as Smith is transferred from different prisons in a police van. In *Runaway*, David Manning, overwhelmed by his debts, is obliged to sell his sports car. In this film, the metaphorical motionlessness of motor vehicles in the city context is embodied by the lawn mower of Manning's father. The lawn mower represents, in fact, the stability and the mediocrity of a suburban life so despised by the protagonist. In *The Quiet Earth*, the deserted streets of Auckland are dotted with immobile motor vehicles. When the protagonist Zac is eventually trapped by Api the city becomes what Carol Clover calls the 'Terrible Place', which is the place of reckoning in every horror movie (Clover, 1989). In *The Quiet Earth*, as in the other films analysed, the narrative path leads the protagonists out of the city towards the countryside. The solution is always to be found elsewhere, away from the city. Usually, New Zealand cities are stripped of their identity to become an anonymous, mythical 'City'. Apart from a brief glimpse of the Auckland Harbour Bridge or the Wellington parliament building in *Goodbye Pork Pie*, the films considered ignore characteristic urban landmarks. Interestingly, while these films are characterised by a proliferation of extreme long shots and aerial views of natural scenery, there is no corresponding use of these technical devices to represent cities or urban settings. This implies two main consequences: on the one hand, it reinforces the anonymous character of the city; on the other hand, it implies the lack of interest in the city as a cultural object.

The perfect counter-example is the opening sequence of *Sione's Wedding* (dir. Chris Graham, 2006) where the aerial views of Auckland landmarks become a celebration of the city and urban values. This radical shift in the representation of the urban setting is in turn a consequence of the political, economic and social changes New Zealand underwent during the 1970s. The main thrust of these changes was towards a more competitive, market-driven and urban-centred society. The results of this national restructuring became more apparent during the 1990s and corresponded to a shift in the visual media towards a greater focus on New Zealanders as an urban population. The clearest example of this representational revolution is that the most popular presentation of an urban version of New Zealand is the soap opera *Shortland Street* (1992–2009), the first episode of which was broadcast at the beginning of the 1990s. Until the 1980s, however, the New Zealand cinematic city was still deprived of its identity or autonomous life. The urban space was systematically set against the wilderness and only acquired meaning within this binary opposition. In summary, the city in New Zealand cinema is a general dystopian space where oppression is enforced in different degrees: explicitly—as in *Sleeping Dogs* and *Goodbye Pork Pie*—or more subtly—as in *Runaway* or *The Quiet Earth*—where the oppressive power of the city corresponds with the unease and solitude of the protagonists.

The New Zealand cinematic city is an integrated space. Even though it often escapes the control of the enunciator, refusing to be encompassed within extreme long shots or aerial views, the urban setting is a tame subject from the narrative point of view. The urban space revolves around the narration, fulfilling its role as antagonist of the film protagonist. The oppressive quality of the city is visually expressed through the use of certain architectural features such as tunnels and narrow streets. In *Goodbye Pork Pie* the plethora of tunnels and lanes represents a constant challenge for the mini and Blondini's driving skills, while at the same time preventing the story from being distracted by other potential narrative detours. In *Sleeping Dogs*, Bullen is trapped by the police in a narrow street, while in *The Quiet Earth*, Zac is trapped by the unknown Api. The urban-scape is an (active) backdrop, a space that encompasses the characters but which is never encompassed by the camera. Unlike the road, the city in New Zealand films does not offer chances for narrative escape. The New Zealand city is thus the mythical badlands repudiated by the film characters in favour of a more authentic and idyllic place: 'nature'.

## Natural places and natural spaces: the mountain and the bush

Transitional spaces, such as the road or the beach, connect mythical spaces: the city and nature. The definition of nature encompasses a broad range of meanings. Nature can be defined as the material world and its phenomena or the forces and processes that produce and control all the phenomena of the material world ('the laws of nature'). Nature is also the world of living things and the outdoors ('the beauties of nature') or a primitive state of existence, untouched by civilisation or artificiality ('return to nature'). The last two definitions of nature are the most useful for our current purposes.

In New Zealand cinema, while the city is defined negatively as a black hole characterised by lack of identity, lack of authenticity, lack of freedom, nature, on the contrary, is equated with national identity. Because nature pre-exists pre-colonial history, it is often a substitute for the past of the nation. Understanding the formation and the socio-political implications of the representation of nature in New Zealand cinema is thus crucial to any discussion of film-induced tourism. Between 1940 and 1990, New Zealand cinema actively participated in the cultural production and consumption of images of nature. In New Zealand films some places appear more 'natural' than others. As the semiotic square reveals, cinematic places, such as the beach or the river, are transitional spaces that constitute the border between nature and civilisation. Other places, such as the ocean, volcanoes, mudpools or other sites of geological instability, are pre-natural places. They represent the pre-history of a powerful and obscure nature, they are seldom directly represented and their potential explosive threat is implicitly embedded within other New Zealand landscape features such as the mountain. The natural places *par excellence* are the mountains and the bush. Early European representations of New Zealand emphasised the majesty of the national peaks. The favourite subjects of artists such as Gully, Heaphy and Earle were Mitre Peak, Mount Aspiring, Mount Taranaki or the Southern Alps. The romantic aesthetic of the sublime attributed particular value to mountains and, as Francis Pound has pointed out, the mountain was one of the favourite subjects of early New Zealand landscape painters such as John Gully (Pound, 1983: 54).

The bush often features as part of the mountain landscape. Bush is a term adopted by Australian and New Zealand settlers to distinguish the local vegetation from English woods and forests. In New Zealand, the bush holds a recognised historical and cultural significance: protected in national parks it represents the foundation of New Zealand beauty and identity. The uniqueness of the bush flora and fauna has provided national emblems such as the kiwi and the fern. The native forest plays an important role in Māori mythology, where it is celebrated as a source of food and resources. Even though Pākehā have seen the bush differently, particularly as a potential source of arable land, they have attributed to it mythological characteristics. From John Mulgan to Barry Crump, 'going bush' is one of the most important themes of New Zealand literature. Stories about rugged (male) New Zealanders taking on a rugged lifestyle in the bush reinforce the multiple connotations of the bush as a threatening though spiritually regenerating environment. The prominence of romantic views of the bush, in both high and popular culture, is reflected in film. The bush as cinematic place is significantly over-represented, in terms of the actual surface area that it covers. Representations of the bush are also produced with great selectivity: it often appears as a collection of pungas, manuka, ferns and cabbage trees, whereas mangrove swamps and wetlands are seldom represented (Le Heron, 2002: 114). New Zealand feature films from 1940 to 1990 emphasise the idea of the bush as refuge. In *Runaway, Goodbye Pork Pie* and *Smash Palace* it is where the protagonists hide from the police. Similarly, in *Sleeping Dogs* and *Utu* the main characters hide in the bush from the army and the British soldiers respectively. In period films, such as *The Seekers* or *Utu*, differences in the use of the bush are made along racial lines. British soldiers or settlers, as foreigners, are uncomfortable and nervous among misty trees. In *The Seekers*, the leader of the settler community, Philip, forbids his fellow countrymen to venture alone in the bush. In *Utu*, British troops get lost in the mist and mystery of the bush. By contrast, Māori soldiers in the same troop are confidently assertive. In *The Seekers*, Moana surprises a defenceless Philip in the bush. Māori are assimilated to nature and are therefore shown at ease and free to dart through the forest to wage war.

Interestingly, the compositional modes of representation of the bush echo those of the city. The gaze of the camera never grasps the whole expanse of the bush. Like the city, the bush is an active landscape, though in this case it often acts as a facilitator (the bush helps the protagonists to escape). The bush is also an integrated space that is constructed around the narration, even though it is characterised by specific marks of identity (the above mentioned ferns or cabbage trees). One cannot escape from the claustrophobic embrace of the bush as its space does not open up to other cinematic places or potential narratives. The gaze of the protagonists, of the camera and the spectator is frustrated by the thick mist and the lush vegetation.

Usually film characters do not spend too much time in the bush, as the bush is a sanctuary that has to be abandoned. In the last sequence of *Sleeping Dogs*, Smith and Bullen escape from the army across the Coromandel Ranges through extensive bush. The men battle against nature and the odds, coming out alive on the other side where they are quickly killed. The ten-minute escape sequence through the bush proved too long and (visually) too green for the test audience. As a consequence, Donaldson reduced the final chase to five minutes and toned the colour down. Interestingly, even if the nation celebrates the individual engagement with the bush, for movie-goers the encounter was more enjoyable if short lived (Le Heron, 2002: 115). In most of the film, the bush provides a temporary refuge for the film protagonists who sooner or later return to civilisation and face 'real' life. The analogy between the construction of the bush as a (temporary) utopian space and the narrative structures of the tourist experience are quite apparent. Like the bush, the tourist destination provides a temporary escape from the obligations and frustrations of everyday life.

While the bush is a consistent narrative space where the protagonists perform their actions, mountains on the contrary, are constructed as cinematic places, pictorial rather than narrative landscapes. Film characters look or point at the mountains but rarely inhabit them. While the camera gaze can never comprehend the bush as a unified whole it can, on the contrary, frame the mountains, compressing the large, dramatic, inspiring landscape into one shot. Until the 1990s, film characters rarely ventured into the mountains and when they did they either died or explicitly challenged death, like the extreme adventure tourists in *Off the Edge*. The last sequence of the spectacular three-screen travelogue, *This is New Zealand*, shows a stunning aerial view of the Southern Alps that is closely reminiscent of the bird's eye views of *LOTR*.[14] As the camera tracks forward, accompanied by the rousing soundtrack of Sibelius' Karelia Suite, the spectator has the impression of physically moving within the landscape. In the final shot, the film suddenly stops as the camera almost crashes against a snowy peak. Similarly, *Off the Edge* and its sequel *The Leading Edge* are characterised by this constant tension between extreme long shots of the mountains and subjective shots from the protagonists' point of view. When the camera ventures into the blinding white body of the mountains, vision is destined to die.

Mountains and bush are positioned in the fourth corner of the semiotic square, as 'Nature'. Nevertheless, they are characterised by a diametrically opposite relation to narration. While the bush is constructed as a cinematic space inhabited by the film characters, the mountain is a filmic place that conflates the gaze of the camera, the protagonists and the spectator. The spectator, in fact, often sees the mountain through a subjective shot. From the enunciative point of view this device could be defined in Francesco Casetti's words as an "interpellation": the enunciator delegates the narration to a narrator who is directly addressing the enunciatee (Casetti, 1998: 138).[15] The identification with mobile, gazing protagonists transforms the spectator into a virtual tourist. Cinematic places develop, in fact, as something fascinating in themselves, a source of visual pleasure, a tourist spectacle.

Even though mountains and other filmic places are often represented in ways which cut against the narrative flow or the explicative meaning, as pure visual surplus, they are sometimes reabsorbed within the cinematic space. In *Sleeping Dogs* a desperate Smith, who is escaping the army, gazes at a peak covered by vegetation. The camera indulges in the pictorial value of the landscape, of its being a pure place, but the narrative rhythm works to transform 'place into space' as the landscape becomes an actant, an obstacle the protagonist has to overcome. This example reveals how thin is the line that divides place from space and how place can continuously emerge or re-enter the narrative space.


**Journey to the centre of the film: the 'cinenauts'**

The analysis of the complex map of New Zealand filmic *topoi* reveals that every place/space establishes a peculiar relation to narration. This analysis of the films selected highlights the recurrence of a specific narrative pattern that moves back and forth through four cinematic spaces/places.

>  integrated dystopic spaces (city)
>  transitional, porous spaces (road, river, beach)
>  integrated utopic spaces (bush)
>  non-integrated utopic places (mountains, volcanoes)

There is in New Zealand cinema a significant tension between utopian and dystopian spaces that, in turn, results in a constant mobility. Furthermore, these spaces and particularly the bush are not simply backdrops. By contrast, they often become the foreground and an active character (actant) in the story. As a dynamic space of action, the utopic space draws in the spectator as a participant. The spectator is virtually mobilised; s/he becomes a 'cinenaut'.

One of the most relevant features of the films analysed is the physical mobility of the protagonists. Consequently, transitional spaces often play an important role as the narrative backbone. The ability of porous spaces to amplify the power of the gaze contributes to the development of a surplus of pictorial landscapes. This surplus of cinematic places in New Zealand cinema is the result, on the one hand, of a mobilised gaze activated by the high reliance of New Zealanders on the car and, on the other hand, by the role of tourist narratives in shaping the identity of the nation. The navigation of the film space offers the cinenaut numerous viewing platforms. The voy(ag)eurs may rely on the power of film to capture images of remote destinations and on-the-camera movements to explore the cinematic landscape. The cinenauts may still benefit from these devices but, in addition, they can identify with the protagonists of the films and travel with them within the filmic space. The narrative mechanism itself implies mobility: the development of narration is in fact determined by the desire to explore, to find out what is missing, to move into a new scene. In this sense every film is a journey. What is peculiar to New Zealand film production from 1940 to 1990 is a different relation between narration and landscape, between the gaze of the spectator, the protagonist and the camera. The travelogues commissioned by the government during the 1920s and 1930s created voy(ag)eurs who imposed an imperialist gaze on empty landscapes ready to be filled with meaning imported from elsewhere. These new films about escape and mobility, on the contrary, enhance the ability of the spectator to move within the filmic landscape. Cinenauts immerse themselves in the dynamic of opposition between utopic and dystopic space, between narrative space and cinematic place. The cinenautic activity is characterised by virtual mobility within the cinematic space and visual pleasure derived by the consumption of the filmic places. The cinenautic experience, therefore, directly anticipates the tourist practice.

There is no evidence that the films analysed in this chapter directly boosted tourism to New Zealand. Their diffusion was mostly limited to New Zealand and in only a few cases they reached a limited audience in Britain or the USA. The importance of these texts for the analysis of film-induced tourism in New Zealand derives from the fact that they prepared narrative patterns, and an aesthetic of the landscape, producing a relation between landscape and narration that influenced successive productions which benefited from a wider distribution. Thus the cinenaut was opening the way to the cine-tourist.

## Notes

1. *Off the Edge*, which was nominated for an Academy Award, also became the first New Zealand feature shown by Home Box Office, the wealthy new American pay-television system which had two million subscribers (Shelton, 2005: 31).

2. The tax shelter used a marginal tax of 66%, allowing financial backers to write off this percentage and receive a guaranteed return even if the film productions were not a commercial success (Churchman, 1997: 62).

3. The reasons that justify the choice of these films are, at once: their historical significance, their success at the box office and their popularity overseas. Because of their limited impact both in New Zealand and overseas this list does not feature films made by women or Māori directors. These productions convey a different representation of the landscape and they might therefore partially contradict my categorisation of New Zealand film geographies which is mainly based on the analysis of works by male Pākehā directors. For a discussion of films by Māori directors and their different perception of the landscape see Chapter 4.

4. Greimas defines the 'seme' as the minimal unit of signification. It is not an autonomous element, as it exists only because of the differential gap that opposes it to other semes. Located on the content plan, it corresponds to the 'pheme', the unit on the expression plan (Greimas and Courtes, 1982: 278).

5. The *topos* 'farm' is present in some of the films not considered in this chapter (particularly *Vigil*, 1984), but its relative marginality in the other texts justifies its exclusion from the list. Recently, in films such as *The Price of Milk* (dir. Harry Sinclair, 2000) or *Black Sheep* (dir. Jonathan King, 2006), the farm has gained prominence in terms of filmic representation as a place radically opposed to the urban space.

6. Rangitoto is a volcanic island in the Waitemata harbour in Auckland. Its distinctive symmetrical silhouette is a dominant landmark of New Zealand's biggest city.

7. Significantly, during the 1990s and the following decade the renegotiation of the settler relation with the land in a postcolonial society is reflected in a new representation of the ocean. In films such as *The Piano*, *Memory and Desire*, *Whale Rider* and *Rain*, the ocean becomes an explicitly threatening force and the recurrent theme of drowning seems to articulate the settler anxiety of a new relation to national identity.

8.    For a wider discussion of the liminal status of the beach see Chapters 3 and 4.

9.    See Chapter 3.

10.   In the South Pacific region the beach also has a historical role as the location of the cultural contract (Pearson, 1984).

11.   Martin Lefebvre has elaborated a very similar distinction between two different representations of space: setting and landscape. For Lefebvre, setting "is the place where the action or events occur" (Lefebvre, 2006: 21) while landscape is the space freed from the narrative and the main focus of the text.

12.   In his typology of the relation between the landscape and the narration, Bernardi also formulates two subcategories: the 'Time of Games' (*Tempo dei Giochi*) and 'The Openness to the Possible' (*Apertura sui possibili*). They represent, respectively, the transitional stages from 'Panorama' to 'Time of Myths' and from 'Time of Myths' to 'Time of Reflection' (Bernardi, 2002).

13.   According to structuralist semiotics theorists, the enunciation is "the domain which governs the passage from (linguistic) competence to (linguistic) performance" (Greimas and Courtes, 1982: 103). In other words, the enunciation is the process by which language virtualities are turned into discourse's utterances. The enunciator is the implicit sender of the enunciation (in a film, for example, the camera). For a more extensive discussion of the notions of enunciation and enunciator see Chapter 3.

14.   For a more detailed discussion of the analogies between *This is New Zealand* and *LOTR* see page 186 in Chapter 6.

15.   For a more detailed definition of 'interpellation' see page 73 in Chapter 3.

3

## The Legacy of *The Piano*:
## Film-Tourist Geographies and
## the Aesthetic of the Sublime

**Introduction**

The camera tracks along a rugged Auckland West Coast beach on a gloomy day. Two women walk along the shore. A blond young man calls out to them and asks (in a broad German accent): "Excuse me… I wonder… could you tell me: is this way they made ze film… ze Pi… ze Piano?" The opening sequence of *Topless Women Talk about their Lives* (dir. Harry Sinclair, 1997) acknowledges the iconic status of Karekare beach that, for more than a decade now, has been the destination of a film-tourist pilgrimage for visitors coming from all around the world (Harvey, 1994; Beeton, 2005). *The Piano* was the first New Zealand film[1] to achieve worldwide popularity. In 1994, one year after its release, it was estimated that the global takings of the film had reached $US 140 million (Crofts, 2000). The extraordinary critical response to Jane Campion's masterpiece was sealed by the winning of a Palme d'Or, three Oscars and several other prestigious international awards. The international success of *The Piano* also contributed to putting New Zealand on the global map for moviegoers who had previously never been exposed to images of the country. Ten years after the release of *The Piano*, another New Zealand global success, *LOTR*, has also made the country one of the world's most popular film-tourist destinations. Most of the critical commentaries about *The Piano* deal with its feminist commitment, postcolonial questions or stylistic issues (Coombs and Gemmell, 1999; Tincknell, 2000; Margolis, 2000). This chapter will draw from some of these works in order to present a conceptual framework for understanding the film tourism induced by *The Piano*.

**Methodological premises**

A textual analysis of *The Piano* reveals the possibility of a 'tourist' reading of the film, that in turn could further clarify the connection of tourist practices to the film locations. In particular, the thesis I suggest here is that the identification of the spectator/tourist with both the protagonist and the camera itself contribute to induce the visit to the locations depicted in the film. In order to reveal the way in which *The Piano* constructs and inscribes an ideal tourist/spectator within the filmic text, it will be necessary to adopt two different, but related, approaches: on the one hand, the semiotic analysis of the film landscapes, on the other hand, the dissection of the enunciative structure that underlines the film.

The second approach is based on the theoretical premises of Greimasian generative semiotics. Greimas defines enunciation (*énonciation*) as the linguistic domain logically presupposed by the existence of the utterance which contains traces (or markers) of the enunciation itself (Greimas and Courtes, 1982: 103). This latter governs the passage from linguistic competence to linguistic performance, from virtual semiotic structures to structures realised in the discourse. The enunciation in its turn involves the domains of the enunciator (*énonciateur*) and of the enunciatee (*énonciataire*). The enunciator is the implied sender of the enunciation and should be distinguished from the narrator (*narrateur*), which is a personification of the enunciator and is explicitly inserted within the discourse. Conversely, the enunciatee corresponds to the implied receiver of the enunciation. Once again, it is essential to distinguish the enunciatee from the narratee (*narrataire*), which is an actant recognisable within the utterance in sentences such as "The reader will understand that…" According to Greimas:

> The enunciatee is not only the receiver of the communication but also the discourse-producing subject: reading is a language act (a signifying act) in the same way as the actual production of discourse is a language (speech) act. The term subject of the enunciation […] in fact covers both actantial positions of enunciator and enunciatee. (Greimas and Courtes, 1982: 105)

It is also useful to remember that the enunciator and enunciatee should not be confused respectively with the film-maker and the film spectator. On the contrary, they are pure virtual positions waiting to be filled by actual 'bodies' (i.e. the real spectator) that can, therefore, renegotiate their role or the reading proposed by the filmic text.

The analysis of the enunciative structure of *The Piano* and the combined semiotic analysis of the landscape will assist in locating the position of the textual spectator within the film, while revealing its strategies of interaction with the film landscape.

## Ada McGrath: a Victorian adventure tourist in New Zealand

*The Piano* opens with a subjective shot; the spectator sees the scene through the eyes of Ada, the protagonist of the film, as she peeks through her interlaced fingers at the world around her (Figures 3.1 and 3.2). The voice-over of the same character provides the audience with the information necessary to start the narrative: she is mute and she has to leave Britain for New Zealand where she will marry an unknown settler.

The opening shot is a clear example of what Francesco Casetti defines as an "interpellation" (*interpellazione*), the moment in which the enunciator delegates the narration to a narrator who is directly addressing the enunciatee (Casetti, 1998: 138). In other words, the interpellation is the recognition by the film, in the form of a narrator or a voice-over, of someone outside the text (the spectator). The most important effect of the interpellation is an emphasis on the enunciation and the enunciative roles: *I* (enunciator) talk to *you* (enunciatee) through *her* (narrator). The second effect is the illusion that the enunciator disappears behind the narrator, who has taken control

Figure 3.1. *The Piano*, CIBY 2000, Jan Chapman Prod., AFC.

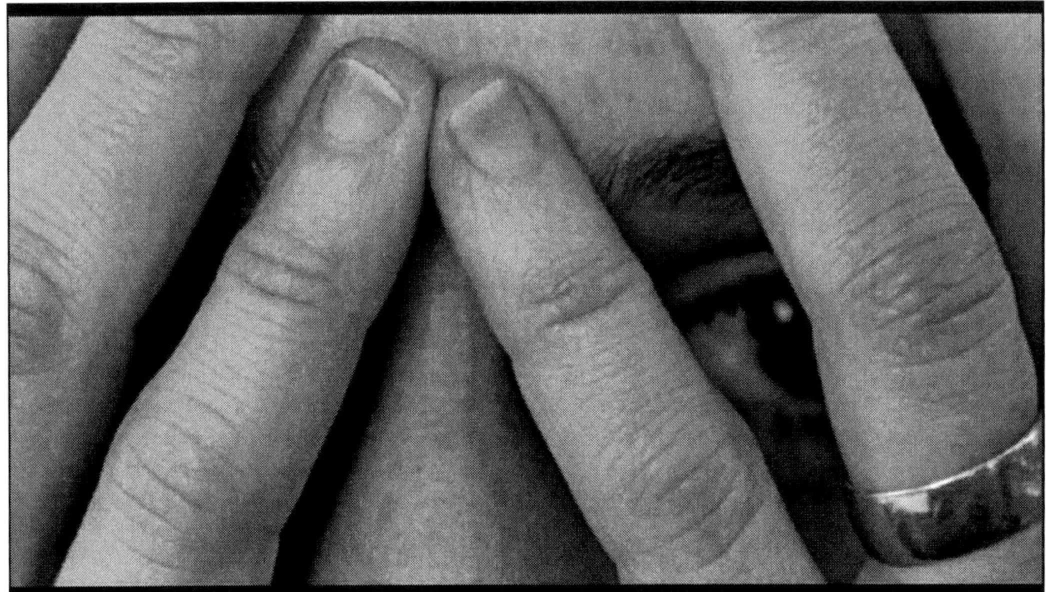

Figure 3.2. *The Piano*, CIBY 2000, Jan Chapman Prod., AFC.

over the narrative trajectory. The third, and final, effect of the interpellation is the identification: *she* (narrator) tells *you* (enunciatee) a story that *you* will see through *her* eyes. The identification, particularly that of the female audience, with the heroine Ada is confirmed by critics' emphasis on feminist readings of the film (Crofts, 2000: 152). The first sequence of *The Piano* apparently defines the enunciative roles and also the relations of power within the narrative: the narrator seems to be in control of the story and the spectator expects Ada to guide him/her throughout the rest of the film. In order to explain the rationale for the rupture of this enunciative structure by the second sequence, I shall discuss in more detail the geography of the filmic locations.

*The Piano* is the story of a journey. The film is characterised by a clearly symmetrical configuration of the places visited by Ada. The narration begins in Scotland, which represents civilisation and the familiar. Then, through the liminal spaces of the sea and the beach, it passes into the exotic and primitive world of New Zealand. Eventually, the heroine leaves, once again across the beach and the sea, for a different civilised place, understood as the settlement of Nelson in the South Island. The first sequence of the film opposes two places and establishes the necessity of a journey. The scene is set in Scotland, where Ada herself announces that she is about to leave for a 'distant country'.

The actual destination (New Zealand) is revealed by the writing on the packing case of the piano, an object which will become a symbol of civilisation and the familiar. The film introduces, from the outset, the distance and fracture between two geographical and psychological places; an opposition which will be reinforced throughout the rest of the film. In terms of a morphology of narrative places, Propp (1968) distinguishes two spaces present in the folktale: the 'own space', where the hero is born and grows up, and the 'other space', where s/he has to perform. Similarly, Greimas points out that every narration is divided into a 'topic space', where the subject acts, and a 'heterotopic space' (*espace hétérotopique*), where the subject stipulates a contract which will ultimately be sanctioned positively or negatively (Greimas and Courtes, 1982: 142). In the case of *The Piano*, the heroine has to deal with an actual contract, the wedding agreement arranged by her father, which obliges her to leave home for an unfamiliar place. As the analysis of the first shot has revealed, Ada gives the illusion of being in control in Scotland. From an aesthetic point of view this sense of control is reflected in the representation of the landscape. As Tincknell points out, the Scottish set is "flooded with shimmering sunlight and brightly lit, Technicolor hues" (Tincknell, 2000: 116). The use of bright colours in the prologue contrasts markedly

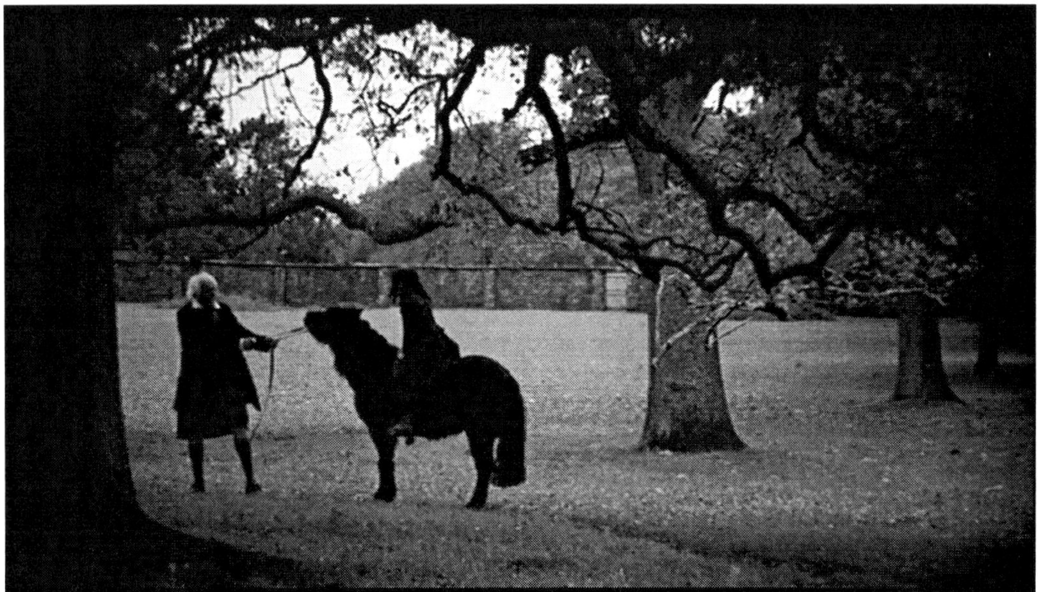

Figure 3.3. *The Piano*, CIBY 2000, Jan Chapman Prod., AFC.

with the palette of dark tones and blues that characterise the forest scenes in New Zealand. Similarly, the composition of the space is rationally and logically organised as is apparent from the first scene observed by Ada (where her young daughter Flora learns how to ride a pony), which is structurally framed by the black silhouettes of the trees (Figure 3.3).

If the analysis of the first sequence shows a narrator in power, whose gaze and voice structure both the space and the narration, the second sequence represents a mini revolution of this enunciative status. The arrival in New Zealand opens with a shot of the hull of the boat that is transporting Ada and Flora to the beach. This shot is what Casetti might define as an 'impossible objective view' (*oggettiva irreale*) (Casetti, 1998: 137). The main characteristic of the impossible objective view is that the scene is represented by an objective perspective that cannot be identified with the gaze of a specific diegetic character. Furthermore, the perspective of the shot is neither 'normal' nor transparent, but rather 'unreal'. This 'unrealism' implicitly emphasises, on the one hand, the presence of the enunciator and, on the other, the omnipotence of the camera (Casetti, 1998: 138). In the case of the shot described, the camera is looking up from the bottom of the sea to the hull of the boat, a perspective that would be clearly impossible for any diegetic character.

The use of an 'impossible objective view' in the very first shot set in New Zealand is particularly meaningful and entails two consequences. First, it highlights a shift in the power relationship in terms of the narration: the enunciator regains possession of the story and dislodges the narrator (Ada), who in the first scene was presented as the spectator's guide. This choice will prove to be consistent throughout the film as we will not hear the narrator's voice-over again until the last scene set in Nelson (heterotopic space of the sanction), which is specularly connected to the prologue (heterotopic space of the contract). The second consequence of the use of the impossible objective view is the establishment of a complicity between the enunciator and the enunciatee. As the enunciator denounces the narrator (Ada) as a fake authority, a sort of impostor, it reaffirms its power over the narration, the characters and spaces—a power which is therefore offered to the enunciatee. The enunciator is in fact proposing to the enunciatee an identification with the power and position of the camera, which has the ultimate control over the story. The shot of the hull of the boat from the deep sea is a trial of the strength of the enunciator. It would be possible to translate the intentions of the enunciator as such: "*I* can show *you* through *my* powerful eye things *you* couldn't see otherwise". Another important function of the hull shot is, of course, to represent metonymically the journey to New Zealand through liminal spaces (the sea and the beach), a shift which is also emphasised by the use of a different tonal palette (Figure 3.4). The presence of the sea, the beach and the very same shot of the bottom of the boat (this time leaving the beach) will recur at the end of the movie, the two shots functioning as the physical brackets of the narrative.

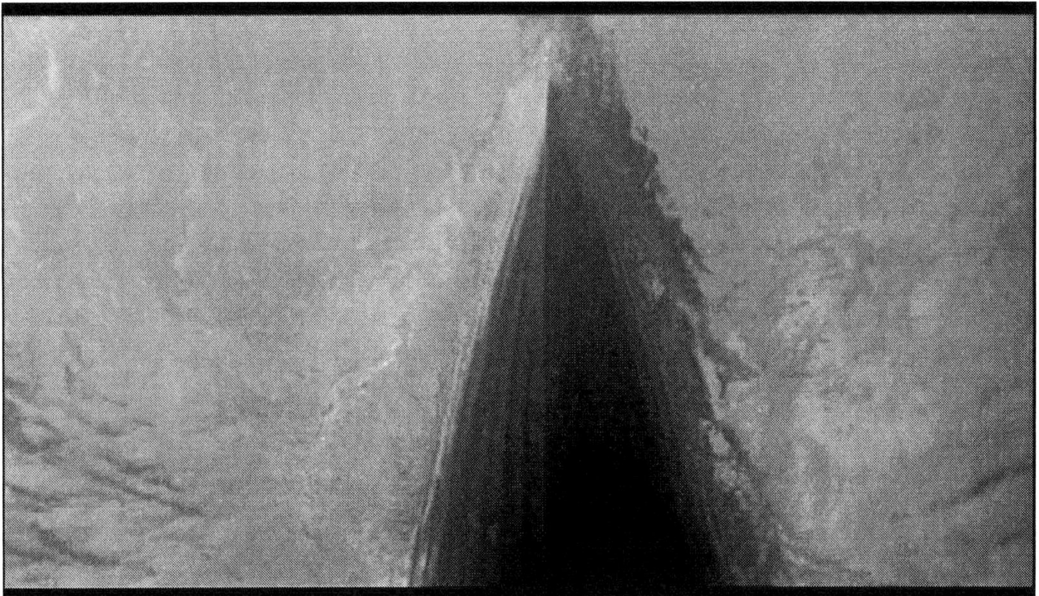

Figure 3.4. *The Piano*, CIBY 2000, Jan Chapman Prod., AFC.

As has been already mentioned, the beach is the place where the enunciator reaffirms its power over the narration and enacts its sadistic revenge on the narrator, Ada, who suddenly and unexpectedly loses control over the story. Thus, the precariously balanced heroine literally struggles when she is transported to the beach by the sailors, but she also struggles from the enunciative point of view as she is gradually erased from the scene by two extreme long shots of the beach (Figure 3.5). These shots celebrate the magnificence of the landscape, while further reducing the power of the protagonist. From this point of view the beach, which has become, along with the piano, the critical icon of the movie and a tourist destination, can be considered as a liminal place in two senses: on the one hand, it is a space of transition from the familiar to the exotic, the space where fear, desire and expectation merge (this is where Ada will wait to meet both Stewart and Baines for the first time), on the other, the beach is also a transition space which marks the passage of power from the narrator to the enunciator. As a result, the spectator may feel both shocked and dizzy, rather like Flora who vomits when she finally gets to the beach. The spectator's allegiance to Ada, established from the first shot through the use of a subjective point of view, the voice-over and the

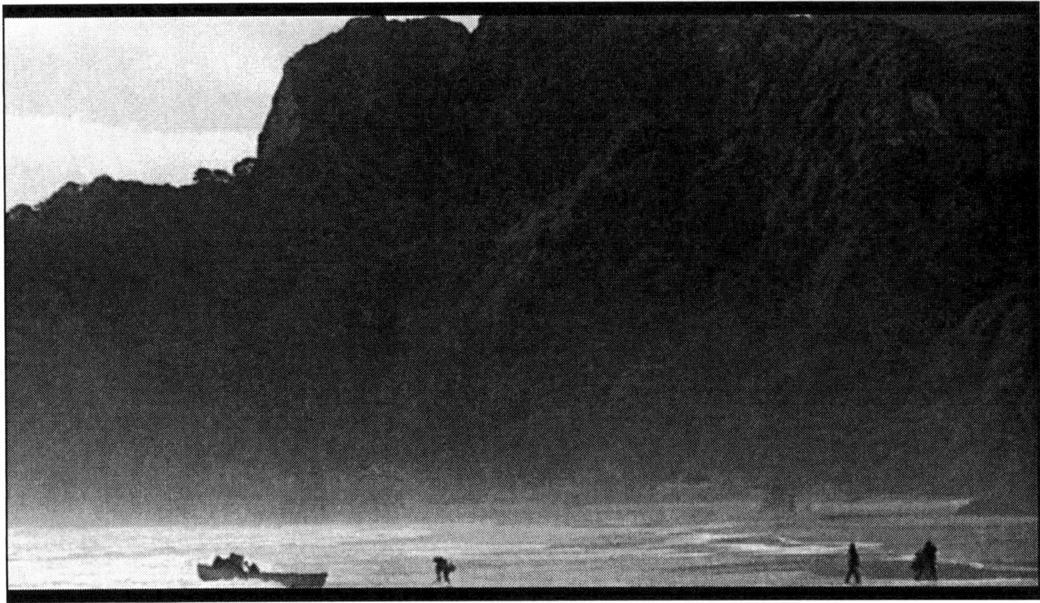

Figure 3.5. *The Piano*, CIBY 2000, Jan Chapman Prod., AFC.

awareness that she is obviously the film's protagonist, is powerfully challenged when she arrives in New Zealand. Both the heroine, and the spectator who identifies with her, are deprived of control over the narrative as Ada is crushed and flattened by the majesty of the landscape.

The similarity between the long shots of the arrival at the beach and eighteenth-century romantic paintings is evident. Both refer to the idea of the Sublime as defined by Edmund Burke, its major theoretician, as that which excites the emotion of self-preservation (Burke, 1998: 79). The favourite object of the Sublime is nature and particularly mountains, oceans, sky and storms, while its major qualities are terror, darkness, the superior power of nature and infinity. The aim of the Sublime is to produce a sort of pleasurable vertigo and delightful horror reflecting man's sensation of smallness in the face of nature's majesty. One of the devices used by romantic artists to enhance such effects was the insertion of human figures within the painting which could provide the viewer with the possibility of identification. In *The Piano*, this possibility is offered visually by the black silhouettes of the sailors and the protagonists (Figure 3.5). In witnessing the beach scene the spectator is caught in an ambiguous position: having recently identified with Ada as the narrator, s/he must share her experience of being deprived of power and shunted back and forth amidst a terrifying, dark landscape.

At the very same moment, however, in which the enunciator deprives the narrator of her privileges, the former holds out a hand to the enunciatee, proposing a safe viewing platform and establishing a new complicity with the ideal viewer. In this way, *The Piano* offers the spectator a double, simultaneous identification with both heroine and camera. The film spectator can be entangled within the diegesis and experience a sort of sublime emotion (as s/he previously identified with Ada) while at the same time observing the story from a distanced, safe position of power. In this position the viewer is able to master and control the elements (rugged sea, vast beach, majestic cliffs) which are threatening Ada. The film gaze in fact replicates a settler gaze which has already tamed the land. This point will be further developed in the next section of this chapter. For the moment it is important to underline the co-existence within the spectator of multiple beliefs, desires and expectations engendered by the film.

The existence of multiple beliefs is characteristic of the nature of cinema spectatorship itself which, according to Christian Metz, has its roots in the unconscious and fetishism in particular. As Metz points out:

> The fetish signifies the penis as absent, it is its negative signifier; supplementing, it puts a 'fullness' in place of a lack but in doing so it also affirms that lack. It resumes within itself the structure of disavowal and multiple belief. (Metz, 1983: 71)

The cinema, fetishist institution *par excellence*, articulates together the imaginary, the symbolic and the real, each of these twists presupposing a division of belief; the film requires then a whole series of stages of beliefs, imbricated together into a chain. Consequently, the spectator is not duped by the diegetic illusion, s/he is aware that the spectacle is fiction and yet for the film to work it is essential that this make-believe is respected (Metz, 1983: 72). It is this co-existence of multiple beliefs that ensures, for the spectator of *The Piano*, the simultaneous identification with both the protagonist and the camera.

The ambiguity that deeply marks the enunciative structure of *The Piano* finds a powerful analogy in the tourist experience itself. Some scholars, such as Boorstin, have defined tourism, and particularly the prefabricated experience of mass tourism, as a popular act of consumption (Boorstin, 1962: 93). Other authors claim that tourism is a form of escapism from the pressures of contemporary life, in that it offers 'new', 'real', 'authentic' experiences. MacCannell, for example, points out that tourists search for experiences that embrace authenticity as an antidote to the shallowness of their ordinary lives (1999: 160). He distinguishes between authenticity as feeling and as knowledge, claiming that tourists are often satisfied by a 'staged authenticity' that can better fit their expectations and desires. More radically, Boorstin points out that tourist experience articulates itself along the lines of a tension between risk and safety, the familiar and the unknown, claiming that tourists prefer their own provincial expectations to authenticity. The tourist experience is thus the complex result of the interaction between desire for (physical, cognitive, emotional) risk and desire for safety (Boorstin, 1962: 87).

This theory could explain the success of theme parks which provide tourists with hyper-real experiences that merge authenticity and illusion whilst also allowing total mobility within a safe and sterilised space, one conceived for the perfect tourist experience. The tourist experience articulates itself along the lines of a tension between risk and safety, the familiar and the unknown. Similarly, *The Piano* replicates this tension at different levels within the text itself. At the diegetic level the protagonist, and the spectator with her, experience risk lost in a foreign land, facing the overwhelming power of a rugged natural world and the threat of an unknown destiny. At the enunciative level, however, the spectator is safe and in control as, in complicity with the enunciator, s/he can replicate its comprehensive, powerful gaze over the landscape.

As has already been mentioned, *The Piano* is the story of both a physical and a psychological journey. Ada's character, therefore, could be read as a simulacrum of the traveller. This is particularly significant in light of the fact that *The Piano* has contributed to attracting thousands of tourists to West Auckland beaches. According to Boorstin (1962: 107), the modern mass tourist travels in guided groups, within the 'environmental bubble' of the familiar, and is insulated from the strangeness of the host environment. Similarly, once Ada is left alone on the beach surrounded by her luggage she creates a simulation of the familiar civilised world: in the surreal scenes of her first night in New Zealand she plays the piano and, like a Victorian proto-backpacker, camps under her hooped skirt. The skirt, a true 'environmental bubble', will save Ada again when Stewart attempts to rape her in the woods. In the latter scene, Ada falls over her skirt and seems defeated, but is eventually saved by her all-enveloping clothes, the symbol of Victorian femininity.[2]

Another interesting analogy between the tourist and Ada is provided by her muteness. One of the most common experiences for tourists overseas is the impossibility of establishing an independent and unmediated communication with the host environment and the local people. This situation is perceived as both the greatest appeal and the greatest risk of the tourist experience: the desire to 'get off the beaten track' and to meet the 'real people' clashes dramatically with the impossibility of communicating with the locals. This is why tourists need surrogate parents (travel agents, couriers, hotel managers) to take responsibility and protect them from harsh reality. In a similar way, Ada needs a 'mediator', a translator, here represented by Flora, in order to communicate with the external world. As Tincknell points out: "Flora in her tiny version of Ada's black bonnet and crinoline appears as a miniaturised mirror of her mother, mimicking her actions, moods and responses and giving verbal expression to Ada's views" (Tincknell, 2000: 111). One of the most significant tropes of the first part of the film is the inability of the protagonist to communicate with the 'local hosts'. For instance, the main problem in the relationship between Ada and Stewart is that the latter does not understand the importance that the piano has for his new wife. This is why the marriage between Ada and Stewart cements the bond between the woman and her daughter. It seems obvious that when Ada will finally be able to communicate with the local hosts, particularly Baines, she will no longer need Flora's translation support. The role of Ada's translator is occasionally transferred to the little notepad used by the heroine to write short sentences. The notepad is strangely reminiscent of the pocket dictionaries that provide tourists with keywords or basic sentences in a foreign language. In summary, the heroine is not in control of the narrative, the communication or the space and, as a consequence, seeks refuge in the familiar, namely the piano and her clothes.

**Nature, space and narrative**

As suggested, after the prologue the enunciator takes advantage of every scene to reaffirm its power over the narration and the space. The most common devices used are long shots of the landscape from a commanding vantage point, 'impossible objective views' or shots taken from unreal perspectives in order to underline the power of the camera, and shots of details of rugged nature in order to prove that the enunciator knows in advance the obstacles the characters will have to go through.

Another clear example of the 'impossible objective view' is the bird's-eye shot of the bush. This 'impossible objective view' holds a triple meaning. First, it is meant to reinforce the sense of complicity between enunciator and enunciatee (*I* can show *you* this and *you* are privileged because no one else is able to see it); second, it signifies metaphorically the journey of the characters as the camera moves forward trying to follow them; finally, it provides the opportunity to introduce a new character— nature—the power of which has been projected during the first sequences (when Stewart says: "Might I suggest that you prepare yourself for a difficult journey? The bush will tear clothing and the mud is very deep in places"). Nature is now presented as having an active role.

The sequence which follows opens with a shot of the mud and the feet of the characters who struggle to find a path through it. The scene confirms Stewart's warnings and the enunciator seems to take his side, as though saying: "Look at this mud, Stewart was right: nature is bad and cannot be trusted". A further confirmation of this concept is made by the Māori porters. In the film Māori are clearly assimilated to nature,[3] and in this particular scene the Māori with a facial moko embodies, for non-New Zealand audiences, the mysterious and potentially dangerous power of an alien nature. He claims that the group has to stop and change route as they are about to cross a *tapu* area. In Māori culture, the tapu area, often a burial ground, is one which is sacred. The explanation sounds irrational to Stewart and to the international spectator who lacks an understanding of Māori culture, as the detour will make the journey even longer and more difficult. After the above-mentioned scenes it seems as if the enunciatee has found in Stewart a new narrator who can align himself with the position of the enunciator. He is a 'local' and he gives the illusion of being in control of both what is good (rationality, common sense) and what is bad (nature).

Greimas (1983) claims that the relation between subject and space is inscribed within deep narrative structures. In this formulation, space could in fact actively oppose the project of the subject and should, therefore, be considered as an actant: a closed door, for instance, is an 'Opposer', an antisubject that is an obstacle to the potential programme of the subject. In the first part of *The Piano* space, and untamed space in particular (the sea and the bush), is constructed as an actant, an actual character of the story. Referring to the importance of the New Zealand bush in the story, Jan Chapman, the film producer, points out that "it was really a major player in the film. And now I also feel that it is very much part of New Zealand, that the relationship to the land is fundamental there" (Bilborough, 1993: 142). The bush, the mud and the mysterious dangers hidden in the untamed land stand between Ada and her main object of desire: the piano. Nature limits her mobility to the extent that she cannot freely move around without the presence of a 'local' guide (either Baines or Stewart). The implicit suggestion by the latter that nature is the actual 'villain' seems, therefore, to be justified. For a moment the spectator thinks s/he has found in Stewart a character who is apparently in control of the space, or at least someone who knows how to deal with it.

Nevertheless, in the following scenes the enunciator immediately undermines Stewart, as it once undermined Ada. The enunciator in fact reveals that Stewart's (and the settlers') attempts to establish control over the surrounding nature are ridiculous and inadequate. The staged photograph of the wedding is a clear example of this failure (Figure 3.6). The idyllic landscape of the painted backdrop, which represents Stewart's desire to establish control over the land, contrasts strikingly with the rugged New Zealand landscape which forms the real backdrop to the scene, as revealed by the real (extra-diegetic) camera. Similar scenes, such as the Bluebeard play with its fake English backdrop or Auntie Morag's failed attempt to establish a protective barrier against nature whilst urinating, have a similar function.

At the figurative level, the most obvious symptom of Stewart's inability to establish a real and positive control over nature is the depiction of the mangled, desert-like land that surrounds his house. The skeletons of the burned trees that inhabit Stewart's

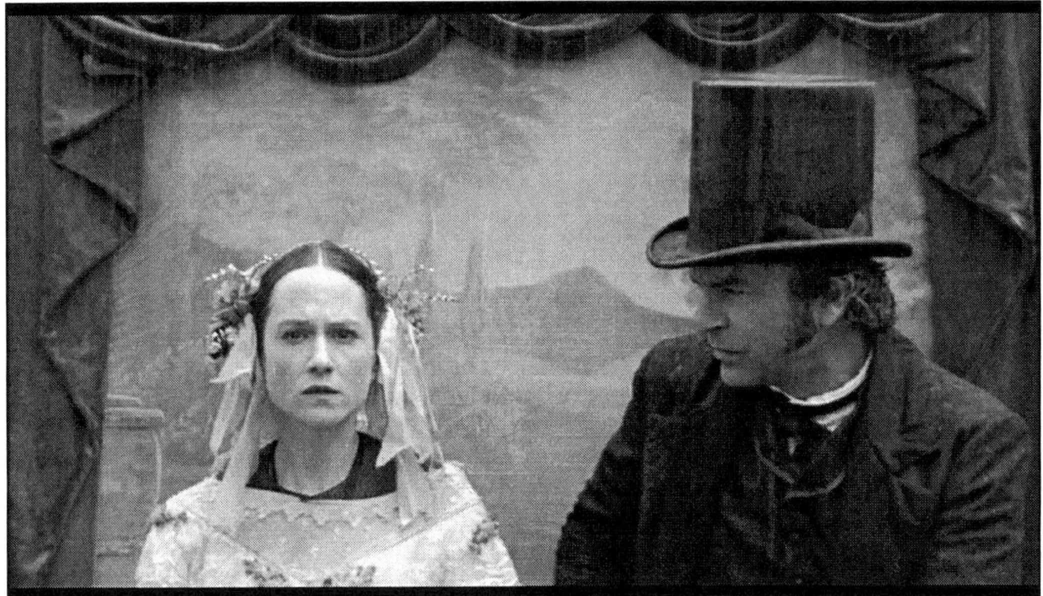

Figure 3.6. *The Piano*, CIBY 2000, Jan Chapman Prod., AFC.

property contrast strikingly with the lush vegetation around Baines' house. Baines has chosen to live with the Māori who are presented as an organic part of the wild New Zealand nature. Andrew McAlpine, the production designer, remembers how the film crew tried to alter the landscape in some way to enhance or heighten the mood of a particular scene. Referring in particular to the visual opposition between Stewart's and Baines' houses, he claims: "I wanted the bride to be seen to be drawn into this dank darkness that is Stewart's and then to step out into this green cathedral of *nikau* and *punga* that is Baines's life: a very gothic landscape surrounded by this cool green light" (Bilborough, 1993: 140). While the narrative unfolds, the balance of the relation between nature (bush, Māori community) and culture (Stewart, settler community) gradually changes. The space that was at first identified as a protection against external threats soon becomes the source of actual dangers. Stewart's house, a surrogate of the civilised world that Ada left at the beginning of the film, becomes in fact the space of enclosure and violence. It is in the very familiar domain of the domestic that Ada is first jailed and then mutilated when Stewart finds out about her true feelings for Baines. By contrast, Baines' home, initially deemed to be a threatening place as part of the untamed space of nature, is eventually revealed as a space of pleasure and liberation.

The relationship between these two spaces is reflected in the evolution of the two male characters. Drawing on Joanna Russ' categories of masculinity in the Gothic genre, Estella Tincknell claims that Baines and Stewart are, respectively, examples of 'Super-Male' and 'Shadow-Male' (Tincknell, 2000: 112). As Modleski summarises: "the former is almost always the apparent villain but the real hero, the latter is usually a kind, considerate, gentle male who turns out to be vicious, insane and/or murderous" (Modleski, 1982: 79). This dichotomy between civilised and natural space could be articulated through other oppositional categories such as sexual repression versus sexual liberation, conformity versus difference, violence versus pleasure.

The viewer of the film follows Ada's journey from the familiar environment to an exotic and hostile space, where she meets the local hosts, Stewart and the settler community. In this new setting, she has lost the control she used to have over the familiar and she is not able to really communicate with the 'hosts'. The viewer soon realises that the settlers are not the real 'hosts' as they have no genuine power over the space. They are, rather, a surrogate of the civilised world that Ada thought she had left behind. The authentic hosts are nature, the Māori and Baines, who is the personification of the host environment. The merging of Baines and the landscape is signified, on the one hand, by the tattoos on his face (that, because they are like unfurling fern fronds, visually blend with the bush) and, on the other hand, by his communication skills, particularly his ability to speak Māori, to read the bush and to understand the emotional, unconscious language of the piano. His organic relationship with 'nature' is also emphasised by his illiteracy, which further separates him from the settler community. Finally, it is also interesting to notice that Baines' character is played by the most famous actor of the cast, Hollywood star Harvey Keitel. The presence of Keitel appeals to the inter-textual memory of the movie spectator and makes Baines a familiar character for the audience. In turn, this familiarity connotes Baines as a positive character.

Ada carries out the encounter with the 'local', exotic world, represented by Baines/ Keitel and epitomised by the growing sexuality that he ignites, in opposition to the civilised, pseudo-familiar space which is actually one of violence and frustration. Interestingly, this latter opposition finds an analogy in the narrative structures of the tourist experience. As has been pointed out by Urry (2002: 11), in much tourism everyday obligations are suspended or inverted. This involves a permissiveness which revitalises tourists prior to their return home. The suspension of normal social conventions, facilitated by anonymity and freedom from collective scrutiny, particularly with respect to the modification of patterns of sexual behaviour, finds an extreme expression in certain forms of sexual tourism. In a sense *The Piano* is the story of a successful tourist experience, where the protagonist, a Victorian proto-adventure tourist, finds escape from the strict social conventions of bourgeois society and the frustrations of everyday life. Ada rejects the surrogate of the familiar represented by Stewart and the settler community (in a way the symbol of the fake tourist experience), preferring the authentic encounter with Baines, originally white and Scottish, but now perfectly integrated into the local environment and in harmony with the Māori.

The end of the film forms the closing bracket to the narrative. Once again the camera presents the 'impossible objective view' of the hull of the boat from below the surface of the sea. Ada leaves from the same beach where she originally landed; this time, however, she is accompanied by Māori rowers and not British sailors. She has accomplished her 'tourist' mission as she has successfully interacted with the local environment and broken through the repressive barriers that characterise the civilised world, in her case represented most powerfully by her desire to remain silent. The familiar environmental bubble represented by the piano is no longer necessary and is therefore thrown overboard. Ada gradually regains control over her life as she first decides to be dragged into the water along with the piano and then chooses to survive. She eventually re-establishes her control over the narration when she is safely back in civilisation, in Nelson. As in the prologue, the enunciator delegates to Ada's voice-over the task of summarising her experiences. Nelson is specularly connected to Scotland as both are civilised places. However, they differ significantly in that while the latter was the space of the contract (Ada has to travel to New Zealand to perform an action: marry Stewart), the former is the space of the sanction where the enunciator, the enunciatee, the narrator and the spectator set up rewards (for Ada and Baines who marry) and punishments (for Stewart). The same distinction between heterotopic space of the contract and heteropic space of the sanction could be applied to the tourist experience. Like the hero of a tale the tourist 'signs up' to a contract (desire or the need to escape the frustration of everyday life) that obliges him/her to leave the familiar space of home and work. At the end of the journey s/he always returns to the familiar space where s/he has to be sanctioned (by friends, family, himself or herself). More specifically, what is actually to be sanctioned is the tourist experience itself. The tourist will talk about his/her journey and express judgements about the quality of the destination, the tourist activities and the travel companions. Eventually, the tourist will display to the public view the physical manifestations of his/her experience (souvenirs, photos, suntan). In a similar, but much more dramatic way, at the end of the film Ada shows off her metallic finger, a physical sign of her tragic, though regenerating, experience.

To conclude this section it is useful to recall the relevance of the symmetrical and oppositional imaginative geography that shapes *The Piano*: the narrative passes from different places, each place being characterised by a different enunciative situation as shown by the following table:

| **Scotland** | **Beach** | **New Zealand** | **Beach** | **Nelson** |
|---|---|---|---|---|
| *civilised place* | *liminal place* | *exotic place* | *liminal place* | *civilised place* |
| Ada (narrator) in control | Enunciator takes control and establishes complicity with the enunciatee | Enunciator constructs landscape as an actual character of the story | Enunciator gradually hands over the power to Ada | Ada regains control over the narration |

It has been noted that, at both the narrative and enunciative level, *The Piano* displays many analogies with the tropes of the tourist experience. Ada's character in particular could be read as a simulacrum of the tourist: she leaves a familiar space on a journey to an exotic, untamed land where she is unable to communicate (for she is separated from the fetish of the familiar: the piano) and where she loses control over the space. She gradually experiences an authentic, dramatic encounter with the host environment (represented by Baines) as she rejects the surrogacy of the familiar world (Stewart and settler community). She eventually goes back to the familiar civilised world where she regains control over her life and the narrative itself. The spectator's identification with Ada has allowed him/her to experience the dramatic loss of control when faced with the overwhelming landscape, while the simultaneous identification with the camera has granted him/her the possibility to observe the story from a safer, 'tourist proof' position.

It is, however, evident that *The Piano* is not the story of a tourist experience. Ada's journey to New Zealand is not motivated by a tourist escapist desire for pleasurable destinations. Rather, she is obliged to leave, as victim of a patriarchal system that has planned her future and ignored her explicit will. Her stay in New Zealand has nothing in common with the leisure activities proposed by tourist brochures and, on the contrary, it ends with the tragic mutilation of her finger. Although *The Piano* is not a film about tourism or a 'tourist experience', it does explore mobility and its limits through a narrative of migration and settlement. Even though the experiences of migration and tourism are marked by profound differences, they nonetheless share some basic tropes such as the notions of travel and the opposition between the new and the familiar. This is particularly true in a postcolonial society such as New Zealand, where the settler gaze is likely to short-circuit the tourist gaze. In her documentary *Wake* (1994), Annie Goldson tells about her experience of migration to New Zealand in the 1960s. In the film, Goldson points out the strict interconnection between tourism, migration and settler enterprise by highlighting the striking resemblance between the amateur tourist footage (filmed by her father in order to convince his family to move to New Zealand) and the New Zealand landscape paintings of early settlers that were produced to be sent back to the metropolitan centre to solicit immigration (Goldson, 2006).

In the following sections I will analyse the way in which the spectator/tourist selects certain film-tourist destinations and excludes others and how, in the particular case of New Zealand, tourist texts absorb and replicate film texts through the mediation of settler culture.

## Locations and national identity

In order to create a filmic landscape which could effectively represent the lush differences of nineteenth-century New Zealand, the producers of *The Piano* had to shoot in various remote locations around New Zealand's North Island.[4] Many scenes were filmed 40 kilometres west of Auckland at Karekare, the location that features in the film as the beach where Ada first lands in New Zealand. Following the film's success, the beach has become both a popular film-tourist destination and a celebrated icon of New Zealand's rugged landscape. 'The beach of *The Piano*' has been referenced by most of the tourist guidebooks about New Zealand and it is considered by several authors as one of the most successful examples of film tourism (Le Heron, 2002; Beeton, 2005). No wonder then that the fame of the beach has recently been ironically acknowledged by a New Zealand movie, *Topless Women Talk About Their Lives*, that features Karekare and '*The Piano*-tourists'.[5]

*The Piano* was the first New Zealand film to generate a significant international tourist spin-off. In doing so, it initiated a film-induced tourism phenomenon which reached its peak a decade later with *LOTR*, the first blockbuster to be entirely shot in New Zealand. One of the main differences between *The Piano* and the *LOTR* tourist spin-off, however, is that the latter concerned dozens of film locations in both the North and South Islands, while the tourism induced by *The Piano* has been concentrated on Karekare beach. The popularity of the beach over other film locations, such as the bush or the settlers' village, is explained by several factors. First, some physical features of the beach (the black sand, the rugged waves, the outline of the cliff) give tourists the possibility of identifying the location as Karekare or at least as one of the West Auckland beaches. By contrast, the representation of the bush, a hybrid creation of distant and neighbouring places jigsawed together, does not provide us with any hint of the actual location of the settlements. Second, the relatively easy access to Karekare, just 40 kilometres west of Auckland, made the beach part of an established tourist circuit even before the filming of *The Piano*. Third, Karekare and West Auckland beaches in general are considered the ideal type of the New Zealand beach: empty, wild and untamed (Matthewman, 2006: 46). The emptiness of Karekare is precisely its appeal for international, particularly European, tourists seeking escape from crowded, metropolitan beaches. Furthermore, the local administrative body, Waitakere City Council, has actively encouraged film productions and film-induced tourism to West Auckland beaches (Thompson, 2000). These are all plausible and complementary explanations for the success of Karekare as a site for the film-tourist pilgrimage. However, the main reason for its popularity may be traced in the use of the landscape in the film and the significance of the beach in the narrative.

The beach represents for Ada an uncertain future in an untamed new world. The landscape in the arrival scene resonates with the protagonist's emotions, namely anxiety and loss of control. This is expressed through a number of technical devices, such as the use of grey tones or the long shots that emphasise the power of nature over the characters. But most importantly the beach is a liminal place, which connects the past and the future, the familiar and the unknown, arrival and departure. These features make the beach the most significant place in the story. At the visual level, the idea of 'liminality' is conveyed by the image of the piano stranded on the beach, an image so powerful that it has become *the* icon of the film. The image's impact derives from the disjunction between a sophisticated musical instrument and the wild beach, invoking a clash between nature and culture, civilisation and the primitive world. From this perspective, it is not surprising that *The Piano*'s landscapes, and the beach in particular, have become such popular icons of New Zealand. The image of the piano on the beach has in fact become a potent visual symbol of New Zealand itself, in its original blend of familiar European culture and 'exotic', wild nature. For the international spectators/tourists, *The Piano* is an imaginative map of the biculturalism of New Zealand society, a visual national monument that summarises the essence of a nation, like the Eiffel tower for France or the Coliseum for Italy.

The landscapes in *The Piano* have helped position New Zealand within the competitive global market for tourist destinations. If countries like England, France or Italy have mainly targeted art and heritage tourists, New Zealand has branded itself as the 'green, clean and wild country'. In discussing how *The Piano* has packaged New Zealand locations overseas, Anna Neill claims that "because of the way the film's luscious footage of remote bushes trades in the exotic, it brings New Zealand right into the global arena, offering its hardly touched landscape up to the tourist's (or foreign investor's) eye" (Neill, 1999: 137). The image of New Zealand that emerges from *The Piano* conforms to the marketing strategy adopted by the national tourism board. Research commissioned by Tourism New Zealand identified the country as rich in four assets: landscape, people, adventure and culture (Morgan et al., 2003). The tourist authorities thus designed a new positioning strategy, according to which New Zealand is "an adventurous new land and an adventurous new culture on the edge of the Pacific Ocean" (Piggott cited in Morgan et al., 2003: 293). The essence of the New Zealand brand, as conceived by Tourism New Zealand, and promoted to the world through the '100% Pure New Zealand' campaign, is therefore the landscape. The national tourism board has targeted the 'interactive traveller' who "seek[s] out new experiences that involve engagement and interaction, and demonstrate[s] respect for the natural, social and cultural environment" (TNZ, 2004: 1). One of the features of the interactive traveller, whose key reason to visit the country is interaction with the landscape, is that s/he is more likely to be a movie-goer and a high user of technology (TNZ, 2004: 1).

The characteristics of the interactive traveller remind one of that category of the 'new petty bourgeoisie' defined by Pierre Bourdieu as the 'intellectuals' (Bourdieu, 1984). The main features of Bourdieu's intellectuals are their preference for 'aesthetic-asceticism' expressed by their characteristic leisure activities (mountaineering, hiking, walking) and their fascination with 'natural, wild nature'. The intellectuals possess a cultural capital which is greater than their actual economical capital. This could partially explain their predilection for "the most culturally legitimate and economically cheapest practices, e.g., museum going, or in sport, mountain-climbing or walking" (Bourdieu, 1984: 267).

Another characteristic of the intellectuals is their constant quest for what Urry defines as the 'romantic gaze'. The romantic gaze emphasises a private and semi-spiritual relationship with the object of the gaze. In Urry's words: "The romantic gaze involves further quests for new objects of the solitary gaze, the deserted beach, the empty hilltop, the unhabited forest […] and so on" (Urry, 2002: 150). Similarly, the wild and untameable beach of *The Piano* is the ideal object of a romantic gaze, as the sense of isolation and remoteness conveyed by the film landscape is reinforced by the significance of the beach in the story. The real Karekare beach matches the expectations of tourists as there is no direct commodification of the site. While practically all New Zealand guidebooks mention Karekare as the beach-setting of *The Piano*, there are no tours dedicated solely to the film locations. Similarly, access to the beach is free and there is no signage on site to reveal its connection to *The Piano*. *The Piano*-tourist wishing to visit Karekare will often be able to reach the destination on his/her own and cast, therefore, a solitary gaze on a relatively untouched and uncommodified tourist site. The feeling of an individual, romantic 'discovery' of the tourist destination will therefore reactivate the memory of the cinematic identification with both protagonist and camera.

Even if the visual elements are essential components of the tourist experience, this cannot be limited to the activity of gazing, but instead involves multi-sensorial engagement and bodily involvement (Perkins and Thorns, 2001: 186). In *The Piano* the roar of the waves combined with the music of the piano plays a crucial role in emphasising the romantic, sublime character of the beach scenes and in enhancing the uniqueness of the Karekare location. From this point of view, further research is needed in order to analyse the impact of the popular soundtrack of the movie by Michael Nyman on influencing travel decisions to the film locations.[6]

## Framing the beach

The New Zealand Film Commission was the first institution to recognise the potential spin-offs generated by *The Piano* for New Zealand. According to film commissioner Lindsay Shelton, even before the triumphal Oscar ceremony where *The Piano* received three Academy awards (Campion, best original screenplay; Hunter, best actress and Paquin, best supporting actress), the film was creating interest in New Zealand with particular benefits for tourism and export (Shelton cited in NZPA, 1994: 24). After the Oscar success, the Trade Development Board and the Film Commission used stills from *The Piano* in a brochure about international investment in New Zealand. Nevertheless, not everybody shared the same optimism about the film's capacity to attract more tourism and foreign investment. Tourist Board chief executive David Beatson, for example, was strongly opposed to using the film as a tourist promotional

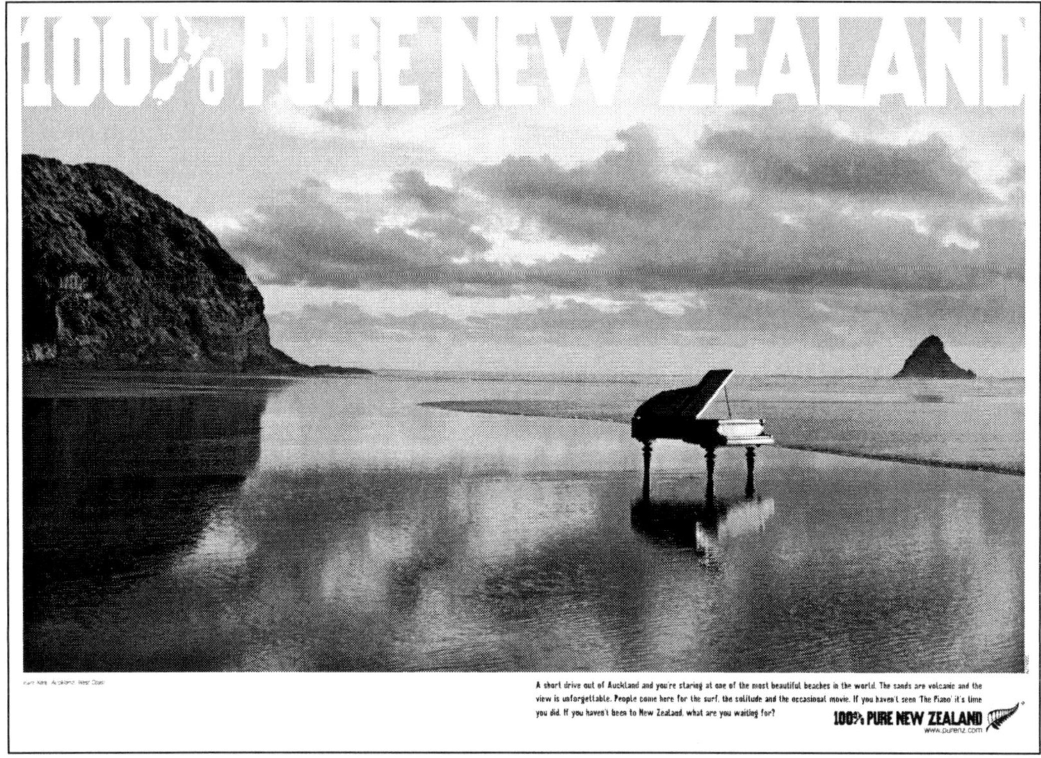


Figure 3.7.  MC & Saatchi for Tourism New Zealand, 2001.

tool on the grounds that the Karekare beach settings and the dense bush images were too muddy and gloomy, unlikely to attract holiday-makers. Furthermore, the film was considered too 'arty' to cash in on, as it was thought that the very people to whom the film appealed would be put off by any attempt to capitalise on it. Managers of other destination marketing organisations were more long-sighted than Beatson. Saatchi & Saatchi chief executive Peter Cullinane, for example, referring to the movie's potential spin-off, claimed that "Some of the best tourists to this country are backpackers, who would relate to the scenery. It would appeal to the environmentally aware tourists" (Hill, 1994: 48). Time has proved Beatson wrong as, on the one hand, Karekare has become a film-induced tourism site and, on the other hand, the Waitakeres have achieved an international profile as a film production area (Harvey, 1994; Thompson, 2000).

In 2001, increasingly aware of the global profile films achieve and create, Tourism New Zealand used an image inspired by *The Piano* in its international advertising campaign '100% Pure New Zealand' (Figure 3.7). The promotional poster created by the Sydney Saatchi & Saatchi agency is not a still from *The Piano*, but is a staged picture that features some elements not present in the original film. A semiotic analysis of the poster will cast new light on the complex relationship between film and tourist language.

The analysis of the signifier of the poster reveals that it is divisible into three horizontal sections. An upper band that contains the logo of the advertising campaign (100% Pure New Zealand), a central section that in technical terms is defined as the 'visual' and a lower band that contains both the 'claim' of the advertisement and the logo in smaller font. The picture in the central section echoes the visual composition of the original scene from the film, dominated by horizontal lines: the clouds, the horizon, the waves and the piano. These lines generate the sense of infinity and untameable power that, in the film, highlight Ada's isolation and powerlessness in the face of nature's primitivism. Unlike the film, though, the horizontal lines are framed by two vertical black silhouettes: the edge of the range on the left and the small rocky island on the right. In the centre of the picture, at the crossover between the beach and the sky, is the piano. The latter, a blend of vertical and horizontal lines, is in turn framed horizontally by two white bands and vertically by two black rocks. *The Piano* is therefore positioned as the focal point of the picture. It is worth noticing that the piano depicted in the poster is different from the instrument in the film in at least two aspects. First of all, it is a grand piano, an even more sophisticated object than the original one; second, the instrument is open and ready to be played: a clear visual invitation to the viewer. Both characteristics contribute to making the presence of the piano on the beach even more surreal than it was in the film. Furthermore, the piano cannot be separated from its reflection on the water which is blurred, almost a dreamlike image or a mirage. Viewers of the poster, although aware that no such piano exists in this location, will be inclined to project onto the real beach its virtual image. The ghost of the piano will inhabit the beach forever.

The textual analysis of the 'claim' in the lower band reveals that the enunciator is directly addressing the enunciatee: "A short drive out of Auckland and you're staring at one of the most beautiful beaches in the world". The first sentence establishes an informal relationship that reminds one of the conversations typical between backpackers. Nevertheless, if we analyse the content of the sentence in relation to the visual composition of the picture, the enunciation becomes more assertive. The enunciator, in fact, is not only suggesting a mode of action (staring), but has already framed the picture, implicitly confirming the right way to view it. In the rest of the 'claim' the enunciator suggests other possible activities ("People come here for the surf, the solitude and the occasional movie") and reinforces the link between *The Piano* and New Zealand ("if you haven't seen 'The Piano' it's time you did") implying that the movie is the first step to the exploration of the country.

Finally, in the left corner of the lower band, the author of the poster provides the reader with objective information concerning the advertisement's location ("Karekare, Auckland, West Coast"). In turn the image includes characteristic features of the beach (black sand, ranges, small rocky island) that make the location recognisable.

The semiotic analysis of the poster could be further extended. Nevertheless, from this introductory examination several points can be made:

- The poster, unlike the film, makes the identity of the location explicit through the use of both textual and visual elements.

- The visual composition of the poster is marked by the opposition between horizontal lines (signifying infinity, remoteness and power of nature) and vertical lines that frame the picture and consequently control this power.

- The surrealism of the icon of the film, the piano on the beach, is reinforced through the use of a grand piano and the simultaneous presence of its simulacrum, the reflection of the piano on the water.

- The enunciator prompts, both through the text and the visual structure of the poster, the right way of experiencing the beach. It has already pre-constructed and pre-packaged a tourist gaze that is now ready to be replicated by the tourist.

The analysis of the '100% Pure New Zealand' poster provides the opportunity to investigate analogies and differences between tourist and film language, particularly as in this case the object represented (the beach) is the same for both media.

The differences between the media arise from the different interests and goals that characterise film and tourism industries respectively. The ultimate aim of the film-makers is to sell their final *product*, the movie, while the destination marketing organisations mainly deal with selling a *location*. In the case of *The Piano*, even when the landscape played an essential role in the story, it was always a function of the film as a whole. The logical consequence of this is that film-makers are not interested in the recognisability of the film landscape. The latter is by definition purely functional to the narrative and often comprises a jigsaw of different real places. The geographical imagination of the film-makers strongly influences the choice of the location: the story has an ideal place associated with it and the location must enhance the narrative. In the case of *The Piano*, it is quite fortunate that Campion's beach has remained quite true to the actual Karekare location. This very fidelity could account for the attraction of visitors to the beach.[7] By contrast, the priority of tourist advertisements is to facilitate the recognition of the potential tourist destination. As noted of the '100% Pure New Zealand' advertisement, the designers emphasised the characteristic features of Karekare: black sand, forested cliff, rocky island and the association with the filming of *The Piano*. The need for commodification implies that the location has to be charged with values and narratives that meet consumers' desires. In other words, in the film the idea comes first and the choice of the actual location is secondary; whereas tourist professionals create a story around an already existing place. The possibility of clearly identifying this place is thereby essential for any subsequent form of the location's commodification.

The second main difference between film and tourist texts concerns the relative emphasis on the narrative and the enunciative structure. In most movies the narration has a prominent role: even within the constraints of seriality and genre categories, the feature film usually tells an original story that involves the action and interaction of one or several fictional characters. Apart from some exceptions, such as the presence of a narrator, the use of voice-over or subjective shots, the enunciative structure of a movie is generally 'transparent'. The enunciator shows the enunciatee a scene from an impersonal point of view. Very seldom does a film stress the enunciative roles: rather, the presence of *I* (enunciator, camera) and *you* (enunciatee, virtual spectator) is hidden or disguised. By contrast tourist texts tend to play down the importance of the narrative. The stories told by tourist brochures or advertisements are inevitably unoriginal as they employ standard recurrent tropes: lying on a beach under the sun, gazing at exotic landscapes, enjoying fine traditional food. Nothing disturbing or dramatic ever happens, as conflict and pain are always removed from the tourist narratives. Rather, the tourist texts play with the visual pleasure generated by the destination image by anticipating and stimulating the hedonistic behaviour of the potential tourist. Similarly, tourist texts emphasise the enunciative roles within the narration: tourist brochures are full of personifications of the enunciator (narrator) and the enunciatee (narratee). This enunciative strategy creates or reinforces the bond between an ideal guide and an ideal tourist: the reader of the tourist text can therefore identify with the narratee, the tourist represented in the brochure, and be more likely to accept the narrator's arguments. The process is not as automatic as it may seem, for the reception of the text will be different for every physical reader.

The '100% Pure New Zealand' poster is a clear example of the traditional enunciative structure of a tourist text. The narrative is predictable as the pattern of activities allowed on the beach is limited by the text of the advertisement: tourists can 'stare' at the beach, enjoy surfing or solitude. Conflict is erased and escapist desire enhanced by the appeal of the picture. In the same way, the enunciator establishes a direct informal relationship with the enunciatee while explicitly constructing an ideal reader/tourist. The ideal tourist prefers 'romantic gazes', is young and likely to engage with the landscape: these characteristics obviously recall the social figure of the 'interactive traveller' described earlier.

The final difference (or partial resemblance) between film and tourism language refers to the compositional modes and frames of the landscape. As has already been mentioned, in most of *The Piano* the enunciator establishes a clear control over the landscape; the film frames the land in a way that draws upon conventional ways of seeing, namely, the classic European figurative traditions of the early British settlers. Laurence Simmons points out the analogies between *The Piano*'s landscapes and paintings by early New Zealand settlers. As Simmons notes, these similarities are evident in the employment of devices such as "a commanding vantage point; the syntax of the sublime; the planar logic of foreground, middle distance with an object of interest, and a light-saturated horizon; its patently staged theatricality" (Simmons, 1999a: 126).

Other signs of the collapse of the film gaze into the settler gaze are present in the depiction of the Māori and the flora. In his work on early New Zealand landscape painters, Francis Pound demystifies the myth of an unmediated representation of New Zealand nature, claiming that access to the pure and original land is impossible (Pound, 1983). The very act of seeing is an act of possession and displays an unequal relationship of power between the seer and the seen. As Foucault reveals in his analysis of medical power, the doctor represents the ideological norms and is permitted to gaze from a position of power at the patient, who represents the deviation from such norms. The patient is the Other, as Foucault argues: "the clinic was probably the first attempt to order a science on the exercise and decision of the gaze [...] it was no longer the gaze of any observer, but that of a doctor supported and justified by an institution" (Foucault, 1973: 89). Urry, drawing on Foucault's theory, claims that the tourist gazes at the visited place and people from a position of power, imposing his/her own ideological norms. The tourist compares what is gazed at with the familiar and in doing so s/he reproduces his/her expectations (Urry, 2002: 1).

The colonial legacy is active in *The Piano* through the influence of European ways of framing the land: the sublime representation of the landscape in the film consistently draws upon the myth of a wild, pure, natural New Zealand, one that vitally underpins New Zealand settler culture. The same rhetoric also appears in the tourist field, particularly in the '100% Pure New Zealand' brand. The film provides the tourists with a controlled image of 'exoticism', which tourists both seek and repossess through the imaginary frame of the filmic souvenir and the actual frame of the camera. The 'hermeneutic circle' is eventually closed: the settler gaze initially possessed the land, the film gaze synthesised the settler gaze and the tourist gaze repossesses the land, looking for the filmic images that were seen at home.

## Return to the beach: *Memory and Desire*

The panoramic views of Karekare's cold tides as depicted in *The Piano* became the distinctive mark of New Zealand for film viewers all around the world. According to Lydia Wevers, the landscape in the film functions as "an authenticating context for a narrative which encoded 'New Zealand' to foreign audiences" (Wevers, 1994: 1). Viewers were struck by the uniqueness of the dark West Coast beaches and the dense, subtropical bush. And yet the film landscape was constructed according to Western modes of representation. The distinctiveness that characterised the film locations did not alienate Western viewers as it was framed within the familiar canon of the sublime. This representation of a 'tamed otherness' was particularly congenial to the tourist industry, which later exploited the image of the country produced by *The Piano*.

Subsequent New Zealand films such as *Once Were Warriors* (dir. Lee Tamahori, 1994) and *Topless Women Talk about their Lives* (1997) implicitly or explicitly commented on the role of film and tourism in the process of landscape commodification. These films acknowledge the global resonance of the image of New Zealand landscape constructed by *The Piano* and other local films. The opening sequence of *Once Were Warriors*, for example, shows an idyllic New Zealand country landscape which fills the frame. However, as the camera gradually zooms back it reveals a gritty urban setting, within which the rural landscape appears only on an advertising billboard. The opening of the film does not simply oppose the tourist imagery of the country with the harsh city-life of South Auckland, it is also an (ironic) reference to the plethora of New Zealand films that begin with establishing shots of the country's natural beauty.

The deep interconnection between film landscape and tourist imagery in the New Zealand context is one of the themes of *Memory and Desire*, directed by Niki Caro. The film tells the story of a Japanese couple, Keiji and Sayo, on their honeymoon in New Zealand. Sayo, a humble secretary, is attracted to Keiji who is both younger and of higher extraction. The couple decide to marry despite the objections of Keiji's mother. In order to escape the constraints of Japanese society the two lovers travel to New Zealand, where they celebrate their marriage and travel through the country on a tourist bus. However, Keiji becomes depressed when it seems he cannot consummate their marriage. During a stop at a wild surf beach he mysteriously drowns. Japanese tradition dictates that Sayo must return to live with her hostile mother-in-law. However, she eventually returns to New Zealand, where she starts living in a cave near the beach where Keiji died. In the cave Sayo suffers mental collapse and has sexual intercourse with a local fisherman, who she believes to be Keiji.

The film is based on the short story 'Of Memory and Desire'[8] by Peter Wells but it makes several amendments to the original text. While Wells' story deals mainly with contemporary gay life in New Zealand, the focus of the film shifts instead to the relation between New Zealand landscape and the love affair of the two Japanese tourists. In Wells' novel, it is clear that the couple does not succeed in making love because Keiji's impotence is a consequence of his homosexuality. The film, however, is not coloured by the question of Keiji's sexuality and the outcome of the last lovemaking scene is deliberately ambiguous. According to producer Owen Hughes, Caro's original plan attempted to follow the linear narrative structure of the short story. The director went as far as shooting a scene where Sayo sees Keiji falling from the rocks and drowning in the sea. In the editing phase, however, the film-makers decided to open the film with a scene of Sayo and Keiji kissing in the cave, thus altering the linear structure of the film and creating a narrative 'hole' between the moment when the protagonists kiss in the cave and Keiji's drowning (Hughes, 2008). As a result, the film implicitly suggests that the couple might have had sex in the cave where Keiji carves the word 'love' just before the tragedy. Keiji's death in the film does not appear to be suicide but simply a surf accident, an interpretation confirmed by the high seas and the reported death of other tourists in the same location. Some film critics and reviewers (Sayle, 1999) did not question the hypothesis of the accident while others explicitly claimed that the couple eventually manages to have sex in the cave (Stewart, 2008).

As in *The Piano*, Caro's film landscape is much more than a background for the film's narrative: the wild landscape directly interacts with the story of the young couple. In terms of Propp's narrative functions, the landscape initially acts as a '(magical) Helper' 'curing' Keiji's impotence and providing the couple with a place (the cave) at the border between nature and culture, a place which is exclusively theirs. Later it becomes an 'Opposer' irremediably tearing the two lovers apart and pushing Sayo to the edge of madness (Propp, 1968).

The film deals with the protagonists' quest for liberation from the constraint of an oppressive society: the unfolding narrative resonates in the aesthetic metaphors of the film's setting. The film features a scene which is completely absent in the novel: Keiji and Sayo's first meeting in a love hotel. The love hotel's contrived wilderness— that attempts to simulate a tropical forest—is the only nature that can be found in the intensely claustrophobic Tokyo. The urban setting of the opening scenes is then opposed to the sublime New Zealand landscape, which represents a radical alternative to the ordinary tourist routes. Similarly, within New Zealand the tour depicted in the film unfolds along the lines of a continuum that goes from the most commodified tourist destinations such as the MOTAT and Rotorua's spa to the 'authentic' place *par excellence*: the wild West Coast beach. Keiji's impotence is reflected in the sterile and anonymous character of the different rooms that the couple stay in every night. The only place where the newlyweds seem to consummate their marriage is the cave near the beach in which Keiji drowns soon afterwards.

Sayo's subsequent return to the cave might be interpreted as a quest for the preoedipal. There, Sayo has a sexual relationship with a local fisherman whom, in her state of mental confusion, she believes to be Keiji. From this point of view, the film's evocation of the preoedipal could be explained by Kristeva's distinction between what she defines as the 'semiotic' and the 'symbolic' (Kristeva, 1985: 216–17). According to Kristeva, the symbolic is "the functioning of the signs and predications. The symbolic is initially constituted in what the psychoanalyst calls the mirror stage and the consequent capacities for absence, representation or abstraction" (Kristeva, 1985: 216–17). Kristeva goes on to observe that "language as symbolic function constitutes itself at the cost of repressing instinctual drives and the continuous relation with the mother" (Kristeva, 1980: 136). In the film the ordained and claustrophobic urban spaces where Keiji is unable to maintain an erection can be read as the repressive places of the symbolic. Furthermore, the film is characterised by a proliferation of windows and screens: the glass doors of the hotel bathroom, the subway and the bus window, the veils of white smoke in Rotorua and the lens of the camera that the protagonists use to film each other. These transparent screens are at once a point of connection with, and a barrier which prevents access to, both the preoedipal landscape and the couple's love. Sayo's passionate kisses to the glass door of the hotel bathroom and to the underground train window reflect the repressive power of the symbolic places (in the Kristevian sense of the word) inhabited by the protagonists.

The meaning of the film's emphasis on the notion of screen/barrier might be better understood within the theoretical frame of Lacan's works on the 'Gaze'. According to Lacan, the screen is the point of intersection between the Gaze and the picture and therefore it is the focal point of desire. Lacan claims, in fact, that the Gaze refers to the uncanny sense that the object of our eyes' look is somehow looking back at us of its own will. The gazer may believe that s/he is in control of his/her glance; however, any feeling of power is always undone by the fact that the materiality of existence, the Real, always exceeds the meaning structures of the symbolic order. By having the object of our gaze *look back at us*, we are reminded of our own lack, of the fact that the symbolic order is separated only by a fragile border from the materiality of the Real (Lacan, 1978).

Lacan goes on to suggest that there is an intimate relationship between the *objet petit a* (which co-ordinates our desire) and the Gaze (which threatens to undo all desire through the eruption of the Real). At the heart of desire is a misrecognition of fullness where there is really nothing but a screen for our own narcissistic projections. It is that lack at the heart of desire that ensures we continue to desire. However, because the *objet petit a* (the object of our desire) is ultimately nothing but a screen for our own narcissistic projections, to come too close to it threatens to give us the experience precisely of the Lacanian Gaze, the realisation that behind our desire is nothing but our lack: the materiality of the Real staring back at us (Lacan, 1978). From this point of view, the cave is not only a physical hole in the rock, or even a narrative hole (in that we ignore what happens between the scene in the cave and Keiji's death) but also a 'hole of desire'.

Sayo's gaze through screens and windows may be read as a projection of her desire to escape from the symbolic order into the preoedipal, identified, in tourist terms, as the 'authentic'. Before reaching the beach where the tragedy will take place the two characters retrieve a postcard from the ground and give it to another member of the tour who is sitting on a bench at the edge of the beach. Throwing away the postcard, the characters symbolically exchange a framed, mediated experience of the place for an authentic one. The protagonists thus attempt to remove the barriers that separate them from the real through a return to the semiotic register. Kristeva defines the semiotic as:

> [T]he primary organisation (in Freudian terms) of drives and rhythms, intonations and primary processes. […] Plato speaks of this in the *Timaeus*, in his invocation of a state of language anterior to the word, even to the syllable, and which, quite different from the paternal name, has a maternal connotation. Plato calls this the chora, the receptacle, the place before the space which is already named, one, paternal sign and predication. (Kristeva, 1985: 216)

The beach and the cave where Keiji inscribes the word 'love' is the chora in Kristevian terms. The only time Keiji is able to perform a (symbolic) erection is hand-standing on the beach as a kid. He briefly repeats the performance in New Zealand just before drowning. Similarly, in the cave Sayo strips herself of any signs of the symbolic order: words, clothes, cooked food. It is as if the New Zealand landscape—with its "eerie prescience, unsoftened by human form" (Wells, 1991: 171)—offers an escape from the symbolic order.

The utopic return to the preoedipal has tragic consequences, however, as it implies the eruption of the Real and the exposure of the lack at the heart of desire. Keiji dies as if driven away by the "hunger and appetite" of Sayo's desire. As she suffers a mental collapse in the 'semiotic' cave, Sayo is confronted with her own lack, or to use the Lacanian terms: 'the materiality of Reality staring back at her'. She eventually goes back to Tokyo where, in the last sequence of the film, she gazes out of the train window to the (imaginary) view of the beach. The barrier between the Real and the symbolic order is now safely restored in her memory.

*Memory and Desire* is a film about the tourist quest for 'authenticity'. The New Zealand tourist brochures promise an escape from the constraint of everyday life which is partially disappointed by the actual tourist experience of the newlyweds. The crowded and claustrophobic space of the bus echoes the contrived urban setting the protagonists were initially trying to escape. Similarly, the commodified tourist attractions of the first days of the tour offer an equally unauthentic encounter with a tame nature. Rotorua's volcanic activity—domesticated by the presence of tourist platforms—reflects Keiji's repressed sexuality. The only chance for an authentic encounter with the "so green so clean so empty" (Wells, 1991: 169) New Zealand landscape occurs when the young couple leave the tour party to wander out on the beach. The location of the beach within the economy of the film narrative is particularly relevant. While the crucial part of Wells' story was set on a generic beach in the South Island, Caro's film was shot at Piha, just kilometres away from Karekare, the location of *The Piano*. Most of Auckland's tourist websites claim that the film was actually shot at Karekare (View, 2008; Tourism Auckland, 2008). The belief that Karekare was the film location of *Memory and Desire* clearly alludes to the film tourist imagery generated by Campion's film: the construction of the landscape as a terrain of otherness depends on the extra-textual reference to *The Piano*. According to Owen Hughes "it's one of those myths that attach to films probably because people wish it had been shot there, it gives them more symmetry" (Hughes, 2008). The 'authenticity' of the beach location is validated by the adoption of another film's setting. Interestingly, the selling of *Memory and Desire* was handled by CIBY Sales, a subsidiary company of the French CIBY 2000 which was in turn one of the main investors in *The Piano*. The manager of CIBY Sales Wendy Palmer (aka Wendy 'Palme D'Or' because of her previous success at the Cannes Festival with *The Piano*) tried to take advantage of *The Piano* spin-offs while marketing *Memory and Desire*. At the 1997 Cannes market, when Caro's film was in post-production stage, Palmer created a poster of the film that did not use any of the stills sent by the New Zealand producers. Instead she used a Don Binney-like[9] image of a West Coast beach that was reminiscent of the Gothic aesthetic of *The Piano* (Figure 3.8).

The similarities between *The Piano* and *Memory and Desire* are not limited to the beach location. Both films display a similar narrative structure. Like *The Piano*, *Memory and Desire* opposes the space of 'culture' (the artificial nature of the love hotel) to that of 'nature' (the dramatic beauty of the beach). Both female protagonists camp on the beach and experience love with a local (Baines in *The Piano* and the

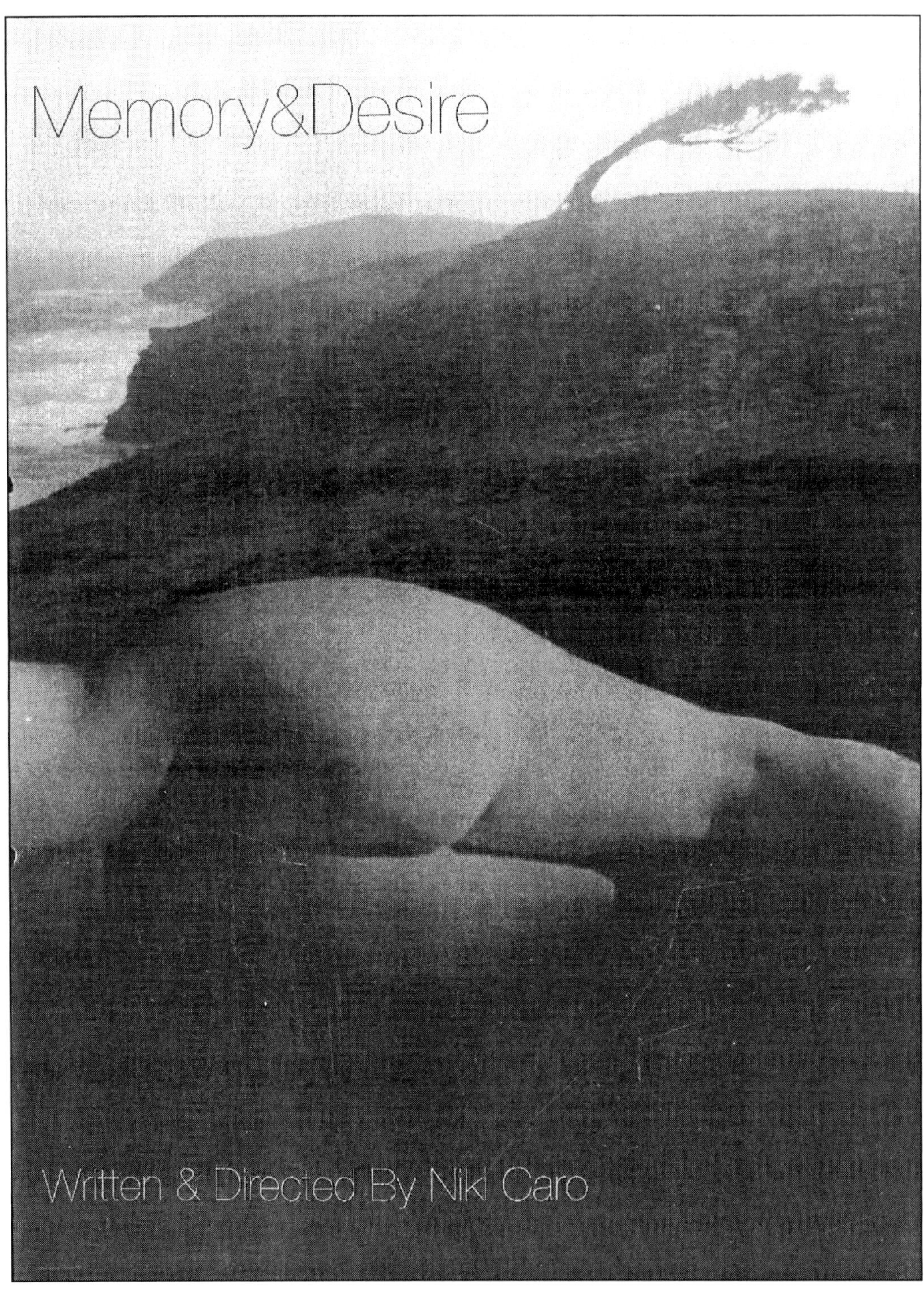


Figure 3.8.  CIBY Sales, 1997.

fisherman in *Memory and Desire*). Significantly, in both cases the male characters are unarticulated and assimilated to nature (the fisherman is always shown on the beach or in the proximity of it). The wholly speechless character of the fisherman, in fact, reminds the viewer of the illiterate Baines. The encounter between female and male characters occurs beyond the register of the symbolic in the preoedipal chora. Eventually, in both films the protagonists return to the civilised world taking back with them a tragic memory of the 'sublime': Ada's chopped finger and Sayo's daydream vision of the beach.

However, Sayo represents an evolution of Ada's character. While Ada is a traveller/settler, Sayo is a tourist. *Memory and Desire* re-presents the same 'hermeneutic circle' suggested by *The Piano*: the film gaze synthesises the settler gaze through the use of a sublime aesthetic, while the tourist gaze eventually repossesses the land. In the last sequence of Caro's film the landscape is safely framed in Sayo's memory. Sayo's geographical origin is also significant. The 'Japaneseness' of Sayo and Keiji reinforces the antithesis between the civility of an industrial country and the wilderness of New Zealand. Indeed, the formality and strict social etiquette that characterises the Japanese characters evokes the austere Victorian social conventions of *The Piano*'s protagonists.

While it is clear that Caro's approach to women's sexuality appealed to female audiences, there was more controversy over which geographic region was the intended target of the film. There was no Japanese contribution to the film. When the New Zealand producers approached potential Japanese investors they received negative answers as the Japanese felt uneasy with the content of the story. Referring to Caro's adaptation of the film, Deborah Shepard claims that "Niki's attempt to portray the culture and customs of the Japanese was an ambitious undertaking, destined to fail if it in anyway demeaned the people it attempted to speak for" (Shepard, 2000: 164). Critics particularly disliked the fact that in the film the Japanese characters speak English even when they are in Japan. CIBY Sales though was fiercely opposed to the possibility of shooting the film in Japanese with English subtitles as this would reduce the potential market for the film (Hughes, 2008). Eventually, the producers managed to sell *Memory and Desire* in Japan but the film never screened in that country. The film was not sold at all in the main Anglophone markets, UK and USA, and only did well in Continental Europe, particularly France, Italy and Germany where it attracted the art house crowds that already appreciated *The Piano*. Finally, in New Zealand the performance of the film at the box office was considered a failure.

The use of an oriental, stereotypical 'Other', that neither appealed to Japanese nor Western audiences, could be interpreted as the veiled expression of a 'self for export' (Turner, 2000). In his analysis of the production of a self-image in former white colonies, Stephen Turner has claimed that "lacking a self sustaining critical mass of population or financial capital, the settler society was shaped by forces dictating that whatever is produced must be also exportable" (Turner, 2000: 218). Turner's argument suggests that the production of the Self in a settler society creates a condition of internal exile, as the place that is lived in is the object of a metropolitan fantasy. Turner goes on to use examples from the Australian and New Zealand film-making tradition where texts, such as *Crocodile Dundee* (dir. Peter Faiman, 1986), *The Piano* or *Once Were Warriors*, which are intended for international audiences. The Australianess or New Zealandness of these films is the result of the acknowledgement and approbation of the global market rather than 'the reality of the lived experience of the place' (Turner, 2000: 219). To be worth producing, local programmes have to exaggerate their New Zealandness. This attitude is encouraged by the policy of public bodies such as the New Zealand Film Commission, that favour the production of features which focus on 'New Zealand content'. In *Memory and Desire*, which received a substantial contribution from the Film Commission, the notion of New Zealandness

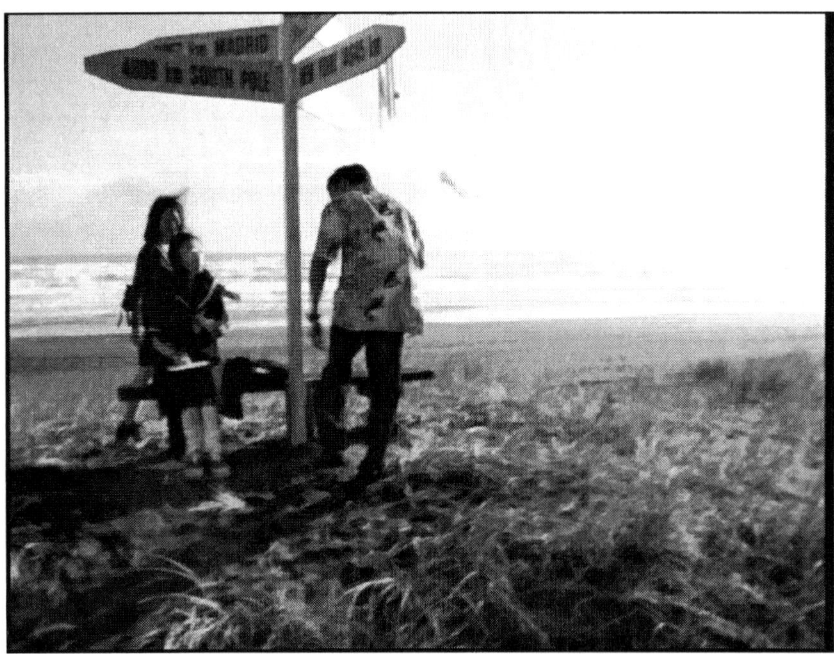

Figure 3.9. *Memory and Desire*, Frame Up Films.

was reduced to the stereotypical West Coast Auckland beach made world-famous by films such as *The Piano*. That international audiences may not actually watch local productions such as *Memory and Desire* does not make any difference, as the local image is always shaped by the desire of the metropolitan gaze. From this point of view, the global signpost[10] (Figure 3.9) in front of the beach in *Memory and Desire* could be read as an allegory of the relation between New Zealand image and global market (Babington, 2007: 221). Everything produced in New Zealand (in this case the wilderness of the beach) is measured in relation to its distance from the main urban centres. According to Turner, living in the export zone of white settler societies implies that New Zealanders are tourists at home. This could explain the proliferation of TV travel programmes and films such as *Memory and Desire* where the theme of the tourist gaze is crucial to the narrative. The production of tourist images in a country such as New Zealand is inextricably bound up with the production of identity. In Caro's film, an exotic Other such as the Japanese, stereotypically considered as the tourists *par excellence*, may be read as a projection of the mentality of Pākehā New Zealanders who imagine themselves as tourists in their own country.

*Memory and Desire* presents many analogies with another antipodean production: *Japanese Story* (2003), directed by Australian Sue Brooks. This film tells the story of Perth-based geologist Sandy and Japanese businessman Hiromitsu. Sandy is forced by her business partner to act as a guide for Hiromitsu in the Pilbara desert, in the hope that he will purchase their product. The cultural differences between Japanese strict work ethics and Australian informality soon result in conflict between the two protagonists. Hiromitsu insists that Sandy drives deeper into the desert, but eventually their vehicle becomes bogged down in the difficult Outback terrain. After a series of increasingly desperate attempts to release the vehicle, they are stranded and forced to spend the night together. The accident results in a liberating experience as the two characters are drawn together. As the journey progresses the couple initiate a sexual relationship, even though Sandy learns that Hiromitsu has a wife and children in Japan. Eventually the pair arrives at a swimming hole, where Hiromitsu suddenly drowns. Sandy returns to Perth with Hiromitsu's corpse, where she is confronted by the grieving widow. As in *Memory and Desire*, the main theme of the film is the liberating and yet tragic encounter with the wild landscape.

*Japanese Story* is part of a long line of Australian films, from *Picnic at Hanging Rock* (dir. Peter Weir, 1975) to *The Adventures of Priscilla Queen of the Desert* (dir. Stephan Elliot, 1994) and beyond, where the Outback setting has a tangible effect on the protagonists. The aestheticised vision of the landscape in Brooks' film is evident in the opening sequence, where the aerial views of the Pilbara desert are abstracted into a series of brown patterns. The abstract patterns are then gradually reduced to human scale. According to Rose Capp this is "a view of the landscape that has a longstanding tradition in Australian cinema, foregrounding as it does, the ambivalent attractions of a vast and at times unforgiving continent" (Capp, 2003: 28). Like his counterparts in *Memory and Desire*, Hiromitsu is made to observe that "Australia has lots of space and no people while Japan has many people and no space". Both films oppose metropolitan centers (Tokyo in Caro's film; Kyoto in Brooks'), intermediate/unauthentic spaces (Perth and Hamilton/Rotorua) and authentic, wild spaces (Outback and West Coast Beach/ Cave). *Japanese Story* proposes a more obvious simulacrum of the white settler/tourist in the character of Sandy. According to *Japanese Story*'s producer Sue Maslin, (aptly named) Sandy's work as a geologist "represents the metaphorical equivalent of her emotional journey" (Maslin cited in Capp, 2003: 31). Sandy/Hiromitsu and Sayo/Keiji literally travel to the heart (swimming hole/cave) of a foreign land seeking a spiritual and material regeneration. The themes of the beach, spiritual regeneration, relation to the land, tension between metropolitan centre and periphery, reoccur in the second film feature directed by Niki Caro, *Whale Rider*. Unlike *Whale Rider*, though, *Memory and Desire* did not boost any relevant form of tourism to its location mainly because the film was a commercial failure, both in New Zealand and overseas. Nevertheless, the analysis of the film reveals how the tourist subtext is inextricably part of the process of the production of a New Zealand self-image: New Zealanders are tourists at home and this is reflected in the way the film landscape is framed and interpreted.

## Conclusions

This chapter has dealt with two major questions: *why* and *how The Piano* has had such a strong impact on tourism, to the extent that Karekare beach, the most significant film location in narrative terms, has become the destination of an international film-tourist pilgrimage. One of the main reasons for the movie's tourist spin-off is its critical and commercial international success. The global diffusion of images of New Zealand landscapes has heightened awareness of the country as a possible tourist destination, for audiences previously unaware of its existence. Nevertheless, the success of the film at the box office cannot alone explain the significant tourist spin-off. The semiotic analysis of the film text reveals that *The Piano* activates many tropes of the tourist experience. The viewer's double identification with both Ada and the camera allows the audience to experience the story respectively from the inside and the outside of the diegesis, in the latter case being granted a distanced, safe position of power over the narrative as well as over the fictional space. This echoes the main feature of the tourist experience, namely the irreconcilable tension between the tourist's desire for risk (or novelty) and safety (or conformity). *The Piano* evokes many other tropes of the tourist experience such as the journey to a distant destination, the opposition between familiar and exotic places, the need for an environmental bubble of the familiar, the inability to communicate with the locals, the quest for an authentic encounter with the host environment. Even if *The Piano* is not the story of a conventional tourist experience, these analogies elucidate the film's success in influencing decisions to travel to New Zealand.

In *The Piano* the opposition between civilised and primitive worlds is central to the narrative and nature gradually acquires the role of an active character. The beach has a particularly significant role within the narrative for it represents the liminal space, the borderline between civilisation and wilderness; the famous image of the piano stranded on the beach dramatises this crucial opposition. Nevertheless, from a tourist perspective, this image could also be read as a powerful symbol of contemporary New Zealand: as both a familiar, civilised country and an exotic, untamed paradise. The piano on the beach is therefore transformed into the icon of New Zealand itself.

The landscape depicted in *The Piano* reflects the myth of a wild, pure, natural New Zealand and this has consistently been exploited by the marketing strategy of the national tourist board. It is not surprising, therefore, that *The Piano* was eventually used in the international advertising campaign '100% Pure New Zealand'. The main analogy between film and tourist texts, such as the advertisement analysed in this chapter, concerns the way in which they both frame and compose the landscape; in particular both the tourist and the film gaze are strongly influenced by the legacy of the settler gaze. This is evident in the prominence of the aesthetic of the sublime as well as in the representation of the landscape from a commanding vantage point, that emphasises an unequal relationship of power between the seer and the seen.

*The Piano* did not merely impact upon tourism and tourist images of the film locations. The representation of a landscape 'for export', characteristic of *The Piano*, has deeply influenced New Zealand's cultural self-image and in particular subsequent local film features. For example, visual and narrative references to Campion's masterpiece are evident in *Memory and Desire*. In this film the representation of a sublime landscape that exists first and foremost for tourist consumption is directly connected to the success of *The Piano* in selling the New Zealand scenery to global audiences. In this sense, therefore, the West Coast beach that features prominently in Caro's film could be read as the inter-textual *memory* and *desire* of the one already depicted and acclaimed in *The Piano*.


**Notes**

1.  Even if the official nationality of the film is Australian, everyone referred to it from the outset as a New Zealand movie. This was acknowledged by the Australians after Cannes when Sydney's *Telegraph Mirror* recognised that "*The Piano* is as much a part of New Zealand as the kiwi or the haka" (Shelton, 2005: 129).

2.  For an analysis of the symbolic significance of the clothes in *The Piano* see Bruzzi (1993: 10).

3.  The assimilation of Māori and nature suggested by the movie prompted critical reactions, particularly from a postcolonial studies perspective. See for example Pihama (2000) and Brown (2003).

4.  Among the locations used by the film-makers are West Auckland, Matakana, Waitakere Ranges, Bay of Plenty and Mount Taranaki (Martin and Edwards, 1997).

5.  See page 71 above.

6.  The importance of the soundtrack is often acknowledged by tourist narratives of the film locations. For example, on a travel website referring to Karekare a tourist comments: "West of Auckland, approx 1 hour + drive, is 'The Piano' country. Remember the movie? Holly Hunter, Harvey Keitel, HH [Holly Hunter] in all her Victorian finery playing the piano on the beach. I can hear the Michael Nyman soundtrack as I write …" (Virtual Tourist, 2007).

7.  This theory is nevertheless quite controversial, as the case of *LOTR* shows that the opposite could be true as well. Often film-tourists find pleasure in recognising and visiting locations that were enhanced by computer graphics or physically manipulated in the film.

8.  The short story itself is derived from a real life news event about a Japanese woman who was found living on a beach in Stewart Island in the Far South of the country and consequently repatriated to Japan (Hughes, 2008).

9.  Don Binney is one of New Zealand's most prominent contemporary painters. Binney's favourite subject is the New Zealand landscape, in particular islands and beaches. His paintings, characterised by strong lines and vivid colours, have been widely celebrated since the 1960s as expressions of contemporary New Zealand identity.

10. The image of the global signpost on the beach echoes a more recent TV commercial by Telstra Clear, where a blonde kid on a rugged New Zealand beach (again Piha) pulls a rope that connects him to an imaginary city-island that lies beyond the horizon.

4

# FROM *NGATI* TO *WHALE RIDER*: THE FILMIC JOURNEY OF THE INDIGENOUS TRAVELLER

## Introduction

Attempts to define the distinctive character of New Zealand cinema have often been limited by the tendency to focus on films produced and directed by male Pākehā New Zealanders. This tendency is exemplified by *The Cinema of Unease* (1995), a documentary written and directed by Sam Neill and Judy Rymer, which is the most influential work to use a single explanatory concept to clarify the peculiarity of New Zealand cinema. Neill and Rymer suggest in fact that contemporary film-making in New Zealand is marked by the 'dark heart' of a 'menacing land'. One of the corollaries of *The Cinema of Unease*'s thesis is the centrality and homogeneity of landscape in local film features. Despite the fact that *The Cinema of Unease* gained a certain recognition overseas, it was criticised at home for overlooking the many exceptions to the mainstream production, in particular films made by women and by Māori (Horrocks, 1999: 130). During the 1980s a series of new films by Māori such as *Patu!* (dir. Merata Mita, 1983), *Ngati* (dir. Barry Barclay, 1987), *Mauri* (dir. Merata Mita, 1988) and *Te Rua* (dir. Barry Barclay, 1991) and by women such as *Mr. Wrong* (dir. Gaylen Preston, 1985) or *Send a Gorilla* (dir. Melanie Read, 1988) undermined the prevailing ideas of 'New Zealand-ness' (Horrocks, 1999: 130). The new Māori film-makers in particular subverted themes, style and subjects characteristic of many earlier local films, which they considered to be the result of a "white neurotic industry" (Mita, 1992: 47). The representation of the landscape in Māori films reflects the significance of certain places in Māori culture and as a consequence it often differs from the traditional patterns of representation proposed by non-Māori film-makers. Barry Barclay, for example, points out how the beach in Māori culture is considered as a workplace and his representation of the beach in *Ngati* is definitely opposed to that offered by many New Zealand films where it is portrayed either as a place of leisure or the liminal space between nature and culture (Barclay, 1990: 49). Māori film landscape therefore often eludes the categorisation and the semiotic relations described in my previous chapter about New Zealand film landscapes.

Films by both women and Māori had a very limited diffusion at the time of their release and their box office takings were insignificant.[1] As a consequence, it is clear that such films did not directly generate any significant tourist spin-off. Nevertheless, the analysis of such films, particularly Māori productions such as *Ngati* and *Mauri*, is productive as they had a strong influence on the Māori film-making community and other successive, larger productions. A film such as *Whale Rider*, for example, defined by many as a Māori film, is said to operate in a similar mediascape as these indigenous films (Walker, 2006: 99).

The first part of this chapter will focus on the analysis of three Māori films: Barry Barclay's *Ngati* and *Te Rua* and Merata Mita's *Mauri*. In particular, the study of these film texts will contribute to determining the way in which they create the figure of the 'indigenous traveller'. In turn, the notion of 'indigenous traveller' is a crucial element that could help explain the success that *Whale Rider* had in attracting tourists to its film locations. The similarities between *Ngati*, *Mauri* and *Te Rua*, on the one hand, and *Whale Rider*, on the other, also concern the representation of the landscape, the Māori community and New Zealand as a whole.


## Fourth cinema

The first problematic issue to acknowledge when confronted with Māori cinema is the very definition of Māori film. To the seemingly obvious question "what is a Māori film?" Barry Barclay, Māori film-maker and theorist, answers: "a film made by Māori and set in the Māori community" (Barclay, 2003b: 16). To define Māori and indigenous cinema Barry Barclay has adopted the notion of Fourth Cinema. Barclay distinguishes Indigenous Cinema from First Cinema, the cinema of Hollywood and the international mass market, and Second Cinema, the art house cinema. Finally, according to Barclay indigenous issues are not adequately represented by the Third Cinema movement either: "I am not in Third Cinema also. I am not living in a Third World nation state" (Barclay, 2003b: 8).[2] Fourth Cinema is specific to societies of second settlement such as New Zealand. The term indigenous refers to the relation between first peoples (Māori) and second settlers (Pākehā) who have appropriated the land of the local people and subjected them to their laws. Fourth Cinema instantiates the (severed) relation between first peoples and the land (Turner, 2002). According to Barclay indigenous film-makers should "seek to rework the ancient core values to shape a growing cinema outside the national orthodoxy" (Barclay, 2003a: 11). Indigenous or Fourth Cinema, as a form of affirmation of first peoples, therefore implies that the aesthetic questions cannot be separated from politics and history.

Barclay's introduction to indigenous film-making in a society dominated by another culture came in the early 1970s, when he directed for television the six-part documentary series about Māori culture called *Tangata Whenua* (1974). Barclay's engagement in political Māori organisations resulted in the creation of a national organisation of Māori communicators called *Te Manu Aute*. The organisation's constitution claimed that "every culture has a right and a responsibility to present his own culture to his own people" (Barclay, 1988: 8).

*Ngati*, Barclay's first film, was defined by Helen Martin as "the first New Zealand feature film made principally by Māori and the world's first feature made by an indigenous culture living within a white majority culture" (Martin and Edwards, 1997: 128). Barclay's political commitment was reflected throughout the production of the film. This engagement resulted in training the crew in order to involve as many Māori as possible and employing culturally sensitive filming techniques. These processes are documented in Barclay's theoretical work *Our Own Image* (1990).

*Ngati* is set in 1948 in the small community of Kapua on the New Zealand East Coast. The narrative starts with the arrival in town of racist Australian Greg Shaw who, during his stay in Kapua, will come to discover that he is actually of Māori descent. The main story is interlocked with two other subplots: the community struggle to save the local freezing works that provides most of the town people's jobs and the relation between young Tione and his dying friend Ropata. The multiplicity of the storyline emphasises the importance of community, which is essential for the individuals as they gain a sense of identity from knowledge of and respect for their ethnicity (Edwards and Martin, 1997: 128). In *Ngati* identity is a crucial issue as being Māori is to understand and accept community, home, namely 'ngati', a Māori term that could be loosely translated as 'tribe'.

The tapestry-like narrative of the film implies a society on the verge of change: the break-up of rural communities through exodus to the city. From this point of view, *Ngati* is not only a film about being Māori: some of the film's main themes revolve around the figure of the indigenous traveller. According to Merata Mita, at the end of the nineteenth century New Zealand had two remarkable attributes: "The first was commonly described as New Zealand scenic attractions, the second was the Māori and both were eminently photogenic" (Mita, 1992: 40). The tourist depictions of the indigenous people conflated Māori with nature in order to attract visitors or settlers and titillate the Western imaginary of the South Pacific. Early New Zealand cinema drew upon nineteenth-century photographers, further restricting the range of Māori images to a limited number of categories: the noble savage, the fierce warrior, the clown, the cute kid and the brown maiden (Edwards, 1989: 20). *Ngati*, as the first Māori film feature, partially subverts these codes and most importantly proposes new ones. Films such as *Ngati* and *Mauri*, in fact, occurred within the framework of the so-called Māori renaissance that took place in the 1970s. During the 1950s and 1960s

Māori lifestyle had been dramatically transformed by the urban drift. The newly urbanised Māori struggled to find employment and preserve a sense of identity in the cities, while country Māori retained a stronger feeling of belonging to their culture and community. Some of the protagonists of *Ngati*, like those of many other films directed by Māori, are indigenous travellers. The indigenous traveller accomplishes a (sometimes metaphorical) journey from an urban, alienating space to the integrated, rural community. This journey is always a return home, the completion of the quest for identity and roots. The desires of the indigenous travellers are spiritual and emotional as well as material: they in fact attempt to reconnect to the landscape as *whenua*. The Māori term *whenua* refers to both the land and the placental afterbirth. According to Geoff Park, the notion of *whenua* evokes the idea of Māori adaptation to the ecosystem on which they depended (Park, 2006: 241). Simmons has further deepened the interpretation of the term, claiming that *whenua* is "landscape as atmosphere, as quality of feeling, that preserves and deepens our sense of living within it [...] and certainly not as early Pākehā understood the treaty—land as a tradable commodity" (Simmons, 2008: 17). The appeal of *whenua* for the indigenous travellers is complemented by their internationalism: they inhabit the 'glocal' position between the literal and the global village. While the indigenous travellers often end up retrieving their identity, the new ideas they have encountered in the city often lead them to clash with the community and even to question the traditional ways.

Similarly, their long stay in the city often wipes out their familiarity with indigenous values and knowledge. As a consequence, the indigenous traveller presents himself or herself as a subject who needs to be taught. Those Māori who have lived too long outside the community need to be reintegrated before they lose their Māori ways. This process implies the necessity of physical and metaphorical travel. Sally, one of the main characters in *Ngati*, gradually retrieves the Māori identity that she had lost from living for too long in the Pākehā cities. Similarly, Greg needs to physically leave Australia, implicitly constructed as a place that corrupts traditional values, in order to discover his individuality through an authentic contact with his ethnic ties. Interestingly, Māori ethnicity is not a necessary condition to access the authenticity of the community values. Liberal Pākehā characters such as Jenny Bennett, the daughter of the town's doctor, escape the simple opposition between community (good) and outside Pākehā world (bad). She is in fact claimed as Māori and can hardly be distinguished from the other townspeople. Thus, the figure of the indigenous traveller is not determined by the exclusivity of racial identity as proven by the case of Jenny and her family.

*Ngati* ends with the process of instructing Greg about Māori practices. The claim of the protagonist "I'm only a new Māori" offers Pākehā viewers the opportunity to connect to the processes of Māori tikanga (practices). As Murray points out "the bigot who discovers his indigenous root is, perhaps, a gesture toward a greater sense of national inclusion" (Murray, 2007: 94). The indigenous traveller is not exclusively Māori, everybody could potentially take on the 'indigenous journey'. The necessary condition is the point of arrival: the recognition of the landscape as *whenua*.

In *Ngati* an essential element of the *whenua* is the community. The community, in particular the rural one, is the repository of Māori identity and customs. The film attempted to achieve on screen that sense of community participation that is the heart of Māori culture. From this point of view Barclay tried to combine style with cultural sensitivity. Referring to his experience as director of *Ngati* Barclay claimed that for him the camera was first of all a listener:[3] "to be any sort of Māori you have to be a listener. You do not interrupt a person who is talking no matter how humble the person might be" (Barclay, 1988: 11). In order to convey a sense of ordinariness Barclay used a long lens for panning shots instead of the dolly. The deliberate renunciation of the dolly implied an observational shooting style that contributes to the documentary feel of *Ngati* (Cairns and Martin, 1994: 110). From this point of view Barclay himself was disappointed by the result achieved by the film. Referring to his desire to translate on film the authenticity of Māori lifestyle, Barclay claimed, "We had what I consider a failure on *Ngati*, one that I did not expect to arise. It has to do with creating a visual tapestry reflecting the physical details of Māori communal life" (Barclay, 1988: 14).

Apart from Barclay's disappointment with the crew's inability to capture certain details of the community life, *Ngati* is a celebration of Māori culture. The scenes that depict communal activities such as sheep shearing, kai moana (seafood) gathering and food preparation are filmed with sunlit colours. The tone and the representation of the landscape in *Ngati* is very different from that of films such as *The Piano*, where the dark and threatening nature of the bush reflects the traumatic nature of the settlement experience. An important Māori film-maker and theorist, Merata Mita, pointed out how the notion of the Pākehā settler at odds with the environment has been the theme of many New Zealand films. According to Mita the whole New Zealand film industry is a white, neurotic one. In her words, local films "repeatedly fail to analyse and articulate the colonial syndrome of dislocation that is evident in such works" (Mita, 1992: 47).

Entering Kapua means accessing a magically isolated community located in a different spatial and temporal dimension. The first sequence of the film, with the old bus that struggles along the weaving coastal road that takes it to the town, is highly reminiscent of the familiar tourist representations of New Zealand (Figure 4.1). The beautiful shots of the coastline and the emphasis of the camera on old cars and people on horseback confirm the stereotypical tourist image of the country. Barclay himself admits that *Ngati* was set nicely within both the Māori world and the national orthodoxy; "an orthodoxy which tells us that—way back then—all summers were everlasting, especially summers at the seaside at the end of that long and dusty road" (Barclay, 2003b: 10). From a First Cinema perspective Barclay would say that the film

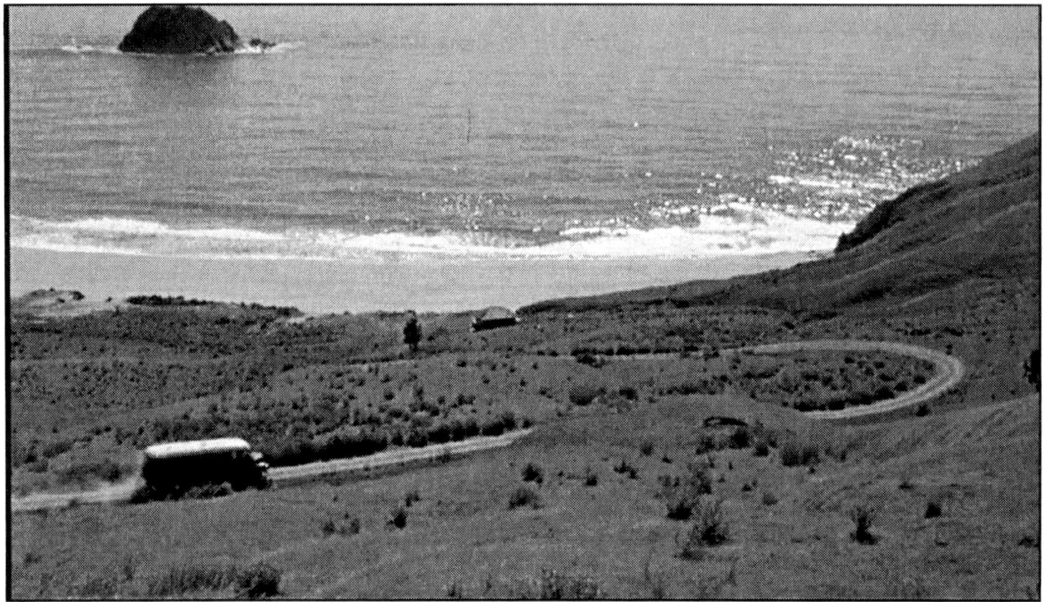

Figure 4.1. *Ngati*, Pacific Films.

is a sweet idyll with ethnographic anecdotes and a touching story. Some reviewers of the film could not see past the summer idyll and compared *Ngati* to the pieces written by the Romantic Lake poets in reaction to the corruption of the landscape invaded by 'the dark satanic mills' during the Industrial Revolution (Paatsch cited in Cairns and Martin, 1994: 109). Similarly, the film reinforces the construction of the city or Western civilisation (Australia) as threats to identity and authenticity. This emphasis on 'authentic values' raises the question of whether *Ngati* can transcend a nostalgic reading. As Martin Blythe puts it in fact: "affirmative and dignified as it is, the film refers to a historical period which is now past and although the problems it portrays persist today, they also need to be addressed in an urban setting where most of Māori now live" (Blythe, 1994: 276).

Even though the idyllic setting might suggest a pastoral nostalgia and a commodification of the landscape, the scenic beauty of nature and the communal activities actually convey a political message. According to Murray, *Ngati* proposes "a politics of image that stresses the contemporaneity of tribal culture. At the heart of this sense of the film is a refusal to present indigenous issues only for non-indigenous audiences" (Murray, 2007: 93). Even though a Western, international audience could be tempted to read the film as a nostalgic opposition between authentic (or natural) community values and corrupted urban setting, in reality Barclay's intentions were less simplistic. This first 'international' and 'touristic' reading of the film should nevertheless be taken into account as it illuminates differences and similarities between *Ngati* and *Whale Rider*.

Both *Ngati* and *Whale Rider*, in fact, are set in Māori villages on the East Coast of New Zealand's North Island and have comparable narrative content. The title of the theme song in *Ngati* is Paikea, the chief from Hawaiki who came over on the back of a whale and whose story inspired *Whale Rider*. But while Barclay's direction and control makes *Ngati* a very culturally specific text, Caro's *Whale Rider* reflects the influences of the global market and Pākehā direction. It will be shown how *Whale Rider* draws from some of the tropes of the Indigenous Traveller but implicitly converts them and adapts them for international tourist export.

*Ngati* undermines the simple opposition nature/culture that characterises the tourist texts, making explicit reference to the social conflicts that mark the relations between the community and the Pākehā world. Throughout the film, it becomes evident that Kapua is not a happy, isolated enclave but a community under threat from the external world. Furthermore, as we anticipated, the representation of certain film places in *Ngati* differs strongly from that of other New Zealand films. The beach is a case in point. According to Barclay, Māori do not see the beach in the same way as Pākehā, as a place of leisure and pleasure or as a 'sublime' location. In *Ngati* Māori are never shown sunbathing or gazing at the landscape, they collect kai moana instead. "I find it hard to recall more than a couple of films in which I have seen an individual, a couple or a family go to the seashore in the way that Māori do—to collect seafood" (Barclay, 1990: 49). Apart from collecting seafood, the protagonists of the film carry out all sorts of work at the beach. In the light of the traditional representation of the beach as a leisure and liminal place, the two sequences of the film where cattle and pigs wander on the sand seem shocking and almost surreal. In some cases, the break with convention is obvious: the scene on the beach where Iwi talks to the farm representatives is shown in mid shot with no establishing shot. In this way, *Ngati* undermines the semiotic categorisation of the beach as a frontier between nature and culture, clearly locating it in the domain of culture. Kapua's beach destabilises the tourist imagery of the New Zealand shore. We will see how the strategies of representation of the beach adopted by *Whale Rider* partially differ from those of *Ngati*.

Another element that encouraged the tourist and summer idyll reading of the film was Barclay's recourse to the tactics of nostalgia. According to the film-maker, for the Māori audience this was not nostalgia, but rather "the tactics of 'immutability and timelessness'" (Barclay, 2003b: 11). What may seem an indulgence in nostalgia is rather a reference to the timelessness and immutability of Māori spiritual values, a reaffirmation of Māori 'long history'.[4] Similarly, the measured leisurely pace of the editing helps to convey a sense of ease and tranquillity. While in Hollywood action films the average shot length is just two or three seconds, many of the shots which make up *Ngati* are as long as 40 seconds. Once again, through this device Barclay attempted to convey on screen the essence of Māori time.

At the beginning of *Ngati*, the audience of the 'majority culture', to use Barclay's terminology, might see Kapua as an apparently ideal tourist destination. In the first sequence of the film the spectator identifies with Greg, the (still unaware) indigenous traveller. The tourist value of Kapua is provided by the seeming purity, inaccessibility and timelessness that characterise the coastal community. As the narrative unfolds, though, it becomes clear that Kapua is a real place; the location is not just a function of a gaze that can impose itself over the 'Other'. *Ngati* fails to produce exotic and potentially commodified views of Kapua because the gaze of the protagonist gradually shifts from the status of outsider to that of insider. Greg's attempts to experience the traditional pleasures associated with tourist activity are frustrated as he is constantly reminded that he is at home. Similarly, Jenny notices as she takes Greg around, to the pub or to visit the sheep shearers, that the visitor is unquestioningly accepted by the Māoris. As the film unfolds, Greg, the indigenous traveller, becomes increasingly aware of his Māori identity until the truth is finally revealed by the grave of his mother. In this way, the 'exotic' gradually becomes the 'familiar'. When he eventually discovers why his father had insisted so strongly on his spending a holiday in this small town, he decides he will make it his new home. The indigenous traveller leaves the familiar only to find out that s/he has never left home.

The tourist experience is based on the fundamental dichotomy Us/Other. From this point of view, *Ngati* has ambiguous effects on the construction of a film-tourist imagination. As suggested, the opening sequence encourages the identification of the spectator with Greg, the Australian outsider. The identification with the protagonist in turn allows the viewer to vicariously travel to Kapua. Nevertheless, as Greg rediscovers his true identity the Us/Other dichotomy gradually dissolves and the viewer (virtual traveller) is unable to cast a tourist gaze over the film locations. Like Greg, the viewer has discovered that there is neither leisure nor pleasure associated with the beach which is rather revealed as a working place. Similarly, the timelessness that characterises the life of the town reflects a different conception of temporality. By the end of the film it is clear that Kapua is not an exotic, disneyesque destination where the rules of culture do not apply. On the contrary, Kapua has become too familiar. Similarly, the anti-idyll and anti-tourist reading of the film is reinforced by the multiplicity of the narrative structure that explores several interlocking stories. While the first half of the film is concerned with resolving Greg's problems of cultural and personal identity, the second part deals with the historical problem of economic survival as expected by the community's resistance to Pākehā corporate power. In the last part of *Ngati* the spectator is disoriented as Greg's character has lost his centrality and almost disappeared from the screen. At this point, Greg is replaced by a multiplicity of characters: Sally, the daughter of a leading member of the community who has just returned from the city; Iwi, the leader; Jenny, the Pākehā daughter of the local doctor; Ropata and Tione, two young friends. In this way, the possibility of an ethnographic reading of the film is frustrated by the co-presence of multiple gazes. The story is never seen and told from a single, dominant perspective; rather, the film jumps between several parallel quests destined to interconnect. Even though *Ngati* features several elements that could potentially appeal to the tourist imagination (remote seaside community, beautiful scenery, recourse to nostalgia, narrative of travel) it does not completely encourage a 'tourist reading' of the film.

The notions of authenticity, mobility and indigenous travel are also crucial elements of *Te Rua*, the second film directed by Barry Barclay. *Te Rua* is the story of two young Māori, Rewi and Peter, who struggle to get back some precious stolen carvings from a German museum. The film carried a strong political message that underlined the necessity for indigenous people to fight for themselves without relying on any external support. Like *Ngati*, *Te Rua* dedicates part of the narrative to the figure of the indigenous traveller. This latter is embodied in the internationally successful Rewi who needs to undergo a personal journey of rediscovery in order to reconnect to his Māori roots.

The second Māori fictional film feature is *Mauri*, directed by female film-maker Merata Mita. The film was made in 1988, just one year after *Ngati*. Like Barclay's first film, *Mauri* is also set in a Māori coastal community and makes extensive use of the New Zealand natural landscape. The reference to the landscape as *whenua* is made clear in the opening sequence where the placental afterbirth of one of the characters of the film is returned to the land. Like *Ngati*, the narrative of *Mauri* is articulated along the lines of the opposition between urbanised, corrupted world and pure, authentic Māori community. The film features several indigenous travellers. The gang members led by Willie, the brother of the protagonist, come back to the native community to temporarily rediscover familial and traditional values and leave again, revealing the corrupting power of the external world. Similarly, the protagonist of the film, Paki/Rewi Rapana, has himself left the city after some troubling events to find redemption in the small Māori community. In the case of *Mauri* the contribution offered by the community to the construction of the Self is even greater than in *Ngati*, as it allows the protagonist to forge an entirely new identity.

During his youth Paki runs into nothing but trouble in white society until one day he picks up a Māori hitchhiker, Rewi, who is going back to his small hometown for the first time after years away. Paki inadvertently kills the man in a car accident, then assumes Rewi's identity in order to escape a bank-robbery charge. After this event he will travel to the dead man's community where he will start an entirely new life. Paki/Rewi embodies the schizophrenia of contemporary Māori culture. At the end of the film, when he is chased down by the police who have discovered his true identity, the protagonist has visions of haka-ing warriors, suggesting the unresolved modern problem of a warrior culture in transition (Babington, 2007: 233). The traumatic condition of the protagonist resonates in the representation of the landscape associated with him. Throughout the film, the protagonist is troubled by the recurring flashback of the real Rewi inside a car falling from a cliff. Similarly, in one of the last sequences of the film, Rewi's escape is blocked by a drop. The alienation of the modern Māori is embodied by a hostile, dangerous and literally broken *whenua*—the cliff where the protagonist finds himself dangerously stuck: a transitory place between land and nothingness. *Mauri*'s narrative is more ambiguous than *Ngati*'s as Mita's film does not offer any definite solution and the journey of the indigenous travellers is tragically interrupted: Willie Rapana's gang life results in his assassination while Rewi is eventually arrested.

The connection between the Māori community and the external world is not as clear and harmonious as in *Ngati*. In Barclay's film, Kapua is connected to the rest of the world through a scenic coastal route and a bus. Likewise, the borders of the town are clearly defined from the outset by the road, the beach and the aerial view of the town. The ordered setting represents the harmony of Māori communal life, in the 1940s, at time when the dramatic experience of the urban drift was yet to come. *Mauri*'s setting, on the contrary, is fragmented. The connection between Pākehā and Māori worlds is marked by tensions and conflicts, as is evident from the opening sequence when Willie Rapana reacts angrily to the mispronunciation of his name by a toll call operator. This separation is obvious even from the visual point of view, as in the scene where a group of Māori perform the ritual burial of Awatea's afterbirth. The centre of the frame (an extreme long shot of a hill with the sea in the background) is occupied by a tree that symbolically divides the group of Māori standing still on the right side of the screen from Steve, the Pākehā, who enters the screen from the left. Steve's entrance in the scene is a visual and metaphorical invasion of the *whenua*. Later, Ramiri accuses him of having disturbed the ritual.

The external boundaries of the community are uncertain and the community itself is divided by internal conflicts and barriers, in particular those set by the old racist Semmens. The film juxtaposes two different conceptions of the land. The old Semmens embodies the Western idea that the land is at once a commodity and the object of the gaze. The surveying power of the gaze conflates with the voyeurism of the old Pākehā racist. The surveillance of the land with his telescope becomes an excuse to enjoy the sight of the naked Ramiri. The gaze is therefore the powerful tool that allows at once the commodification of the land and the objectification of the native as the stereotypical 'dusky maiden'. The film conveys a strong critique of the Western conception of the land. The 'vital force' of the title (Mauri) is linked to the *whenua* but opposed to the land of the Pākehā which is dead and sterile. This is particularly apparent in the surreal scene in which the old Semmens, disguised as a scarecrow, stands in the middle of a barren, ploughed field. From that position Semmens is able to enforce his control over the land while being unseen. When Awatea points to the scarecrow, telling Willie that it is actually the Old Semmens, Willie (and the spectator) are initially quite sceptical. The scarecrow looks too still to be actually a living being. Semmens will reveal his disguise only when provoked by Awatea.

The film uncovers the neurosis of the white settlers, proposing two point-of-view-shots from old Semmens' perspective before the marriage of Steve to Ramiri. The two handheld camera POV shots emphasise the spatial disorder of the old racist's house thus revealing his madness. The grotesque character of Semmens is associated with fences and protective barriers that symbolise the commodification and separation of the land from nature. The issue of land ownership is central to the narrative. Ramiri marries Steve in order to get back the land that was gained by the old Semmens in questionable circumstances. The tight connection between the land issue and the marriage is evident in the scene in which the two newlyweds smile at the guests behind a fence. While the neurotic conception of the land by white settlers evokes symbols of private property (fences), the landscape's association with other characters is more ambiguous and multilayered, particularly in the case of Willie and the gang. When the gang members work to clean the local cemetery, the recovered connection between the urban Māori and the *whenua* is emphasised by the beauty of the landscape in the background. By contrast, in the scene in which Willie and the other gang members threaten Steve, the characters are surrounded by darkness, a possible symbol of the moral void and lack of traditional values that characterise the gang. Finally, the betrayal and murder of Willie by his friends takes place in an anonymous cityscape that swallows the rest of the gang.

The beauty of the landscape is consistently associated with the only entirely positive characters of the film: the old Kara and Hemi and the young Awatea. The indigenous journey is here represented by the transmission of knowledge from the older Māori generation to the youngest members of the community—Awatea and Ramiri's daughter. In *Mauri* the notion of the indigenous traveller finds a metaphorical expression: the flight of the white heron, which is a recurrent image throughout the film, is at once the symbol of Kara's soul flying to Hawai'iki and the transition to the next Māori generation represented by Awatea's birth. The connection to the land is emotional rather than materialist: Kara claims, "I'm very fond of that hill". In the last sequence of the film Awatea will climb the hill identified earlier by Kara. The new generation of indigenous travellers thus accomplishes the journey to the core of the *whenua*. The last shot is a mobile aerial view of the ancestral land: at the top of the hill the silhouette of Awatea runs after the white heron. As Geraldene Peters pointed out: "this sequence clearly alludes to the spiritual bond between Kara and Awatea being part of a continuum that exists beyond material life" (Peters, 2007: 113). The ending of the film acts as a catalyst that binds different thematics of the film: Māori identity, relationship to the land, the rhythms of life and death. The circularity of the narrative suggests a cyclic notion of temporality. Once again, it is interesting to notice differences and similarities between *Mauri* and *Whale Rider*. Both films begin with a birth (Awatea in *Mauri*, Paikea in *Whale Rider*), a death (Kara in *Mauri*, Paikea's mother and twin brother in *Whale Rider*) and end with another birth (Ramiri's daughter in *Mauri*, Anna's in *Whale Rider*). In *Mauri*, despite the interracial marriage, the new baby is a pure Māori (biological daughter of Paki/Rewi and Ramiri). In *Whale Rider*, on the contrary, the Māori baby is the child of a German tourist. Even though formally *Mauri* and *Whale Rider* feature a similar narrative structure, Caro's film proposes a different scenario in which Māori future is inextricably connected to the global arena.

### *Whale Rider*: indigenous locations and global imaginary

The elements common to the first three Māori films made by the two most representative Māori film-makers, are, on the one hand, the notion of indigenous traveller and, on the other, the omnipresence of the small Māori community. Both elements are present in *Whale Rider*, directed by Niki Caro and based on the 1987 novel by acclaimed New Zealand writer Witi Ihimaera. The film tells the story of Pai, a young Māori girl who struggles to gain the approval of her grandfather and her people. According to tradition the first born male of the chief is to carry the name and role of Paikea, a character in Māori mythology who leads his people to the land on the back of a whale. Pai's twin brother, destined by gender to become a future chief of the tribe dies, along with her mother, during Pai's difficult birth. Pai's father, however, bestows the name on her despite her gender and leaves for Europe, renouncing the role and responsibilities of the chief. Pai's grandfather attempts to find a new leader for the community, teaching the young boys of the village the traditional customs, but, even though he excludes his granddaughter, he is constantly reminded that Pai, a female, is destined to become the chief.

Eventually, Pai's intimate connection with the ancestral spirits is revealed as she rides a whale stranded on the beach back to the ocean. The film has been discussed as the antithesis of the mega production of *LOTR* (Message, 2003: 86). While *Whale Rider* focuses on the local environment, encouraging national identification and balancing localised authenticity and magic, *LOTR* is concerned with the otherworldly that transcends the New Zealand landscape. Like Peter Jackson's masterpiece, *Whale Rider* generated international awareness of, and interest in, New Zealand's scenic beauty. Witi Ihimaera himself, the author of the novel and executive producer of the film, claimed that he hoped that the film would make people want to go to the places where the story was filmed: "I'm hoping that the Prime Minister will think of making a minister for *Whale Rider*, a film that comes out of our country's own f----ing myths, for God's sake" (Matthews, 2003: 20). As Ihimaera hoped, since its release the film engendered positive responses from film critics and people from the movie industry. In May 2003 Ian Stuart wrote that "even before its US release *Whale Rider* is being used to help to attract American tourists to New Zealand" (Stuart, 2003: B6). Tourism New Zealand was responsible for funding some of the costs of the American premieres and Tourism Minister Mark Burton himself was present at the pre-release screening for the US travel media. In Burton's words, "films such as *Whale Rider* will continue to increase our profile internationally and help develop a better understanding of us. *Whale Rider* proved to be a superb vehicle for promoting New Zealand to this discerning and influential audience" (Coventry, 2003: 1). As a direct result of the travel media pre-release, the American National Geographic Channel decided to shoot five five-minute documentaries about New Zealand, two of which focused on whale-watching and *Whale Rider*. The potential tourist spin-off of *Whale Rider* was also spotted by Qantas, which supplied tickets for the cast to the American premieres and launched a co-marketing advertising campaign on New York taxis. Other forms of international promotion came from the press coverage of international newspapers and magazines, such as the London-based *Daily Telegraph* which sent journalist Sheila Johnstone to learn and write about *Whale Rider*.

After the release of the film *Whale Rider Tours* led by a cultural liaison person escorted tourists from Gisborne to Whangara where the movie was filmed. Even though neither Tourism Eastland nor other tourist stakeholders in Gisborne designed a strategy to explicitly promote the *Whale Rider* site, the exposure gained by the film was sufficient to attract tourists to the region. Karena Gaukrodger, Marketing Executive of Tourism Eastland, commented that the local tourist board wanted tourists to Gisborne to find other reasons to stay in the region, in Gaukrodger's words "*Whale Rider* is a hook to get people here" (Gaukrodger cited in Hammond, 2004: 12). Research about the effects of *Whale Rider* on tourism in Gisborne and Eastland revealed that even though there is no evidence that the flow of tourists to the region has increased as a direct result of the *Whale Rider* release, 20% of all tourists (domestic and foreign) surveyed in Eastland at the time had been to Whangara. Another 21% indicated that they planned to go. Furthermore, the majority of the Eastland residents surveyed (85%) indicated that they perceived the effects of *Whale Rider* on Gisborne to be positive (Hammond, 2004: 18). One year after the release of the film, Hone Taumanu, Whangara resident and cultural advisor for *Whale Rider*, commented positively on the tourist flow to the Marae that was one of the film's most significant locations: "The people have been very respectful, they come in groups of 3 or 4 [...] we've had a lot of people through ... Alaskans, Dutchmen, Germans" (Hammond, 2004: 11). There is widespread evidence of the fact that the film appealed to international audiences and boosted Whangara, the East Coast and New Zealand as potential tourist destinations. The front page of the *New Zealand Listener* of February 2003 announced: "The Making of *The Whale*

*Rider*: Turning a New Zealand Classic into an International Hit Movie". The article confirms that the film had become an agent of the global commodification of cultural difference.

*Whale Rider*'s emphasis on the authenticity of the local environment intersects with the trajectories of postcolonialism and globalisation. Māori culture is thrown into the global market where it functions like any other commodity. The film, in fact, uses local signifiers, myths and landscapes to tell a universal story that may appeal to the global public. The invocation of universal values, such as the struggle between tradition and innovation or intergenerational and gender conflict, co-exist with the celebration of Māori culture and the small community of Whangara. *Whale Rider* is an international, German/New Zealand production that appealed to the global market through the deployment of the 'global popular', a concept defined by Simon During as what produces "a mood in which exoticism, normality and transworld sharedness combine, and in which consumption warmly glows" (During, 1992: 342). From this point of view, *Whale Rider* is more akin to *LOTR* than it would seem at first glance. Indeed, it is possible to refute the claim that Caro's film is the antidote to Peter Jackson's mega trilogy. The comparison of the two films has been a recurrent theme in the New Zealand press, and the similarities between the two productions are not limited to their coincidental release. In reality, both films are based on "a logic of franchise capital that is constitutive of the business of settlement" (Kavka and Turner, 2009: 231). Both productions were backed up by Tourism New Zealand which guaranteed a rapid process of commodification of the films' locations. Finally, both films deal with heroic, personal quest stories and narratives of magic and collective mythology.

## Whangara: between reality and hyper-reality

*Whale Rider* proposes a magical escape from the ordinariness of the everyday life precisely by locating magic and fantasy in it. Caro and Ihimaera adopt one of the tropes of Māori film—the celebration of the rural community—profoundly altering some of its characteristics. Unlike Barclay's Kapua, which actively struggles against the white capitalist outsiders and that, despite its remoteness, is anchored to a specific socio-historical context, Pai's community is obviously a fantasyland, the hyper-real copy of Kapua. Whangara is a community frozen in time, as Antje M. Rauwerda points out: "seasons are largely omitted in the film, in which the weather and scenery are consistently wonderful (so much so that it is no surprise that the New Zealand Tourism Board website has links to the movie and the Gisborne/Whangara area in which it was filmed)" (Rauwerda, 2004: 2). With the loss of the novel's emphasis on seasons, Caro's film loses the sense of the circularity of time.

*Whale Rider* infuses its illusory fiction with markers of 'authentic reality', in

Hokowhitu's words:

> Caro populates Whangara the fantasyland with extras from the actual Whangara community. This fact was highlighted in the film's hype and marketing campaign. For global audiences less familiar with Māori culture, *Whale Rider* depicts a more anonymous but authentic primitive culture and place, grounded in kinship relations, fossilized ceremonies, and traditions of totemism. (Hokowhitu, 2008: 126)

The construction of a staged authenticity is enhanced by the realist mode of direction that encourages an ethnographic gaze. One of the film reviews, for example, highlighted how Caro's film is a successful representation of an exotic Other for the international audience: "*Whale Rider* gives us clear-eyed glimpses of rural Māori society, from the old women smoking and playing cards, to the local kids in their American-branded T-shirts, kicking their heels until they're old enough to leave" (Morris, 2003: 18). Ihimaera, Caro and the whole production have been criticised by influential people in the Māori film industry, such as Barry Barclay, who claim that *Whale Rider* is not a Māori film. Even though Māori film-makers and theorists acknowledged the effort made by the production to guarantee a culturally plausible *mise en scene*, they claimed that the film does not 'talk in', that is 'talk to' Māori in cultural and linguistic terms.[5] Furthermore, *Whale Rider* is an ahistorical text that does not address the consequences of the colonising process and the implications of these omissions. Caro is accused of colonial amnesia as she removes any signs of the history of colonisation. While Māori films such as *Ngati* or *Mauri* explicitly engage in a critique of the postcolonial regime represented by the white capitalists in *Ngati* and by the police in *Mauri*, by voiding the film set of Pākehā *Whale Rider* has relegated Western colonial guilt to the realm of the unconscious (Hokowhitu, 2008: 128). The causes of the crisis that affects the local community are never really made explicit and they are attributed generally to the lack of spirituality and visionary leadership. No scenes are shot outside the village or the neighbouring region and Whangara is presented as a self-contained place, very much like a Disney theme park: a timeless space free from the hegemony of the capitalist, global society. The construction of an ethnographic, neo-colonial gaze is directly related to the emergence of a tourist gaze. The film removes any traces of the white people just to emphasise their presence on the other side of the screen. Once again this radically differs from *Ngati*, for example, where the representation of the Pākehā is much more complex. In Barclay's film, in fact, the members of the doctor's family are considered 'locals' despite being Pākehā. In *Whale Rider* the absence of Pākehā characters provides the sense of experiencing the 'authentic' Maoridom. In this sense, *Whale Rider* is not much different from early New Zealand travelogues which reinforced the myth that Happy Māoris lived in a land spatially and temporally separated from actual New Zealand. Like these early tourist films *Whale Rider* suggests that Māori lead a timeless, traditional way of life. This idea suggests a neo-colonial stand: the perception of Māori culture as stagnant is related to the colonial belief that Māori society was inferior as it had failed to evolve into a civilised state.

The main obstacle to Pai's quest is the 'traditional' belief that a girl is not allowed to become chief. *Whale Rider* deploys a key element of the fairy tale: the use of a young or adolescent girl as the protagonist. From *Cinderella* to *Little Red Riding Hood* or more modern fairytales such as *The Wizard of Oz* (Baum, 1996), pre-adolescent female characters are central to the narrative. Their prominence could be partially justified by the societal definition of both youth and femininity as weak, which makes the pre-adolescent female the ultimate symbol of vulnerability. The boundary space between childhood and womanhood is connected to the emergence of the power of procreation and the consequent access to a higher form of knowledge. Referring to the character of Pai, Message points out that "not only does she occupy or symbolize a boundary space, she also signifies the role of process and transition in the production of meaning" (Message, 2003: 90). In *Whale Rider* Māori culture is depicted as occupying an undefined space between adulthood and childhood. The community of Whangara is permitted to enter the adult world only under the condition of adopting the enlightened norms of the West. Pai represents the transition of Maori-ness from the pre-adolescence of a backward culture to the adulthood of modernity. As noted by Garcia, "Pai's actions are those of an enlightened being, of a person who knows her place in the world […] she smashes hierarchies, just as she shatters the classic notions of leadership" (Garcia, 2003: 43). Pai acts as a guide who eases the Māori community into liberalised global values. This, in turn, could explain why *Whale Rider* was so successful in commodifying local culture and landscapes for tourist purposes.

The film encourages the identification of the spectator with the agent of this liberalisation, the protagonist Pai. This identification is established from the outset. The film begins with a shot of blue water and the superimposed credits. The voice-over of the narrator is, by the second scene (the birth of the protagonist), associated with Pai. This scene also contributes to our understanding of the first sequence: the water and the floating whale evoke the uterine world inhabited by Pai before her birth. The uterine is therefore related to the world of magic and dreams. In semiotic terms the enunciator relies on a narrator (Pai) to tell the story. The spectator literally sees the world from the narrator's point of view and this is evidenced by a series of subjective shots from the perspective of baby Pai. Therefore, the first two sequences establish the opposition between two worlds: uterine/magic world and real world. Furthermore, they also potentially produce the identification of the spectator with the narrator. It is relevant that in this respect the film radically differs from the novel where the story is told mostly from uncle Rawiri's perspective. As Rauwerda points out, this implies that in the film Pai is "prematurally gifted and acts as though older and wiser than the adults around her" (Rauwerda, 2004: 2). The Western audience identifies with an enlightened child thus being reassured about the superiority of its values. The very existence of a pre-modern enclave such as Whangara in the global era does not seem plausible. The spectator is aware of the necessity for Whangara and its villagers to evolve and conform to the liberal norms represented by Pai. The Western viewer perceives that impending globalisation will inevitably destroy the 'authenticity' of the village, but s/he still enjoys the suspension of disbelief provided by the film. Whangara is a sort of Disney-style theme park which offers an exotic escape from everyday life. The fictional nature of Whangara, and Māori culture in general, is confirmed by the fact that the villagers are literally suspended between a gloomy reality—the hospital where Pai's mother and brother die—and the imaginary represented by the water, also associated with the uterine and the subconscious (Figure 4.2).

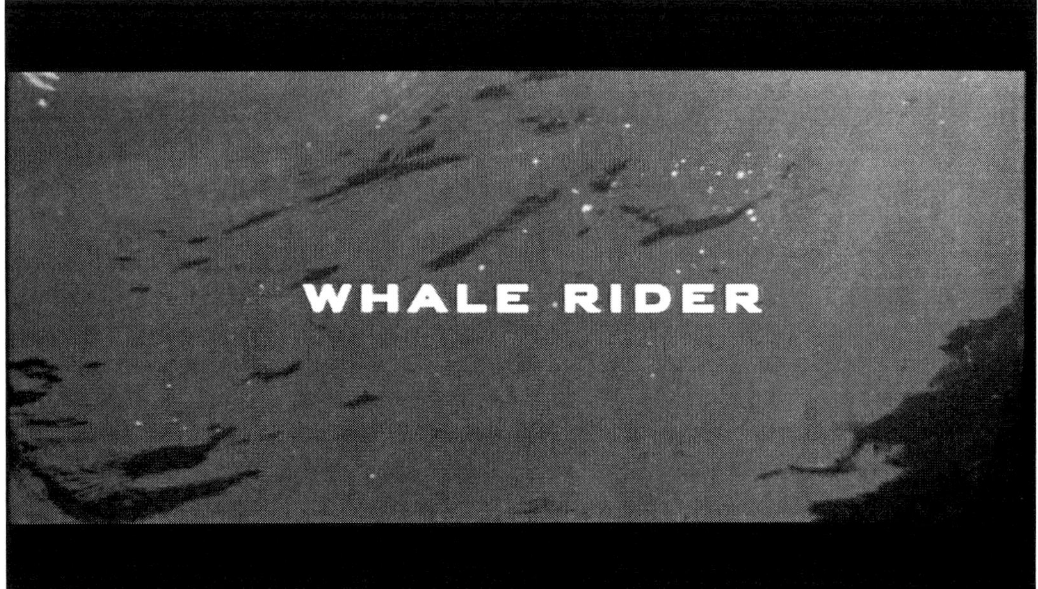


Figure 4.2. *Whale Rider*, South Pacific Pictures, Pandora, ApolloMedia, NZFC.

## Ethnographic, neo-colonial and tourist gazes

Throughout the film the interplay between real, magic and imaginary overlaps with the pleasures derived from the virtual tourism of the film location. For example, as Prentice suggests, the scene in which Pai stares at the ocean out of the car window "builds to another assertion of her spiritual connection to the place through the whales she senses far out in the ocean, while simultaneously participating in the marketing of panoramic beauty combined with convenient accessibility" (Prentice, 2006: 261). This is, of course, not the only example of commodification of the local environment and culture. After the hospital sequence, where Koro refuses to acknowledge his granddaughter, the narrative moves to Whangara several years later when Pai is now a pretty adolescent girl loved by her grandfather. The sequence starts with a tracking shot of the wheel of a bicycle and the feet of Koro pedalling. The shot might be defined as an 'impossible objective view' (Casetti, 1998).[6] One of the main effects of the impossible objective view is the identification of the spectator with an omnipotent camera. The spectator at this stage is prone to a double identification with both the narrator, who is still in control of the narration as underlined by the voice-off that links the two sequences, and the camera. The camera slowly tilts up revealing Pai sitting on the crossbar of the bicycle and holding Koro's necklace. The film then cuts to a close-up of Pai's face and the whale tooth which will acquire a special relevance later in the film. This is followed by a long shot of Koro and Pai on the bike advancing towards the camera. The couple rush past the camera, which pans left eventually resting on an extreme long shot of the beach. The shot focuses for few seconds on the view of the shore, forgetting the two protagonists. The first three shots of the sequence reveal the alternation of the ethnographic and the colonial gaze. The omnipotent camera records meticulously the details that characterise life in Whangara: Koro's jandals, Pai's bare feet, an old bike, an exotic necklace, the Polynesian features of the two protagonists (Figures 4.3 and 4.4). The camera and the spectator become amateur ethnographers engaged in collecting data concerning an exotic culture.

No attempt is made to deepen the knowledge of Māori culture, or to critically approach its relation to the globalised world. These details are consumed for their pure visual beauty and the exoticism they evoke. From this point of view, Huggan's definition of exoticism as "an aestheticizing process through which the cultural other is translated, relayed back through the familiar" (Huggan, 1991: ix) is particularly appropriate. The exotic appeal of Whangara and its inhabitants is based on the evocation of the natural and naturalness. The Māori community in the film is opposed to the world of the metropolitan audience. Here people walk barefoot or enjoy bicycle rides instead of driving in the congested traffic of London or Berlin, thus escaping the pressure of the consumerist lifestyle. Similarly, the individualism of globalised capitalism is opposed to the communal values shared by the villagers (Prentice, 2006). *Whale Rider* conveys

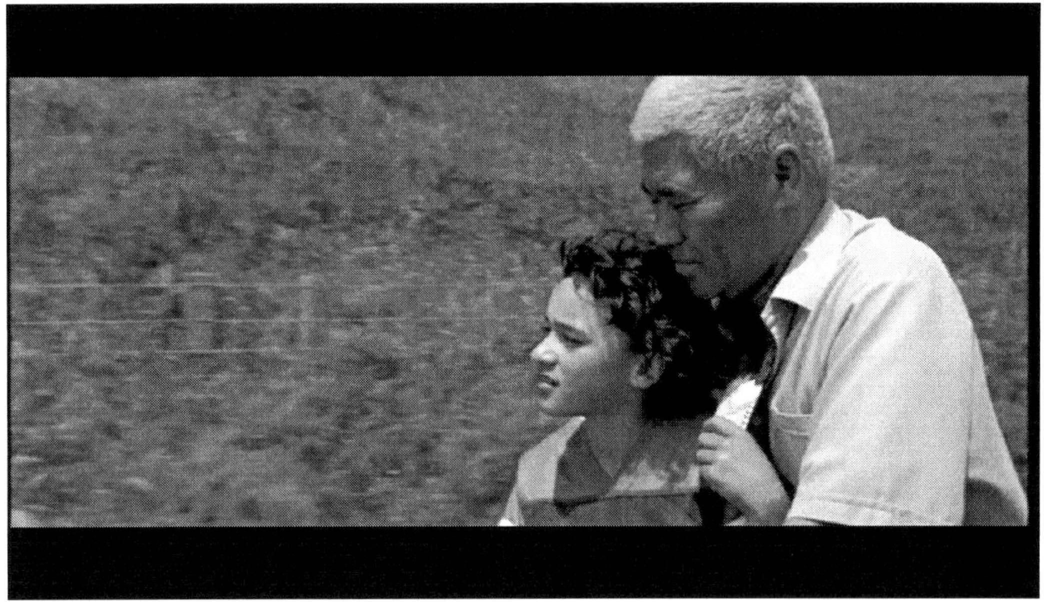

Figure 4.3. *Whale Rider*, South Pacific Pictures, Pandora, ApolloMedia, NZFC.

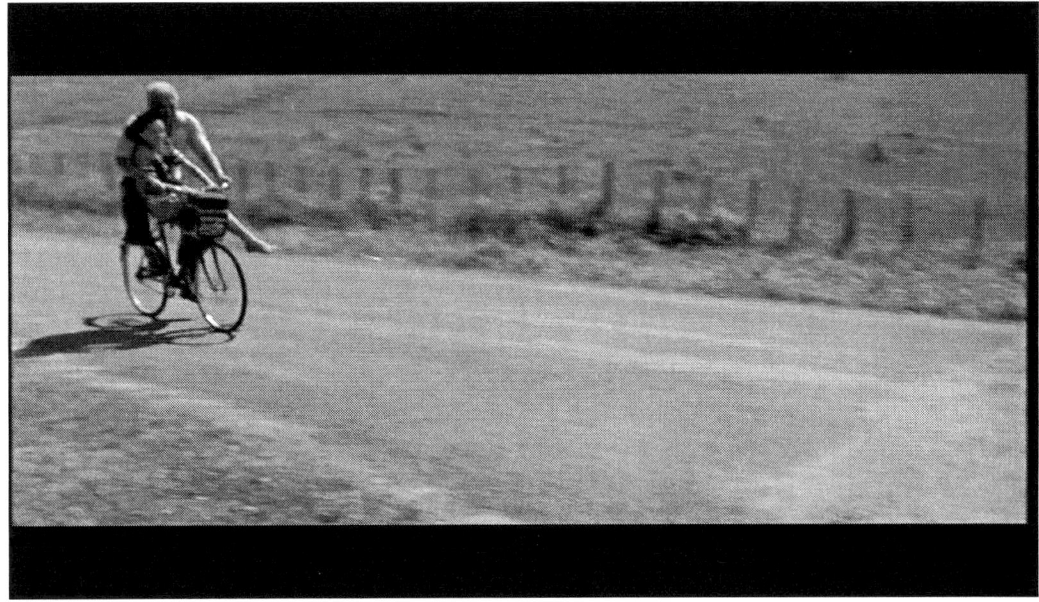

Figure 4.4. *Whale Rider*, South Pacific Pictures, Pandora, ApolloMedia, NZFC.

a message which is absolutely consistent with the '100% Pure New Zealand' campaign orchestrated by the national tourist board. Both the film production and New Zealand Tourism cater for the contemporary nostalgia for naturalness and simplicity exhibited by the global market. The physical remoteness of New Zealand from the centre of the Western capitalist world is one of the essential factors that supports this strategy. Referring to the special character of New Zealand's antipodean location, executive producer Witi Ihimaera claims that the country is the place that "dreams are made of, and this is what cinema goers respond to when they sit in a dark theatre in the more urbanised countries of the world claimed by a universal reality and synthesis" (Ihimaera cited in Coventry, 2003: 2). According to Ihimaera, films such as *The Lord of the Rings* have revealed to the rest of the world a place that offers international audiences unique types of beauty and adventure. *Whale Rider* can go even further since when audiences watch the film "they are rediscovering the intimacy of family, of belonging in an extended way to kin and the kind of yearning for reconnection that is within all of us" (Ihimaera cited in Coventry, 2003: 2). The celebration of the 'natural' and 'simple' lifestyle of the Whangara villagers does not, however, subvert in any way the consumerist ideology that characterises the

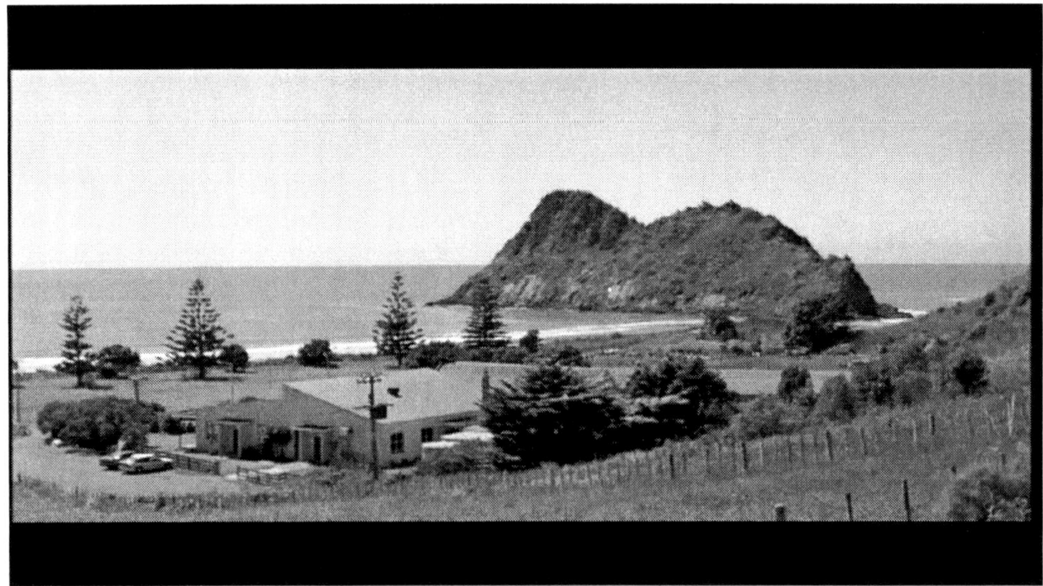

Figure 4.5. *Whale Rider*, South Pacific Pictures, Pandora, ApolloMedia, NZFC.

global market. First, as already mentioned, the 'enlightened' character of Pai represents an implicit critique of the system of values held by the members of the community. Eventually, the protagonist will solve the crisis that affects the community by challenging the dominance of traditional Māori patriarchy embodied in Koro's inability to accept modern times. Second, the exotic sought and enjoyed by the international spectator refers to ideas and values associated with a lost past. The representation of the Other, in this case Māori, offers a "compensatory displacement from the present" (Prentice, 2006: 260). As Prentice points out: "the local is disseminated as a 'value', reproduced as a 'sign' suspended between exoticism and primitivism, fetishised as an image that resolves the anxiety of its loss in the technology of its reproduction" (Prentice, 2006: 260). The film not only commodifies Māori culture for the consumption of (virtual) tourists but it also risks celebrating the poverty of the community as its representation is voided of any political criticism.

The commodification of the landscape is a corollary of the historical decontextualisation of the representation of the Māori. The third shot of the Whangara sequence ends with an extreme long shot of the beach (Figure 4.5). After the camera has employed the ethnographic gaze on the two main characters it turns to an appropriation of the land. The three shots equate the visual pleasure associated with the consumption of the 'ethnographic' details (necklace, bicycle, exotic physical features) with the beauty of the scenic view. In this way, *Whale Rider* generates at the same time images of the postcard and the museum's shelf. Both constructs are inextricably bound up in the process of the production of meaning involved by the tourist experience.

The representation of the beach in Caro's film differs radically from that of Barclay's *Ngati*. Here, the beach is once again a liminal place between the mysterious world of the imaginary and reality. The beach in *Whale Rider* is far from being a mere workplace as in *Ngati*. Instead, it encapsulates the intermediate, boundary state that characterises the local community trapped between modernity and primitivism, culture and nature. In this way, the beach is Whangara itself. Significantly, the climax of the story represented by the distressing scenes of the whale stranding will take place on the beach. On the beach Pai will become aware of her innate, magic power, riding the whale back to the sea and salvation. From this point of view, *Whale Rider* shows a striking resemblance to *The Piano*. In both cases the beach is a liminal place and witnesses extraordinary events. In Jane Campion's film it is the piano, symbol of culture and civilisation, that is stranded on the beach. The surreal superimposition of this sophisticated object from the Western world on a rugged location has contributed to make Karekare, one of the most beautiful West Auckland beaches, a very popular film tourist destination. Interestingly, the *Whale Rider* tourist spin-offs did not particularly emphasise the location of the beach where the stranding takes place. Rather, it was the community of Whangara as a whole that was subjected to the media exposure which, in turn, attracted the international tourists. While space in *The Piano* is an actant that actively opposes the actions of the protagonist, this is not the case in *Whale Rider*, a difference which may account for the contrasting response to the films' locations. In Caro's film, the 'Opposer' is embodied by traditional Māori values and culture and therefore by the Whangara community itself. In *The Piano*, the Māori are represented as an integral part of the landscape, a mere accessory to the wild New Zealand nature. They are a component of the background and signify a potential threat which is never realised. According to Māori scholar Leonie Pihama: "the perception of Māori people given in 'The Piano' is that our tipuna (ancestors) were naive, simpleminded, lacked reason, acted impulsively and spoke only in terms of sexual innuendo" (Pihama, 2000: 128). Campion depicts the Māori as essentially passive as they are subordinated to nature. *Whale Rider* confirms this construction of the Māori as having privileged access to nature, but in this case Maori-ness is presented as an active force, albeit one which opposes the intentions of the protagonist, Pai. Sometimes the members of the village act without explicitly opposing Pai's behaviour, as shown by the sequence of the stranding where the community attempts in vain to free the whales, but even in this case the narrative reveals how the protagonist has a deeper and more enlightened knowledge of what has to be done. In both films the Opposer (physical space in *The Piano* and Māori traditional values in *Whale Rider*) is eventually subjugated, becoming the object of the commodification process imposed by the global market. Finally, both films appeal to the imagination of (virtual) tourists as their narrative is structured around the necessity of a journey. Despite the fact that the *Whale Rider* journey is metaphorical, Caro's movie articulates film geography in three different spaces: reality, the imaginary and Whangara. The characters, and the spectator with them, move back and forth across these spaces throughout the narrative, simultaneously producing the meaning of the different film places.

**The indigenous traveller**

*Whale Rider*'s narrative features three kinds of travellers: indigenous, hybrid and Western travellers. Drawing upon classic Māori films such as *Ngati*, *Mauri* and *Te Rua*, the film constructs the figure of the typical indigenous traveller embodied by Porourangi. Like his homologues in Barclay's and Mita's films, Pai's father represents the crisis of identity experienced by contemporary Māori who has lost or betrayed his roots under the veiled threat of Westernisation. Porourangi is the symbol of a general crisis that affects the Māori world. Indeed, as Pai comments during the film: "he went away, everybody else did". The alienation of Porourangi from his cultural roots is represented, on the one hand, by the incomplete waka that represents the dormant state of Māori identity and, on the other, by his modern, anti-traditional art that provokes sceptical reactions from the members of his family. Like all the other indigenous travellers, Porourangi eventually completes the journey of rediscovery towards his cultural identity. At the end of the film, the spectator sees him paddling with his brother towards the horizon in the waka that he has finished carving, a symbol of a revived Māori tradition. Porourangi's character also provides the viewer with an indirect representation of the Western world through postcards and accounts of his travels. France, Germany and the other places briefly evoked by Poururangi are never shown directly, though the spectator is well aware of the physical and cultural distance that separates them from Whangara. This distance is emphasised by Koro Paka's ignorance when he defines the French landmark depicted in the postcard as a "bridge or something …". A similar lack of European cultural knowledge is revealed during Porourangi's presentation of his artwork to his family. The ignorance of Koro and the other villagers is part of their exotic appeal. They are pure as they are not corrupted by knowledge of the Western world and precisely for this reason their otherness is more valuable and precious to the global audience. Porourangi is the interface that suggests the transformation of the Māori into a generic Other necessary to the reinforcement of the Western Self. Significantly, Porourangi's character is played by Cliff Curtis, an actor whose extra-diegetic connotation is that of 'global Other' (Wilson, 2006). The construction of Porourangi as the generic Other is in fact reinforced by Curtis' association with his former film roles as 'brown guy'—either Middle Eastern, Hispanic South American or Polynesian. Similarly, *Whale Rider*'s emphasis on the representation of authenticity has to be distinguished from an interest in the actual specificity of Māori culture. In the global arena Māori are interesting as long as they provide an opportunity for the commodification of cultural difference.


**The hybrid traveller**

The indigenous traveller Porourangi, who has been exposed to new ideas in the city, is the father of Pai who will actually solve the crisis of the pre-modern community by introducing them to liberal values. Pai is not a traveller in the normal sense of the term. She is physically unable to leave Whangara, despite wanting to go with her father, who also feels compelled to return to the town on a regular basis. Nevertheless, she is mobile as she is able to cross the borders between magic and the real world. She is also the carrier who enables the spectator to move back and forth from one realm to the other. In this sense, Pai is a hybrid traveller. She is hybrid as, despite her physical features, she is not entirely indigenous. Because of her mystical access to the magic world and enlightened values, the film constantly reminds the spectator of Pai's superiority over all the other characters. Even Porourangi is indebted to his daughter's example. Furthermore, the identification of the viewer with the protagonist (suggested by her role as narrator and a number of subjective points of view) paradoxically changes the girl's nature.

Pai shares one of the essential characteristics of the tourist/spectator: the constant awareness of being different from the 'locals'. In the film, the heroine's name changes from Kahu to Paikea, the ancestral whale rider. While the new name has the benefit of simplicity one cannot help but notice the similarity between Paikea and Pākehā. The young protagonist is different from the villagers as she knows more and knows it better. At the same time, however, she enjoys the authenticity of life in Whangara and she never physically leaves the town. Similarly, the tourist and the metropolitan spectator are always aware of the difference that separates them from the exotic Other. One of the pleasures of the tourist experience consists precisely of the comparison of the object of the gaze with the familiar (Urry, 2002: 12). The experience of a 'simple', 'natural' lifestyle is pleasurable because it implies an escape from the frustrations of everyday life, but it is only enjoyable so long as it presupposes a return home. In most cases, the tourist experience is successful when it expunges the social and political causes of the poverty of the locals. Similarly, the hybrid traveller Pai and the film tourist overlook these causes and are aware that their stay in Whangara is limited by the length of the film. Their virtual journey is concluded by an irrational happy ending which consciously ignores the historical context that determined the crisis of the community.

Some scholars (Thorner, 2007) have noticed the similarities between Pai and Daisy, the protagonist of the Australian film feature *Rabbit Proof Fence* (dir. Philipp Noyce, 2002). The film tells the story of three young aboriginal girls—Molly, Daisy and Gracie—removed from their families and installed in a special centre established by the Australian government to civilise the aboriginal half cast and to prevent the creation of a 'third race'. The three girls escape the centre and engage in an epic journey to return home by following the rabbit-proof fence, a structure that divides the Australian continent in two halves from north to south. Like *Whale Rider, Rabbit Proof Fence* deals with the journey of a young indigenous girl who overcomes apparently insurmountable obstacles to eventually meet her destiny. The narrative and the production of the two films bear striking resemblances. Both films were released in 2002; both were adapted from novels by indigenous writers, but directed by white film-makers; both generated a significant tourist spin-off and most importantly both "construct stories that are profoundly local, yet widely resonant" (Thorner, 2007: 137).

Even though both productions have ethnographic ambitions, they produce a "staged authenticity" that aims to please the spectator/virtual tourist (MacCannell, 1999: 98). The producers, for example, decided against filming in Western Australia where the narrative takes place, shooting instead in the Flinders Ranges of South Australia which offered a greater variety of landscapes. This diversity of landscape helped the production to translate into images the enormity of the journey for an international audience not familiar with Australian geography.

## The Western traveller

Unlike *Rabbit Proof Fence*, however, *Whale Rider* offers a visual simulacrum of the Western spectator/tourist. This is in fact embodied by Anna, Porourangi's pregnant girlfriend who arrives from Germany at the end of the film. She is the only non-Māori character in the story and the only one, apart from Pai, with whom the international audience can, at least visually, identify. Interestingly, Porourangi's wife is a very different character in Ihimaera's novella where she is Ana, a Māori woman from the South Island. The appearance of a white Anna is probably a consequence of the involvement of Apollo Media, a German film production company, in the making of the film. The success of the film in Germany reinforced the message of the '100 % Pure New Zealand' campaign. As its second biggest European tourist market after Britain, Germany is highly significant for the New Zealand brand. In 2006 visitors from Germany increased to a total of 58,781 with an expenditure that reached $NZ 239 million (Durr, 2007: 7).

More importantly, Anna's pregnancy with Porourangi's son represents the creative power of the Western tourist who is now able to literally reproduce the Other. Pai and Anna are the only two characters (apart from Pai's mother) who seem to have privileged access to the act of birth, which is, in turn, associated with magic and the imaginary. Pregnancy is associated with the divine and creative act of the demiurge, and so the Westerner, embodied by Anna, literally becomes a creator of worlds. However, Anna's pregnancy also represents the ambiguous relation between the Self and the Other. In his *De l'ospitalité* (*Of Hospitality*, 1997) Derrida claims that a good host is one who decides as a master, *chez lui*, whom to invite into his home. The role of host therefore implies the right and the need to discriminate between good and evil others, that is between the hostile (*hostis*) enemy who invades and the benign host (*hostis*) who welcomes (Kearney, 1999). The law of hospitality always implies a relation of power and a certain degree of violence. In Derrida's words:

> Sovereignty of the self [...] can only operate by filtering, choosing and therefore excluding and doing violence. A certain injustice ... is present from the outset, at the very threshold of the right of hospitality. This collusion between the violence of power and the *Gewalt* (the force of law) on the one hand, and hospitality on the other, seems to be radically integral to the very inscription of hospitality as a right. (Derrida cited in Kearney, 1999: 259)

The ambiguous status of the Other as potential invader or welcomed guest is embodied by the figures of filmic pregnant mothers such as Lieutenant Ripley in *Alien 3* (dir. David Fincher, 1992) where Sigourney Weaver is at once the mother and the host of the alien that invaded her womb. Lieutenant Ripley decides to enforce her power of host by killing herself and the alien inside her womb. In *Whale Rider* of course nothing as dramatic happens; the stranger inside Anna's womb is a good Other and she will become the mother of a Māori child. Nevertheless, her right of hospitality implies a relation of power over the Other. Pai has destroyed patriarchal traditions and democratised the tribe, allowing for Anna's unproblematic assimilation into the family (indicated by her inclusion in the group which gathers at the launch of the waka). Anna thus becomes the new guarantor of the community's ethnic identity. In a sense, Paka Koro's acceptance of Anna represents the triumph of liberal Western agendas over the tradition of the community.

In this reading, Anna's character represents the ultimate evolution of early depictions of Westerners in New Zealand. At the beginning of the twentieth century, white voy(ag)eurs were shown either filling empty landscapes or peeking at scenes of Māori 'primitive' life. Hokowhitu comments on Anna's character, the new Western traveller, pointing out that "menacingly, the hybrid child symbolizes the tribe's sealed destiny of becoming an indigenous component of global culture" (2008: 132). Porourangi's offspring in this sense is like his artistic creations, exposed in the European galleries, but initially rejected by his family: in both cases the artist's creative power is subordinated and exists as a function of Western agendas.


**Conclusions**

"'Pure New Zealand' means that you don't have to deal with the problems of the people in this country [...] you get the pure country, your dreams or wishes exactly delivered". Thus Peter, a German psychologist by training, retrospectively comments on his three-month stay in New Zealand (Durr, 2007: 9). *The Whale Rider*, directed by Niki Caro, reinforces the tourist imagery of the country providing a decontextualised representation of the Māori. The film encourages the virtual tourism of a Māori community, emphasising its purity which in turn resides precisely in its remoteness and isolation from the global arena. The people of Whangara do not have real, tangible problems; the town is a disneyesque oasis subjected to the ethnographic and neo-colonialist gaze of the Western spectator. The commodification of Māori culture in *Whale Rider* does not contradict the film's explicit attention to indigenous practices and languages. From this point of view, *Whale Rider* shows striking resemblances to the ethnographic and travel films about Maoriland shot at the beginning of the twentieth century. Like those travelogues, *Whale Rider* implies that Māori live in a place spatially and temporally separated from the contemporary world. Nevertheless, Caro's film also reveals a crucial difference from early tourist films about Maoriland. Early cinema, like the museum, was concerned with the preservation of the historically and spatially distant, in particular the presentation of indigenous, colonised people. These cultural institutions were active agents in the maintenance of the empire somehow suggesting that the Māori race was eventually destined to disappear. *Whale Rider* on the contrary, grants the Whangara people the possibility to survive, albeit as a mere "indigenous component of the global market" (Hokowhitu, 2008: 132). The survival of the Other depends on its difference from the metropolitan Self but also its willingness to comply with Western enlightened values.

*Whale Rider* has been considered by some to be a Māori film and it does evoke some of the tropes of indigenous cinema: on the one hand, the opposition between remote Māori community and metropolitan centre, on the other, the figure of the indigenous traveller. However, Caro's film subverts these elements, transforming them as part of the process of commodification of Māori culture and landscape. Māori films, such as *Ngati*, occasionally indulge in scenic shots of the landscape, but the potential tourist reading of these films is structurally limited by their political commitment to 'talk to' the Māori audience first. The commitment of these films to the Māori audience is part of a political strategy that is absent in *Whale Rider*.

Similarly, in Caro's film the indigenous traveller, Porourangi, closely reminiscent of the characters of Greg in *Ngati*, Rewi in *Mauri* or Peter in *Te Rua*, is unable to reach redemption autonomously. Rather, he requires the support of the hybrid (Pai) and Western (Anna) traveller. *Whale Rider*, unlike films by Māori directors, boosts the dichotomy between Us (spectator, indigenous, hybrid and Western traveller) and the Other (the community and the traditional Māori values). It is interesting from this point of view to notice that even though the film offers several scenic shots of natural beauty, most of the *Whale Rider*-induced tourism has been concentrated on the Whangara Marae. The Other, namely Māori, tradition is the Opposer of the protagonist's actions and desires. Once this latter has been tamed, however, it paradoxically becomes the main object of the commodification process. International tourists have flocked to New Zealand and Whangara seeking the 'authentic Māori experience'. The tourist gaze has thus attempted to replicate the postcolonial and ethnographic gaze boosted by the film.

Even though the film-makers' attitude was characterised by a genuine desire to hear the Other, dedicating attention to authenticity and respecting the sensitivity of the community, the film was explicitly packaged for the global market. For this reason, tourist institutions have been readily able to capitalise on the hype generated by this film. In this postcolonial age the representation of otherness and its relation to tourist practices is a crucial issue. More research is needed to clarify the relation between *Whale Rider* and Māori cinema and, more importantly, its contribution to the representation of indigenous identity.

**Notes**

1.  In New Zealand *Ngati* recouped $NZ 143,000, *Mr. Wrong* $NZ 67,000 and *Mauri* a mere $NZ 35,000 (NZ Film Commission, 2008).

2.  See Solanas and Gettino (1986) for a further discussion of the notion of Third Cinema.

3.  Some works by Pākehā film-makers have attempted to reconcile style with respect to Māori cultural sensitivity. This is the case in Vincent Ward's documentary, *In Spring One Plants Alone* (1980), which tells the story of an elderly Māori woman's efforts to look after her mentally challenged son. The documentary was filmed over eighteen months, during which Ward lived with the pair in a remote Māori community in New Zealand's North Island. The total absence of narration in the film reflects the director's attempts to become a 'listener' in Māori terms. Ward's life experience in the midst of an alien culture eventually inspired the subject of *The Last Samurai* (see Chapter 5).

4.  Stephen Turner has formulated the notion of 'long' and 'short' history to describe the process through which non-Māori settlers have substituted their shorter history for long Māori history. According to Turner, settlers 'break' with long Māori histories as making a new country and resettling it involves putting an older, longer history of place away (Turner, 2007).

5.  Barclay claimed that the film-maker working within the majority culture is caught between the need for 'talking in' and 'talking out'. In Barclay's words: "On the one hand there is [...] a right and responsibility for any culture to present itself to its own people—'to talk in'. On the other hand, there is an awesome communications structure already established by the majority culture, which [...] seductively pleads to find out more about Māori culture [...] It's 'talk out' brother" (Barclay, 1990: 75).

6.  See page 81 in Chapter 3 for a definition of this notion.

# 5

## From Mt. Fuji to Mt. Taranaki: Dépaysement and Celebrity Worship in *The Last Samurai*

*The opposite of a place. If place is cognate with destination*
(Jean-François Lyotard, *The Inhuman*)

### Introduction

Thus Lyotard defines the relationship between landscape and place: landscape stands as a sign of the absence of place and the erasure of physical support. Lyotard further elaborates on the notions of estrangement and landscape in a passage which is worth quoting in full:

> There would appear to be a landscape whenever the mind is transported from one sensible matter to another, but retains the sensorial organization appropriate to the first, or at least a memory of it. The earth seen from the moon for a terrestrial. The countryside for the townsman: the city for the farmer. Estrangement [*dépaysement*] would appear to be a precondition for landscape. (Lyotard, 1991: 183)

For Lyotard, landscape is intimately connected to the inner feeling of 'being outside', the estrangement from the place.

New Zealand has achieved worldwide fame as a producer and exporter of landscapes, which in turn have been used by global media as transposable exotic settings for stories produced elsewhere. This phenomenon has become apparent since the 1980s, when New Zealand featured as the backdrop for films as different as *The Rescue* (dir. Ferdinand Fairfax, 1988), *Midnight Run* (dir. Martin Brest, 1988) and *Willow* (dir. Ron

135

Howard, 1988).[1] It reached its apex at the beginning of the new millennium, when a plethora of international film productions (particularly Indian and American) used New Zealand as a film location; the versatility of the landscape of Aotearoa was exploited in popular blockbusters such as *Vertical Limit* (dir. Martin Campbell, 2000), *Without a Paddle* (dir. Steven Brill, 2004) and *The Chronicles of Narnia* (dir. Andrew Adamson, 2005). Drawing on Lyotard, Thierry Jutel points out how, in these kinds of productions, Aotearoa/New Zealand becomes a "space of radical *dépaysement*" (Jutel, 2004: 60). Jutel translates *dépaysement* as 'out-of-nationess' claiming that this notion "represents the simultaneous attraction of geographic defamiliarisation, and the separation of the lost homeland" (Jutel, 2004: 60). As has been discussed in Chapter 1, the use of New Zealand landscape as a transposable otherness for export might be explained by the logic of the settler franchise, which in turn is a legacy of the colonial history of the country (Kavka and Turner, 2009). More recently, other socio-cultural factors have contributed to the transformation of New Zealand into a 'space of radical *dépaysement*'.

First, the international outsourcing and high mobility of production and post-production processes encouraged by globalisation has favoured the emergence of the so-called American runaway productions. These are defined as those productions originally conceived for release and broadcast in the US but filmed in another country for economic reasons. Statistics reveal that during the 1990s there was a clear tendency towards an increase of the phenomenon. A study conducted by the US Department of Commerce in 2001 shows that "from 1994 to 1998 the rate of US developed film and television productions produced abroad almost doubled from 14% to 27% while economic losses from runaway production increased fivefold from $US 2 million to $US 10 million" (US Department of Commerce, 2001: 4). Anglophone countries (such as New Zealand, Canada and Australia) that offer quality crews, cheap facilities and appropriate locations have been some of the favourite destinations of these runaway productions (O'Regan and Goldsmith, 2005).

Second, recent developments in New Zealand's political economy have placed emphasis on the importance of the creative industries, in particular sectors such as IT, design, video and film-making. In 2003 the New Zealand Minister for Economic and Regional Development, Jim Anderton, claimed that "For the first time Government regards screen production as an economic force in its own right" (Screen Production Industry Taskforce, 2003: 1). The government focused on the commercial side of the local film industry development as part of the larger process of rebranding the nation. In terms of film-making policy the government launched a $NZ 22 million Film Production Fund that aimed to bridge the gap between low-budget films, traditionally subsidised by the New Zealand Film Commission, and fully commercial products. Furthermore, Prime Minister Helen Clark saw runaway productions as a means of raising the profile of New Zealand industry and in 2003 she launched a Grant Scheme for large-budget films, under which film productions spending $NZ 50 million or more in New Zealand would qualify for a 12.5% recoup of the money spent in the country. As in the 1980s, when the film industry benefited from generous tax breaks thus generating a huge wave of film production in New Zealand,[2] the early 2000s saw Clark's Grant Scheme attract numerous runaway productions to the country. Within this context, the success of *LOTR* served as a guarantee of the quality of New Zealand production and post-production facilities for foreign producers willing to invest in the country.

Clark and the government hoped that New Zealand could profit by the various spin-offs generated by runaway productions and in particular their alleged positive impact on tourism. Expectations surrounding the American production of *The Last Samurai* in 2003 exemplify the general enthusiasm that characterised the New Zealand film industry at the time. More than any other runaway production, *The Last Samurai* raised great expectations about its potential tourist spin-off.[3] Indeed, the film was released at the end of 2003 in the wake of the fever for *LOTR*-themed tourism and this context encouraged the attempt to leverage *The Last Samurai* locations around the Taranaki region where it was actually filmed. A report on the economic impact of the filming of *The Last Samurai* in the region, commissioned by Venture Taranaki in 2004, confirmed the possible interest the movie could generate in terms of visiting the film locations.

This chapter will analyse the impact of *The Last Samurai* on the construction of tourist narratives and practices around the Taranaki area. In *The Last Samurai* New Zealand stands in for nineteenth-century Japan, the landscape in the film is therefore a typical example of a 'space of radical *dépaysement*'. In order to succeed, the film has to empty the land of its original features and replace them with meanings imported from somewhere else. Similarly, the tourist narratives that attempted to capitalise on *The Last Samurai* have stripped the tourist site of its 'destination', to use Lyotard's term, proposing new layers of meaning: on the one hand, the glamour associated with Hollywood stardom, on the other, the 'Japaneseness' of the film setting.

Both the tours and the guidebooks that refer to *The Last Samurai* emphasise the 'auratic' character of the film locations.[4] Tourist advertisements encouraged visitors to perform a pilgrimage to the locations where the stars of the big screen, such as Tom Cruise or Ken Watanabe, actually worked. The New Zealand landscape portrayed in *The Last Samurai* was imbued with the celebrity of its American stars, thus becoming the destination of a secular pilgrimage. Indeed, local destination marketing organisations tried to appeal to potential tourists by branding Taranaki as the place where 'Tom Cruise stayed'.

This strategy has been accompanied by the veiled attempt to market Taranaki as a 'Little Japan', a campaign which emphasised the similarities between the film setting and the film location. Due to the blurring of the boundaries between cinematic representations and everyday life, the film-tourist renegotiations of cultural icons and identities require a theoretical reformulation of notions such as hyper-reality and authenticity. The reception of the film conflates the spaces of otherness which belong in the diegesis (Ancient Japan and the American West) with the actual film location. The mythology of a primeval land of beauty and adventure conveyed by the narrative of the film resonates with the tourist imagery of New Zealand. This is particularly evident in the tourist narratives that brand Mt. Taranaki as Mt. Fuji. These narratives cannot elude the sacred importance the mountain has in Māori culture, an importance which, in turn, echoes the heightened significance of Mt. Fuji in Japanese culture.

The rebranding of the region as either 'Nakiwood' or 'Old Japan' seemed to be successful. In 2004, the year following the shooting of the film, tourism in Taranaki experienced the highest percentage growth for any region in New Zealand. However, by 2006 local tourist authorities recognised that the direct impact of *The Last Samurai* on Taranaki tourism had in fact been minimal. The gradual lack of interest in film-induced tourism in Taranaki raises further theoretical issues concerning the measurement and the duration of the impact of runaway productions on tourist destinations. This chapter will attempt precisely to answer the following questions: Why did *The Last Samurai* raise hopes of a tourist spin-off and why were these hopes destined to fail?


### *The Last Samurai* in Taranaki

*The Last Samurai* was a $NZ 170 million production by Warner Bros. studios, starring Tom Cruise and Billy Connolly. The Taranaki region was chosen as the main location for the movie as the result of the combined promotion efforts of Venture Taranaki, a regional development agency, and Film Venture Taranaki. In 2002, film commissioner Peter Avery, commenting on the film location, pointed out: "Everybody assumes that they're here because of the similarities of Mt. Taranaki and Mt. Fujiama, but that is only one part of the mix when it comes to choose locations. Some of the key locations have no view of the mountain but provide stunning backdrops with easy access to make a production of this scale workable" (Venture Taranaki, 2002). Seventy-six per cent of the movie was shot around the Taranaki region, with significant economic and social impact on this area. According to a report on the economic impact of the film commissioned by Venture Taranaki in 2004, *The Last Samurai* spent approximately $NZ 85.5 million in New Zealand. Of the total, an estimated $NZ 50 million (58% of total) was spent directly in Taranaki; a significant amount for a region relatively undeveloped in film infrastructures (Venture Taranaki, 2004).[5] The film's impact has been important in terms of both the economic boost and the wave of optimism it brought to the region.

According to the report, one of the most important effects has been that the perception and awareness of the Taranaki region improved greatly as a direct result of *The Last Samurai* project. The extensive media coverage experienced by Taranaki raised the profile of the region as a tourist and business destination, both nationally and internationally, and the study explicitly recommended the adoption of a tourist marketing strategy that could leverage off the film locations. The research recognised that "there is a possibility that the film itself may generate interest in terms of finding out more and actually visiting where it was filmed, particularly in regard to Japanese audiences" (Venture Taranaki, 2004: 35). A survey of a sample of the Taranaki businesses involved in the film's production revealed that a considerable number of local entrepreneurs considered the idea of marketing the region as a tourist destination. Some respondents proposed branding Taranaki as "the place where Tom Cruise stayed" or "the heart of *The Last Samurai*" (Venture Taranaki, 2004: 35).

The local enthusiasm about the potential of film-induced tourism was echoed in the local and national press. *The National Business Review* claimed that "tourism arrival figures for industry late-starter Taranaki are segmented into periods described as pre- and post-Tom Cruise" (Kennedy, 2003: 34). These expectations were confirmed by the Regional Tourism Organisation report on Taranaki visitor trends for 2004. The year following the filming of *The Last Samurai*, Taranaki experienced a remarkable increase of 14.6% of visitors in commercial accommodations, the highest percentage growth for any region in New Zealand (Venture Taranaki, 2005: 1). Nevertheless, this growth corresponded with a significant decrease of 24.8% in the number of international guest nights compared to 2003. The decline in international visitor nights (Asian in particular) is likely to correlate with the large number of visitors to the region that were involved in the production of *The Last Samurai* in 2003. The dramatic decrease in North American and Asian visitors was partially counterbalanced by a 34.5% increase in Australian tourists (Venture Taranaki, 2005: 3).

There is no evidence that the making of *The Last Samurai* has led to a tourist increase in Taranaki as no research has directly measured the impact of the movie in terms of visitor numbers. Furthermore, the interpretation of the tourist visit reports is complicated by the fact that in 2003 the region hosted many other events such as the opening of the Puke Ariki museum, the opening of the coastal walkway and several regional festivals. However, interviews with local tourist stakeholders (Radcliff, 2006) confirm that both during and after the shooting of the movie some film locations, which previously held no particular tourist interest, had become the destination of a significant tourist pilgrimage. Also, the extensive media coverage of *The Last Samurai* that emphasised the potential of Taranaki as a tourist destination could be considered as a proxy of the interest in the region generated by the movie. An analysis of the construction of filmic space and the centrality of celebrity involvement in *The Last Samurai* illuminates the potential for tourist spin-offs generated by the film.

### *The Last Samurai* and tourist imagination

Set in the 1870s, *The Last Samurai* tells the story of troubled Captain Nathan Algren (Tom Cruise), an American veteran of the Indian Campaigns. After his role in the war against the Native Americans ends in disillusionment and sorrow, Algren is hired by the advisors of the Emperor of Japan to train his country's first modern, conscript army. Algren travels to Japan and soon receives the order to eradicate the traditional warrior army of the samurai in preparation for a more Westernised and trade-friendly government. The new, unprepared army is defeated by the rebel samurai led by Katsumoto (Ken Watanabe), and Algren is captured and taken to the isolated village of the insurgents. The American finds himself unexpectedly impressed and influenced by his encounters with the samurai. Haunted by the memory of the massacre of a village of Native Americans conducted by his regiment, Algren attempts to redeem his honour by joining the cause of the samurai. Katsumoto and the samurai are ultimately defeated, but the example set by their death convinces the emperor that the pro-Western reforms suggested by his advisors are not in the best interests of the country. The film ends with the American captain returning to the mountains of the samurai village where he will lead a new quiet life with Katsumoto's sister, Taka, and her children.

The story revolves around the figure of Algren, who moves from familiar to unfamiliar spaces literally as a 'tourist'. Apart from the prologue, narrated by the translator Graham, Algren features in every scene of the film. The choice of a movie star such as Tom Cruise for the role of protagonist reinforced the centrality of Algren's character in the narrative. According to Barry King, Tom Cruise excels in roles that render interiority through action, particularly if, as in the case of Algren, these characters are written with his involvement in mind (King, 2008: 126). Algren/Cruise features prominently in all the posters and the ancillary products of the film such as DVDs, books and T-shirts. In the Australasian edition of the DVD the name of Tom Cruise is given the same emphasis as the title of the film, therefore inextricably linking his persona to *The Last Samurai*. Film stars are an integral component of the cultural industry of which Hollywood is the paradigmatic expression. Stars perform an important market function as their presence in a film is an attempt to maximise the lucrative power of the production. The economic importance of the stars is just one aspect of their influence on society. Thus Morin claims that while the growth of the culture industry was central to the development of celebrity worship, movie stars filled a psychological and even spiritual need in a century in which the influence of religion is steadily declining, at least in Western countries (Morin, 2005).

By contrast, Lasch draws a parallel between the emergence of celebrity worship and the culture of narcissism which he sees as a typical quality of modern individuals. Lasch argues that narcissists constantly seek heroes and see them as an extension of themselves. The identification of modern individuals with celebrities would be therefore explained by the need of the former to vicariously experience the glories of the latter (Lasch, 1979: 85).

The most common star type, in fact, is a plausible, likable and subtly strong average guy who matches the aspirations of the time; thus, according to Dyer, stars are cast and sold as "contemporary ideas of what it is to be an individual in the culture" (Dyer, 1986: 8). Tom Cruise's success is guaranteed by his ability to embody the stereotype of the young, white, American male. Referring to Cruise's career Bingham argues that he developed "the persona of a callow but cocky young man whose excess of confidence [...] makes him attractive but also suggests that he needs tempering and maturing" (Bingham, 2004: 253). The narratives of most of Cruise's films, from *Top Gun* (dir. Tony Scott, 1986) to *Rain Man* (dir. Barry Levinson, 1988), as well as *Minority Report* (dir. Steven Spielberg, 2002), work to undermine his character and make him earn back his confidence in a more mature setting. Cruise is a desirable model of middle class, white, American masculinity, whose persona is oriented towards goal and action, experience and authority (Bingham 2004: 253). *The Last Samurai* encourages the viewer's identification with Algren/ Cruise and the presence of Cruise plays an important role in this identification process, particularly because, as King points out "Cruise's acting has projected a persona that is youthful, energetic, attractive to the opposite sex especially, but also to men as a 'regular' guy" (King, 2008: 126). Cruise's embodiment of Western masculinity reinforces the ideological constructs of 'whiteness' that inform the film. Thus, *The Last Samurai* appeals to Western audiences through the representation of the supposed ethnic superiority of the protagonist. During the six months Algren is held prisoner, he learns to speak Japanese and master local customs, such as dressing himself in Japanese clothing without any assistance. He also gains in-depth knowledge of the art of the samurai, to the extent of being acknowledged as equal to his instructor Ujio, who has studied the skill his entire life. As Tierney points out: "the ability of the White practitioner to defeat Asians, using an Asian skill, in Asia, propagates the theme of a ubiquitous, even inevitable White supremacy of global proportions" (Tierney, 2006: 614). The film celebrates both the extraordinary ability of Algren to learn foreign customs and his stubborn determination to intrude into a cultural space in which he is clearly not welcome. In a way, *The Last Samurai* satisfies the tourist fantasy of accessing the 'authentic', overcoming the barrier of cultural differences and ultimately controlling the space of the Other. The ideology at work in *The Last Samurai*, in which the Japanese are merely ancillary to the white subject, reflects a colonialist mindset in which "the colonial subject functions only to consolidate the self of the colonizer" (Young, 1990: 162).

Interestingly, even though the narrative of *The Last Samurai* does not make any explicit reference to Aotearoa and its colonial history it is nevertheless connected to the New Zealand film tradition. The film was inspired by a project developed by well-known New Zealand director Vincent Ward. Ward worked on the development of a project called East/West (and later 'West of the Rising Sun') for nearly four years and, after approaching several film-makers such as Francis Ford Coppola and Peter Weir, he eventually interested American director Edward Zwick. Ward was credited as executive producer and his involvement in *The Last Samurai* was instrumental in the decision to shoot the film in New Zealand (Ward, 2009). The narrative of the film itself was influenced by Ward's personal experience of 'otherness' in New Zealand:

> Years ago, I lived in a little Māori village, and I was the only European there. I had no water, no electricity, nothing. That experience basically gave me a bit of a compass. I ultimately came up with a story, set during the colonial wars, of a woman living among the Māori. Now, I also came up with another story, this time about a European man going into Japan—and that ultimately became *The Last Samurai*. (Webwombat, 2006)

The Chief Executive of the New Zealand Film Commission, Ruth Harley, went as far as to argue that *The Last Samurai* could not be considered a simple runaway production because of Vincent Ward's creative involvement (Harley cited in Conor, 2004: 90). Most importantly, however, the basic structure of the narrative is influenced by very local discourses of race relations between Pākehā and Māori. The story of *The Last Samurai* is based on a real tourist and ethnographic experience within a Māori community and it is informed by a Pākehā point of view. The core of the narrative is the experience of a white man in the midst of a physically and culturally alien environment. The cultural specificity of the Other is irrelevant as long as it provides an exotic background which amplifies and validates the Western Self.

In *The Last Samurai*, in fact, Algren takes on the functions of both 'Subject' and 'Object' of the narrative. Greimas' development of Propp's structuralist analysis of the morphology of traditional folk tales elucidates this double position. Greimas schematises six actants, which can be defined as the figures that perform an action in a given narrative: the Subject is he who seeks, desires, undertakes, and the Object is what is sought; the Giver sends the object and the Receiver is the place to which it is sent; the Helper aids the action and the Opposer blocks it (Greimas, 1983: 201). These six logical modes transcend the notion of character as they can be embodied in one or several characters throughout the story, thus forming the bases of every narrative. Throughout the film, Algren aspires to reconnect with his inner self, to the values of courage and honour that he can find only inside himself, thus becoming at once the Subject and the Object of the narrative. Similarly, power over self and self-actualisation are persistent themes in leisure activities and these form the primary motivations for the adventure tourism for which New Zealand has become well known. Like other protagonists of New Zealand films, from David Manning in *Runaway* to Ada in *The Piano*, Algren is a 'tourist' for whom the alien landscape is a means through which s/he can rediscover his/her inner Self.

## From Mt. Taranaki to Mt. Fuji: negotiating the meaning of place

Throughout the film, Cruise/Algren is often represented gazing intensely at the distant land. The core narrative of *The Last Samurai* is strongly reminiscent of the tourist experience: the opposition between familiar and unfamiliar spaces, the journey to an exotic land and the constant interaction between the protagonist and the environment. The structure of the film itself is founded on the juxtaposition of contrasting environments. In terms of spaces, the narrative of *The Last Samurai* is based on a triple opposition between Far West versus Metropolitan America, America versus Japan and Modern Japan versus Traditional Japan. Similarly, Algren's loyalty shifts from 'otherness' (he befriends the Native Americans) to 'sameness' (he is ordered to destroy a Native American village/crush the revolt of the samurai defined as 'savages') and back to 'otherness' again (he joins the samurai revolt). The protagonist is irresistibly attracted to otherness, to the extent that one of the American officers hired by the Japanese asks him "what's in your own people that you hate so much?" However, the specificity of this otherness is irrelevant as long as it validates Algren's Self. The different spaces of the film can be organised within the categories of nature and culture; sameness and otherness. In the story, the urban spaces of both America and Modern Japan are equated with moral and physical corruption while the rural settings inhabited by Native Americans and the samurai are the expression of a harmonic life within an idyllic nature.

A semiotic square of the spaces in *The Last Samurai* based on the opposition 'nature versus culture' reveals the inner geography of the film (Figure 5.1).

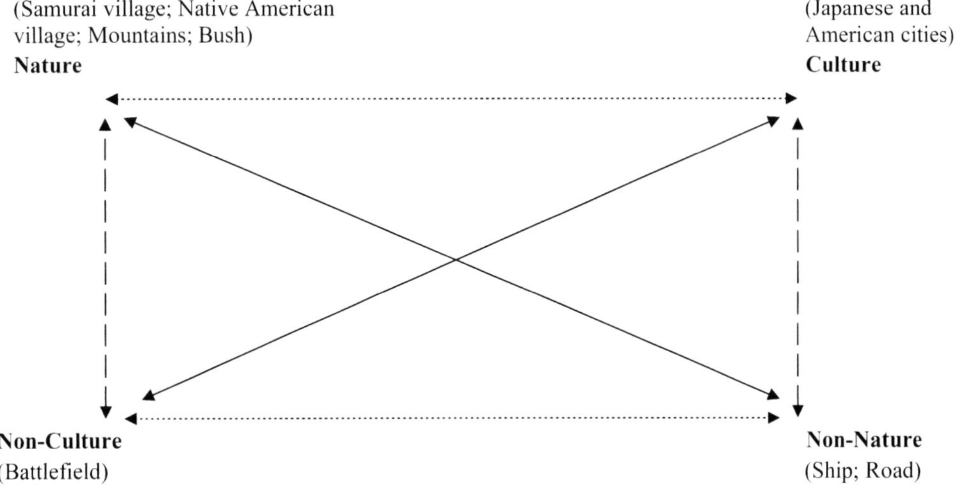


Figure 5.1. Semiotic square, *The Last Samurai*.

Both the Japanese and the American cities belong to the category of Culture while the mountains and both the samurai and the Native American village can be positioned on the opposite side of the square as expressions of Nature. The 'pastoral narrative' is one of the main appealing factors of the film, according to Wilson (2007). Indeed, the success and the coincident release of both *LOTR* and *The Last Samurai* is explained by the demand of city dwellers for pastoral film narratives. In the story, nineteenth-century Japan explicitly represents the myth of a new West at a time when the original American frontier had been tamed. Significantly, as is revealed by the map that appears on screen when Algren leaves America, he travels westward from California to Japan in his quest for freedom and adventure. Similarly, the actual film location, New Zealand, is itself considered, at least from a European and American point of view, as a 'space of frontier' where civilisation has not yet corrupted nature. In *The Last Samurai*, the representation of scenic and adventurous 'places of otherness' is consistent with the tourist imagery of New Zealand as an adventure playground. A reception of the film that is informed by a knowledge of the identity of the actual film location therefore balances three intermingling spaces of frontier: New Zealand/ Ancient Japan/American West. These form a consistent liminal space between tradition and modernity; sameness and otherness; the urban and the rural.

Significantly, *The Last Samurai*-related tourist narratives have emphasised the resemblance of the actual place (New Zealand) to the fictional one (Japan). The

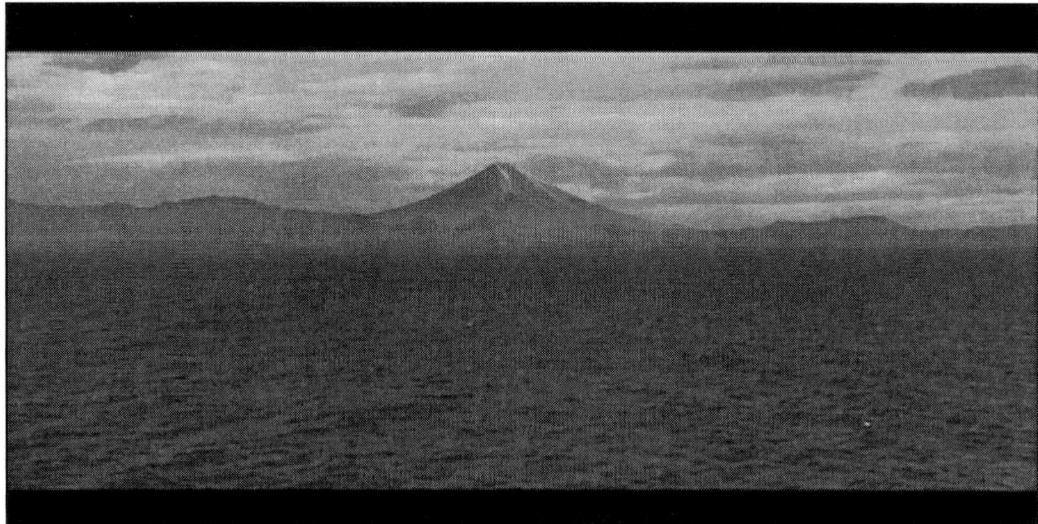

Figure 5.2. *The Last Samurai*, Warner Bros.

New Zealand Tourism website suggests that the region underwent an ontological transformation: "Taranaki became Japan for the making of *The Last Samurai*" (TNZ, 2006). GoAustralia, an American-based travel website, brands Taranaki as the "Land of *The Last Samurai*" and comments:

> If you were in Japan and heard the word Taranaki, you'd think it was a Japanese word. It does sound Japanese, but no, it's not a Japanese word but the name of a picturesque region on New Zealand's North Island. (GoAustralia, 2006)

The fusion between the setting of the film (Japan and Far West) and the actual location (New Zealand) is possible because the appeal of both spaces is founded on the canons of the picturesque.

The opposition of contrasting environments in *The Last Samurai* is not the only element reminiscent of the tourist experience. The journey across an exotic and unfamiliar landscape is another important component of the narrative: the boat and the road in particular play a prominent role and, in the semiotic square of the film geography, they constitute the category of Non-Nature. They are both spaces of transition that often open up new narrative possibilities represented by Nature: for example, from the deck of his ship Algren gazes at the imposing silhouette of Mt. Fuji, an iconic expression of the power of Nature. Similarly, when the American is captured by Katsumoto and taken to the samurai village the road is dominated by the spectacular presence of the Fujiama (Figures 5.2 and 5.3).

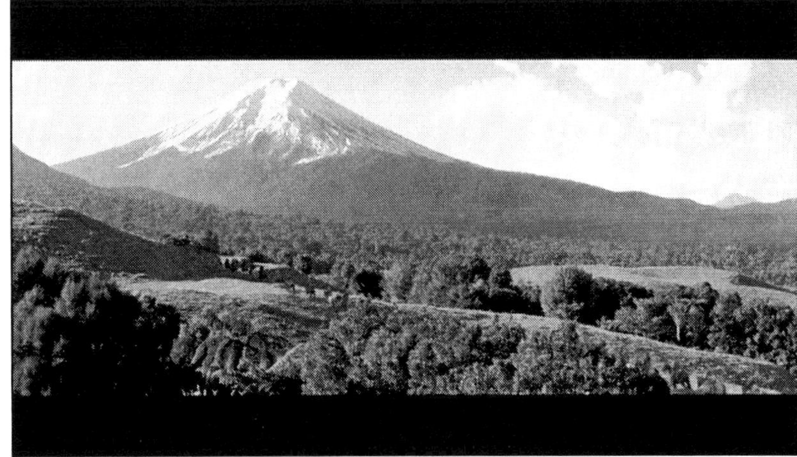

Figure 5.3. *The Last Samurai*, Warner Bros.

Spaces of transition such as the boat and the road activate an aesthetics of spectacle, as they are often associated with extreme long shots of the landscape. Significantly, this landscape is highly symbolic, because of Mount Fuji's association with 'Japaneseness', purity and tradition. The mountain thus embodies the final destination of Algren's existentialist quest and, because of its highly symbolic value, can be considered as the 'icon' of the film in the sense given to the term by Riley and Van Doren (1998). According to Riley and Van Doren an icon can be a single event, a favourite performer, a location's physical feature or a theme that represents all that is popular and compelling about a movie. Icons, abstract or tangible, become the focal point for visitation and the location itself becomes evidence of the icon (Riley and Van Doren, 1998: 924). One of the most frequent issues in the film-tourist narratives that brand Taranaki as the place of *The Last Samurai* is the similarity between Mt. Taranaki and Mt. Fuji. The New Zealand government immigration website, in a section entitled "The world in one place", emphasises the 'versatile beauty' of the country and claims that Mt. Taranaki has been chosen as the film location of *The Last Samurai* because of its striking resemblance to Mt. Fujiama (NZembassy, 2006). This connection has often been emphasised by the media and the destination marketing organisations, despite the fact that it is virtually impossible to catch sight of the mountain from the main set of the film in the Uruti Valley, and consequently the mountain was never shot from this location. In fact, Mt. Fuji features just twice in the film: during the scene in which Algren arrives in Japan and during the journey to Katsumoto's village. In the former instance the mountain was actually digitally recreated. The actual Mt. Taranaki appears in only one three-second long shot, suggesting that the presence of a Fujiama-like mountain in the area was not essential for the production. Warner Bros. chose New Zealand for financial reasons, and not because of Mt. Taranaki. Indeed, the location managers initially focused on the South Island and eventually chose Taranaki because of New Plymouth's proximity to the rural locations. The overestimation of the connection between Fuji and Taranaki implicitly recognises the sacred importance the latter has in Māori culture, an importance which, in turn, echoes the heightened significance of Mt. Fuji in Japanese culture. Nevertheless, what is most relevant about the construction of the myth of the interchangeability of Mt. Fuji/Taranaki is the celebration of New Zealand's versatility. In an effort to attract runaway productions to the country, Film New Zealand recently promoted this versatility in a booklet entitled *The Production Guide to the World in one Country* (Film New Zealand, 1999), claiming that New Zealand has been able to reproduce extremely diverse countries such as Italy, Scotland, Korea or Greece (Film New Zealand, 1999: 21).

It is significant that Mt. Egmont/Taranaki has already been the subject of a cultural conflict between Māori, who believe the mountain to be the god Taranaki, and the European settlers who adopted the name given to the mountain by Captain Cook. The conflict remains unresolved as both nomenclatures are still used, signifying the traditional biculturalism of New Zealand society. The gradual shift from farming and dairy production to an emphasis on creative industries and the film industry in particular, implying a liberalisation of the market and the opening of the borders, is shaking the foundations of New Zealand culture. The creation of a mythical 'glocal' icon, Mt. Taranaki/Egmont/Fuji, is a symptom of the complex renegotiation of national identity experienced by New Zealand during the last few decades. The expectations surrounding the development of a 'Nakiwood' were, therefore, part of a wider project that targeted creative industries as the core of a new economic development strategy.

Mt. Fuji/Taranaki, as an expression of national identity construction in process, is not the only trace of New Zealand that remains in the film. The film in fact conveys a sense of colonial guilt towards the treatment of indigenous people, and Ward's involvement in the production of the film had a deciding impact in this sense.[6] *The Last Samurai* equates the extermination of the Native Americans with the uneven struggle led by the samurai against a modern, Westernised power. Both Native Americans and samurai, defined by the negative Western characters of the film as 'savages', share traditional values such as courage, honour and, most of all, a keen appreciation of war. There is a clear resemblance between the characteristics of the 'indigenous Other' as represented in *The Last Samurai* and the Māori. Significantly, the story is set during the late 1860s, and thus corresponds historically with the Māori Wars between the indigenous people of New Zealand and the British settlers. Referring to the colonial attack on the pacifist Māori settlement of Parihaka in the Taranaki region, Alice Te Punga Somerville suggests that "for the viewer of *The Last Samurai* who retains an identification with Taranaki and the history of Parihaka it is impossible to ignore the messy spectral presence of the bloodshed and violence of Parihaka" (Te Punga Somerville, 2009: 252). The story of *The Last Samurai* therefore resonates with images of the colonial conflict between white Europeans and Māori. Zwick's film goes as far as borrowing some of the conventions of New Zealand films about Māori Wars, in particular the representation of the bush. As in *Utu*, where Māori warriors are represented as at ease in the thick, native bush, the forest is a familiar environment for the samurai. It is by taking advantage of the mist of the bush, in fact, that Katsumoto is able to defeat the imperial army led by the American officers. Similarly, in New Zealand, the bush, into which men travel to create a civilised and colonial order, is feared precisely because of the threat represented by indigenous bodies (Te Punga Somerville, 2009: 256).

Notions of travel and conflict play a crucial role in the film as they offer the protagonist an opportunity for redemption and regeneration. The battlefield fills the fourth corner of the semiotic square as it is a space of Non-Culture. Non-Culture (battlefield-conflict) and Non-Nature (ship, road-travel) are in semiotic terms 'sub-contraries'; they are not strongly opposed and together they form a neutral term. Both ship/road and battlefield connect sameness and otherness, nature and culture. Spaces of both Non-Culture and Non-Nature represent the connective tissue of the narrative. More importantly, their role in the film is emphasised by their association with spectacle. In both cases, this connection is founded on the notion of spectacle; one of the principal appeals of the film is the visual pleasure conveyed by the battle scenes. The regenerative power of the battlefield invariably leads to the idyllic space of nature, as after each battle Algren travels back to the village up in the mountains. As with all the other spaces in the film, the battlefield and the road are active characters in the story. In terms of Greimas' schematisation of the actants, these spaces could be considered as Helpers: it is through the experience of travelling and fighting that Algren is eventually able to reconnect to his inner Self. Similarly, the city or in a broader sense 'Culture' is the Opposer to Algren's quest; while Japan as mythical space of purity (represented by Mt. Fuji and the samurai village as synecdoche) is the Receiver, the place where the protagonist needs to travel to in order to 'solve' the narrative. As in other successful tourism-inducing films, such as *LOTR* or *The Piano*, the environment is an active character of the story in *The Last Samurai*. Riley and Van Doren point out that the interest generated by many Australian movies in the country, particularly the Outback, was explained by the interaction of man with the environment (Riley and Van Doren, 1992: 273). In a similar way, drawing on the works of Tooke and Baker (1996), Beeton claims that tourists want to experience at least part of what is depicted in the film as opposed to merely gazing at the site (Beeton, 2005: 24).

Nevertheless, the construction of space is not the only element that appeals to the viewers' tourist imagination. Tom Cruise himself was another powerful 'icon' of the film and his association with the film locations had a direct impact on tourist visits to these sites. The contemporary cult of celebrity, particularly in relation to film stars, produces what could be defined as the 'Midas syndrome', namely the power of the stars to add value to all they touch, and this is particularly relevant to tourist destinations.


**Celebrity worship**

As Beeton points out, "the concurrent development of mass travel and mass media propelled the twentieth century into the era of celebrity tourism" (Beeton, 2005: 32). The study of the relationship between celebrity worship, film and tourism is particularly relevant to the analysis of phenomena such as the Hollywood tours of celebrity homes, or the tourist fascination with the stars' footprints on Hollywood Boulevard (Beeton, 2005: 32). As suggested by much literature on tourism (MacCannell, 1999; Reader, 2007), the construction of meaning linked to the visits of celebrity-related destinations shows an affinity with the spiritual experience of the pilgrimage.

An important component of *The Last Samurai*-induced tourism has been a manifestation of the worship of the Hollywood 'circus', in particular Tom Cruise. A recent study about the relation between celebrity and the perception of destinations dcmonstrated that celebrity involvement, defined as "the tendency to develop a heightened affection and attachment to a celebrity" (Lee et al., 2008: 813), can have a positive effect on intentions to visit a place related to the celebrity. According to Lee, the visit of a location associated with a celebrity is an act of consuming the qualities that the celebrity signifies. Furthermore, the same study revealed that the level of celebrity involvement has positive effects on the cognitive and affective images of the destination associated with the celebrity (Lee et al., 2008: 815).

During the making of *The Last Samurai* in the Taranaki region, national newspapers and magazines commented on the phenomenon: "Tom-watching and Billy [co-star Connolly]-spotting have become the region's most popular diversion" (Kennedy, 2003: 34). New Zealand Prime Minister Helen Clark even visited the set of the movie in order to meet Tom Cruise, Hollywood's highest-paid actor at the time (West, 2003). At the end of the filming in April 2003, *The Edge Radio* organised a gathering of 1200 people, assembled in formation to spell the word 'Tominaki', in an effort to give the Hollywood star a memorable farewell from Taranaki. The emphasis on the fact that different locations in Taranaki are the 'actual' places visited or touched by the movie stars inflects Walter Benjamin's famous thesis on the loss of 'aura' in the age of mechanical reproduction (Benjamin, 1979). The presence of the American star in Taranaki has created 'auratic' places, namely the film sets and the locations somehow connected with Cruise and the other film stars. Three years after the filming of the movie, local businesses still use Tom Cruise as a marketing tool. Both Taranaki and New Zealand tourism websites mention the presence of the Hollywood star in the region. Several shops and restaurants in New Plymouth display Cruise's autographed picture; the Nice Hotel advertises that "several celebrities and showbiz greats have [...] slept between the Nice's crisp bed sheets over the years: Tom Cruise (several times before and during filming of *The Last Samurai*) [...] and Hollywood director Ed Zwick, to name a few" (Barrett, 2006: 120). The phenomenon of celebrity worship is intertwined with the notions of authenticity and backstage experience. MacCannell elaborates a model of frontstage/backstage authenticity that could be applied to tourist sites. According to this model, the tourist site is divided into regions that provide visitors with different degrees of authenticity. The frontstage is usually represented by public areas such as roads, restaurants and theatres while the backstage is identified with off-limits places, such as private living areas that can offer the opportunity to experience authenticity. According to MacCannell, tourists constantly seek the possibility of accessing the backstage area, and this is particularly evident in the analysis of the tourist rhetoric of 'getting off the beaten tracks' and 'meeting the real people' (MacCannell, 1999: 94).

The application of MacCannell's model to film tourism could explain the great number of visitors attracted to the Taranaki region during the filming of *The Last Samurai*. Tourists sought the opportunity to experience the backstage area, in this case represented by the film set of a Hollywood production. Following the end of the filming, 'Samurai Village Tours', a local tourist company, began offering visits to the main film location. The tour of the set, the display of pictures of the making of the movie and the comments of the guide involved in the film production, provide visitors with a limited insight into the backstage of a Hollywood production. Furthermore, both the film locations and the guide benefit from a 'celebrity-through-proximity' as a result of having played host to film stars. The principle of fame-by-association is reinforced by the use of anecdotes and the display of pictures of Tom Cruise at work on the set. The guide to the Samurai Village claims personal and direct access to the authenticity of the film production by challenging and subverting mass-mediated narratives. Contrary to media gossip, for example, Tom Cruise is defined by the Taranaki residents involved in the production of the film as a "very nice and generous person", who is also "reasonably tall" and "doesn't wear heels" (Radcliff, 2006). The film locations are still invested with the 'aura' of celebrity and the guide of the set provides a mediated access to the reality of Hollywood. Nevertheless, after the shooting was complete, the status of the Taranaki film locations shifted from 'backstage' to 'midstage' where the possibility of grasping the authenticity of the film production is extremely limited.

From another perspective, referring to Riley and Van Doren's definition of film-induced tourism, it is possible to consider *The Last Samurai* as a 'hallmark event'. Riley and Van Doren draw their definition from Ritchie, who describes the hallmark event as:

> Major one time events of limited duration developed primarily to enhance the awareness, appeal and profitability of a destination in the short and/or long term. These events rely for their success on uniqueness, status, or timely significance to create interest and attract attention. (Ritchie cited in Riley and Van Doren, 1992: 268)

Riley and Van Doren claim that because of its characteristics a feature film can be recognised as a hallmark event. Its uniqueness and status make *The Last Samurai* a prime example of a hallmark event. However, as Sue Beeton points out, films (unlike hallmarks) are not created to specifically promote the locations they portray or to attract tourists (Beeton, 2005: 9). Furthermore, as was later recognised, even by Riley and Van Doren (1998), the simple depiction of scenic landscape in successful movies does not guarantee tourist interest in the film location. The sheer popularity of a movie does not explain why certain commercially successful blockbusters fail to generate any form of film-induced tourism, while other minor productions have a much bigger impact in terms of tourist spin-off. According to later works by Riley and Van Doren (1998), other elements of the film such as storyline, themes, relationship between the characters may also cause the public to visit the film locations.

As suggested, the making of this film had a significant economic and social impact on Taranaki. It also enhanced the credibility of Taranaki as a tourist destination and boosted community pride, to the extent that the region has been renamed 'Nakiwood'. However, by 2006 expectations generated by *The Last Samurai* had been disappointing. This confirms Riley and Van Doren's claim that, although destinations depicted in the movie are enhanced by special effects, association with famous actors and highly attractive settings, the awareness, appeal and profitability of film diminishes over time. The movies can, nevertheless, become recurring events if re-released in cinemas, on television or DVD, and the repeated viewing may reinforce the initial effect of enhancing interest in the destination (Riley and Van Doren, 1992: 269).

Research undertaken in 2006 suggests that the direct impact of *The Last Samurai* on local tourism has been minimal. This contradicts the enthusiastic forecasts of the report on the lasting effects of *The Last Samurai* commissioned by Venture Taranaki in 2004. Tourist professionals and local authorities alike claim that the expectations of a relevant *Last Samurai* tourist spin-off have been disappointing. The film has led to the development of just three *Last Samurai*-related tourism businesses. 'Freewheelings', an Auckland-based tour operator, runs one-, three- or seven-day tours of North Island main film locations such as Hobitton (*LOTR*) and *The Last Samurai* set. 'Gumboot Gully movie stunt Horses', formed after the film, provides stunt shows as seen in *The Last Samurai*. Finally, 'Samurai Village Tours' provides visits to the main set of the movie, which is on private land.[7] The production of the film has not led to the development of film infrastructures and no other Hollywood production has chosen Taranaki as a film location. As Pratt points out, *The Last Samurai* was merely a "minor salve to local employment" and the development generated by the movie "is not sustainable (unless another film of this size were to follow on)" (Pratt, 2007: 137).

## The management of film-induced tourism: critical factors

According to Venture Taranaki CEO Stuart Trundle, the main reason for the minimal impact of *The Last Samurai* on local tourism was its disappointing result at the box office. The film, released in 2004, was not considered a failure, but its gross receipts of $US 456 million were less than half that of its direct competitor, *LOTR—The Return of the King*, which took $US 1.118 million. Furthermore, unlike Jackson's trilogy, *The Last Samurai* could not benefit from the type of complementary literary tourism generated by an extremely popular book such as *LOTR*. The movie was based on an original script and could not appeal to a wide and well-established community of fans.

Another problematic issue was represented by the difficulty of recognising the film's locations. In *The Last Samurai* Taranaki was a stand-in for a nineteenth-century Japan. Sets were accurately reconstructed by the American production which was extremely concerned with the 'authenticity' of settings and costumes. According to Warner Bros. the aim of the production designer Lilly Kilvert was to recreate "the look and the atmosphere of late 1860 Japan as authentically as possible" (Warner Bros., 2004). *The Last Samurai* is a typical example of the way in which New Zealand is constructed as *dépaysement*. In his analysis of the tourist impact of runaway productions in rural areas, Pratt claims that

> [i]n the majority of films the background is just that: background [...]. Within the constraints of continuity 'real' spaces may be mixed and matched to create the effect that the director is seeking; worse still, for the locale seeking to capitalise on its starring role, 'the actual countryside' might be digitally enhanced. (Pratt, 2007: 131)

The film begins with the depiction of stunning views of a lush, untouched nature, which is supposed to be Japan. An awareness of the fact that New Zealand is the actual location of the movie, achieved by reading reviews of the film or watching 'making of' documentaries, allows the spectator to read the first scene as a display of the beautiful scenery of New Zealand. But if this awareness is lacking, the landscapes portrayed in the first scene are read as 'standard' exotic icons, the only function of which is to provide a counterpoint to the corruption of the Western world. In the words of Bernard Smith, the exotic is "a category of accommodation by means of which the European perceived and interpreted the Other according to the limits and constraints of European understanding" (Smith, 1992: 10). The notion of exotic cannot be separated from the historical experience of colonialism, as the former describes fantasies of otherness that attempt to contain it within the intellectual and real boundaries of empire. The exotic is therefore a discursive formation that handles the Other, and particularly the East, by constructing it as a counter-image to the Occident/the West. The boundary formation between *Them* and *Us* is based on a notion of European identities as superior to non-European people and cultures. As such, the exotic is the result of a Eurocentric perspective that upgrades European culture and splits the world into "the West and the Rest" (Shohat and Stam 1994: 2).

Even though the film carried some residues of the specificity of New Zealand culture and history (significance of the mountain, problematic relation with the indigenous people and appeal of remoteness and otherness) the landscapes used in the movie were almost completely emptied of their features and replaced with an 'imported nature'.[8] Even if the website of the movie briefly mentions New Zealand as the most important film location, the production did not create any strong association with the country and refused any possibility of co-marketing (Venture Taranaki, 2004). The main agents of promotion for New Zealand as the location of the film have been both the media reports about the movie and destination marketing organisations such as Tourism New Zealand and Tourism Taranaki.

After the end of filming, the local authorities realised that marketing issues concerning the film locations should have been resolved prior to shooting. This was a crucial mistake that limited the subsequent exploitation of the tourist spin-off. The most direct consequence of this attitude has been that virtually all the movie sets were dismantled and all the props auctioned or brought back to the Warner Studios in the USA. In a similar way, the main Taranaki film-related business, 'Samurai Village Tours' has not been allowed to use the title of the movie for marketing purposes. However, the copyright policy has not been extremely strict, as the owner of the Village has managed to reconstruct the set and use pictures of the making of the film, despite the fact that these were officially forbidden, for the tours.

Even though part of the set was reconstructed by the owner of the 'Samurai Village Tours' according to the original production designers' plans, this raises questions about the 'authenticity' of the set as most of its components have lost their 'auratic' character. Furthermore, as most of the locations were enhanced by digital effects, all the props and landscapes, both original and reconstructed, look very different from the film and could not meet the expectations of the movie-goer/tourist. Many scholars (Boorstin, 1962; Baudrillard, 1983; MacCannell, 1999; Eco, 1986) have suggested that visitors could find the actual movie-making process boring and disappointing, thus preferring a 'staged authenticity' or a hyper-reality which matched their expectations, to the actual midstage or backstage experience. Part of the appeal of the 'Samurai Village' lies in its association with celebrities, but even though the 'aura' of stardom briefly survived the departure of the film crew, the international fame of a movie star such as Tom Cruise was already associated with other places such as Hollywood or the USA. It was therefore not plausible to establish a durable connection between *The Last Samurai*'s celebrities and the Taranaki region.

Another factor that limited the tourist spin-off of *The Last Samurai* was the role of the landscape in the film. The landscape is often a character in all respects, playing an active role in the narrative and this is believed to be a factor that appeals to the tourist imagination of the spectator, possibly influencing his/her travel decisions. Nevertheless, the emphasis on landscape in *The Last Samurai* cannot be compared to other tourist-inducing films such as *The Piano* or *LOTR*; the focus of the film is Algren/Cruise and every other aspect of the narrative revolves around his figure.

A further important issue was the ambiguous marketing strategy adopted by the local tourist stakeholders. Even if a tourist advertisement of the Samurai Village in a Japanese tourist guide describes *The Last Samurai* as "the story that was filmed in the beautiful scenery of New Zealand", most of the tourist discourses were concerned with the promotion of the celebrity worship or the resemblance between Taranaki and 'authentic' Japan. The title of the above-mentioned advertisement in fact claimed "The place of *The Last Samurai*: it reminds me the good old times of Japan". These kinds of tourist narratives are based on the appeal of New Zealand as an idealised, uncorrupted

Japan but they risk undermining the uniqueness of New Zealand positioning in the tourist global market. This strategy in fact positions the Taranaki-based Samurai Village in the same market niche as the actual Japanese destinations that signify 'tradition and Japaneseness'. According to Beeton (2005: 10), *The Last Samurai* belongs to the category of 'Mistaken Identities' film tourism, defined as visits to the locations where the movie was filmed, but not set and vice versa. Even if just a minimal part of *The Last Samurai* was shot in Japan, the movie has been used by some Western tour operators as a marketing tool to promote Tokyo and other Japanese cities as tourist destinations. In a similar way, another Hollywood blockbuster, *Braveheart* (dir. Mel Gibson, 1995), generated tourism both to the place where it was filmed (County Meath, Ireland) and set (Scottish Highlands). However, Scotland benefited much more from the tourist spin-off generated by the movie, which also had implications for the negotiation of the Scottish national identity.[9] According to the Scottish Tourist Board, which has promoted the image created by *Braveheart*, the movie, along with other film features set and shot in Scotland, is estimated to have attracted between 7 million and 15 million pounds in extra tourist revenue (Busby and Klug, 2001: 320). From this point of view Tooke and Baker's conclusions on film-induced tourism are adamant:

> If the film location is the true setting the visitor visits the location; if the film location represents a fictional setting, the visitors go to the location; but if the film location represents a different actual setting, the visitors go to the place represented. (Tooke and Baker, 1996: 93)

Apart from such issues of recognition, publicity of the 'Samurai Village Tours' was self-limited by the fear of contributing to an overcrowding of the 'Village'. The movie set is in fact located within a farm and is managed by the owners, who dedicate most of their time to farming activity. Venture Taranaki did not make any effort to market the other film sites in the region, while Warner Bros. was not interested in promoting the New Zealand film locations.

Finally, all the tourist stakeholders targeted the Asian market, as they relied on the word of mouth of the Japanese crew that worked in the region for several months. A Japanese film production used the set of the village to shoot a documentary about Ken Watanabe, one of the stars of *The Last Samurai*, but apart from this, in 2006 the survey of local authorities and businesses revealed that the number of Asian, or even just international tourists attracted to Taranaki by *The Last Samurai*, was minimal.

## Conclusions

Being a small society highly reliant on the growth of export, New Zealand is a dependent economy and, as a consequence, also a very open and free one. New Zealand is fundamentally interdependent on the capitalist system as the prosperity of the country is closely associated with trade prospects with OECD countries. As foreseen by Franklin, the anxiety derived by the country's dependence on the fortunes of international trade has stimulated the development of a more responsive, adaptive and innovatory society (Franklin, 1978: XVII). An example of this is the implementation, by the New Zealand government, of policies aimed to attract runaway productions to the country and capitalise on their tourist spin-offs. The limited budget available for tourism marketing has obliged the New Zealand tourist board to capitalise on the images of the country created by external agents, particularly media and film. As revealed by the case of *LOTR*, this strategy has proven to be extremely profitable and Tourism New Zealand has tried to replicate this success by marketing the connections between the country and other film productions.

The making of *The Last Samurai* in 2003 around Taranaki had significant economic, social and cultural effects for both the region and New Zealand as a whole. Aside from the direct benefits, such as employment opportunities and huge profits for commercial accommodation, Taranaki and New Plymouth received an important boost in media attention due in particular to the presence of the 'Hollywood circus' in the region. More importantly, local authorities and stakeholders hoped to profit from the tourist spin-off generated by the film and *The Last Samurai* became a test bed for the tourist potential of runaway productions in general.

The influence of *The Last Samurai* on tourism could be divided into two stages. The first stage, the shooting of the film and the period immediately following its release, were characterised by a high level of media interest in the region that, in turn, attracted tourists to Taranaki. *The Last Samurai* represented for Taranaki a 'hallmark event', simply because of its scale and its association with the centre of the mediatic empire of Hollywood. Tourist discourses in post-*The Last Samurai* Taranaki focused on the 'celebrity-through-proximity' gained by the region, thanks to the presence of Hollywood stars such as Tom Cruise. Cruise's fame has been used as a marketing tool by local stakeholders who emphasise the 'auratic' character of places or objects somehow involved with the film-making process or with the life of the stars. Furthermore, the film narrative itself, concerned with notions of travel, mobility and inter-cultural encounter, stimulated the tourist imagination of the viewers; possibly influencing their travel decisions. The core of the story exists precisely in the interaction between the protagonist and the environment, which highlights the importance of the landscape and in particular the iconic value of Mt. Fuji. Tourist narratives emphasised the linguistic and physical similarities between

Japan and New Zealand and overestimated the role of Mt. Taranaki as a stand-in for Mt. Fuji, thus creating a connection between the imaginary setting and the actual location. The subsequent attempts to rebrand Taranaki as either 'the place where Tom Cruise stayed' or as 'Little Japan' point to the process of renegotiation of New Zealand national identity. More specifically, they can be considered as creative expressions that seek to satisfy an urgent need for local identity assertion and celebration. As noted by Bell and Lyall, since the early 1990s New Zealand, particularly the rural districts, has witnessed more assertive activities in the bid to gain attention and mark place. For Bell and Lyall:

> With spreading global homogeneity and international processes that ignore the parochial, the lack of recognition or acknowledgement of one's own local place and the contribution it makes can be disturbingly undermining. (Bell and Lyall, 1995: 10–11)

For a short period of time *The Last Samurai* provided the rural region of Taranaki with the opportunity to assert a local and distinctive identity at both the national and international level.

The second stage of *The Last Samurai*'s impact on tourism, the years following the release of the film from the end of 2004 to the present day, is characterised by a steady decline in tourist flows to the film locations. This confirms Ritchie's thesis that the impact of the 'hallmark event' on the tourist destination is destined to diminish over time. The main reason for the failure of *The Last Samurai* to generate a long-term tourist spin-off is the discrepancy between the imaginary setting (Japan) and the actual one (New Zealand). This supports the thesis of scholars such as Tooke and Baker, who suggest that tourists are attracted to places where filming is only believed to have taken place (Tooke and Baker, 1996). It is not clear whether *The Last Samurai* has induced any form of tourism to Japan and this should be the object of further investigation. What is most relevant here is that the partial success of the film in attracting visitors is due to the survival of residues of New Zealand specificity in the film: the association of the film locations with Hollywood celebrities; the symbolic significance of Mt. Taranaki which echoes that of Mt. Fuji; the narrative centrality of notions of purity, nature and frontier, defining characteristics of New Zealand's tourist image.

However, the connection with the uniqueness and history of the actual place is repressed by the film-makers, who attempted to transform the film locations into an 'interchangeable otherness'. Thierry Jutel aptly describes the historical process of construction, commodification and virtualisation of the New Zealand landscape. Jutel detects four categories of this transformative process, here are the first three:

> First, the discourse around New Zealand is firmly grounded in the
> imperialist projection upon the colonised land. Second, as postcolonial
> society Aotearoa produces multiple and often contradictory discourses
> about the landscape. Third, the landscape of New Zealand has come to
> represent a transposable 'otherness'. (Jutel, 2004: 55)

Aotearoa/New Zealand can stand in as 'Other places' precisely because of its
difference and emptiness. This is the ultimate stage of an imperialist project that
has erased the traces of the original inhabitants of the land: the Māori. Referring to
the disappearance of 'Maoriland' from cultural representations of the country, Alice
Te Punga Somerville claims that "the transition from [...] a specifically populated
landscape at the beginning of the twentieth century to a depopulated and repopulated
landscape at the end of that century can only be marked as colonial" (Te Punga
Somerville, 2009: 253). This radical process of taming of the land, which eventually
transforms the latter into a 'transposable otherness', simultaneously reduces its tourist
appeal. In order to be attractive a destination needs to maintain its—in some cases
hyper-real—uniqueness and specificity.

The crucial difference between *The Last Samurai* and *LOTR* is that even though
the landscape is highly manufactured in both cases, in *LOTR* place is invested
with a sense of distinctiveness which cannot ever be fully realised in *The Last
Samurai* simply because Japan already exists, in a more defined and complete way,
somewhere else. Ancient Japan is a prosthetic mask that is removed at the end of the
shooting leaving only feeble traces of its connection with the actual landscape. By
contrast *LOTR* represents the last stage of the process of virtualisation of Aotearoa's
landscape. Indeed, according to Jutel, "New Zealand [...] as it is recognised as
Middle Earth, offers its land as a commodity, which inscribes it in the forces of the
global economy" (Jutel, 2004: 54). In this reading, New Zealand actually becomes
Middle Earth; in comparison with *The Last Samurai*, *LOTR* has been instrumental
in reforging the national identity, contributing to the repositioning of the country
in the global scenario and eventually reinvigorating the tourist appeal of Aotearoa/
New Zealand.

**Notes**

1.  Sometimes the talent of local film-makers attracted Hollywood to New
    Zealand. This is the case for *The Bounty* (1984) by New Zealand director Roger
    Donaldson, or *The Frighteners* (1997) by Peter Jackson featuring popular US
    movie star Michael J. Fox.

2.     For a story of the 1980s tax breaks in New Zealand see page 37 in Chapter 2.

3.     A typical example of the hype that surrounded the release of *The Last Samurai* is this statement by critical scholar Lisa Wong who, in October 2003, claimed: "I have good reasons to assume that the Nippon Travel Agency or other Japanese travel agencies will launch a special theme tour for their Japanese clients to come to New Zealand to tour 'Mt. Fuji' following the release of *The Last Samurai* later this year. From then on, there will be two Mt. Fujis and no one will be able to tell which one is real and which one is a simulacrum" (Wong, 2007: 102).

4.     For a discussion of the notion of 'auratic perception' as the faculty through which Western civilisation would regain a lost appreciation of myth see Walter Benjamin (1979).

5.     The filming of the movie pumped money into thirteen key industry groupings in Taranaki, with the motion picture, radio and TV sector reaping $NZ 40 million nationally and $NZ 12.9 million in Taranaki alone (Venture Taranaki, 2004: 15).

6.     The theme of a white protagonist split between loyalty to the settler and the indigenous camps reappears in one of Ward's latest films, *River Queen* (2005), where a young Irish woman Sarah and her family find themselves on both sides of the turbulent wars between British and Māori in 1860s New Zealand.

7.     Even if the 'Samurai Village' is advertised on the Internet, in some guidebooks and in brochures available at the tourist office and commercial accommodations, the tour runs only occasionally, based on bookings. According to the manager of the company, who is also the owner of the land used as one of the sets of the movie, the average number of tourists to the 'Village' is limited to 20–30 visitors per week, mostly Asian, independent travellers or school groups. The decision to open the 'Village' in 2004 was motivated by the need to regulate access to the film set, which is on private land, after several tourists tried to visit the film location independently. Since then, the flow of visitors has been steady but small, this also being influenced by the explicit concern of the owner to limit the number of visitors for privacy reasons.

8.     More than 150 cherry trees were built by the production, constructed as wooden trunks on portable stands, each tree had sets of removable 'seasonal' branches so it could be dressed for different times of the year during the same day of shooting (Radcliffe, 2006).

9.  The recent unveiling of a statue of William Wallace, that has the features of Mel Gibson, in Stirling has been particularly controversial and does raise questions about problematic notions such as authenticity and hyper-reality (Edensor, 2005).

# 6

# 'WELCOME TO NEW ZEALAND, HOME OF MIDDLE EARTH': HETEROTOPIAN IMPULSE, WESTERN ANXIETY AND SPATIAL IDENTITY IN *THE LORD OF THE RINGS*

*"I sit beside the fire and think of people long ago,*
*and people who will see a world that I shall never know."*
(J. R. R. Tolkien, *The Fellowship of the Ring*)

## Introduction

At the beginning of the twenty-first century the dominant theme of New Zealand cultural discourses was the *LOTR* film trilogy, the cinematic adaptation of the celebrated novel by English academic John Ronald Reuel Tolkien. Shot back to back during a fifteen-month period by New Zealand director (and later national hero) Peter Jackson, the trilogy was released worldwide between 2001 and 2003. According to film scholar Kristin Thompson, the *LOTR* trilogy is to be considered among "the most historically significant films ever made" (Thompson, 2007: 8). The three films have won more Oscars than any other film franchise in the history of world cinema and *The Return of the King* (2003), the concluding episode of the series, alone picked up a staggering eleven Academy awards, equalling the record of *Ben Hur* (dir. William Wyler, 1959) and *Titanic* (dir. James Cameron, 1997). The staggering success of *LOTR* paid off a gamble by New Line Cinema, at that time a subsidiary of Time Warner, which invested between $US 280 and $US 310 million dollars in the ambitious project. The failure of previous film adaptations of Tolkien's epic novel, in particular those by Ralph Bakshi (1978) and Rankin/Bass (1980), represented for years an exemplary warning for film-makers seeking to translate the adventures of Frodo and his fellowship to the screen. The challenge of capturing the quality of the original novel demanded a concerted effort by Peter Jackson and his collaborators: *LOTR* required a cast and crew of more than 2500, while Weta Workshop, Jackson's special effects company, produced thousands of props, particularly weapons, armours and costumes for the mass scenes of the battles. The production of the films was revolutionary not just in scale but also from the technical point of view, as new digital technologies played a crucial role in the realisation of the films. For example, the film-makers set up a digital network so that Peter Jackson would be able to monitor and direct the work of as many as six units shooting simultaneously (Thompson, 2007: 38). Digital technologies had a significant impact on the film itself as the director made extensive use of CGI to generate large crowd scenes and enhance the film landscape.

Another crucial difference between *LOTR* and other successful blockbusters was that the trilogy was almost entirely produced outside Hollywood, as it used the physical landscape, the studios, the post-production facilities and the crew available in New Zealand. Of course it was not the first time that Hollywood had taken advantage of cheaper labour and exotic locations, though in these cases the most critical stages of the film-making process were always located in Hollywood, the centre of the American movie industry. In the case of *LOTR*, the involvement of the national government, the use of local film-production facilities, the participation of a substantial sector of the New Zealand population and, most of all, the leadership of a charismatic local director were among the factors that contributed to the global perception of the trilogy as a 'made in New Zealand' product.

In turn, the massive scale of *LOTR* had a considerable impact, both in the short and long term, on the country. It is possible to identify at least four major contributions made by the *LOTR* production to New Zealand as a whole. First, the film production had a direct positive impact on the economy of the country. A report commissioned by the New Zealand Film Commission in 2002 entitled *Scoping the lasting effects of The Lord of the Rings* (Yeabsley and Duncan, 2002), claimed that at least three quarters of the film budget (estimated at $NZ 350 million) had been spent within New Zealand. The level of expenditure produced a peak period of employment of around 1500 people per week. Secondly, these one-off economic benefits were complemented by long-term positive effects on the local film industry, in particular the elevation of the international profile of New Zealand production and post-production facilities and the up-skilling of the screen production industry at both technical and management levels. A third important contribution of *LOTR* to New Zealand concerned the rebranding of the country. Since the 1970s, when Britain broke its privileged relations with its former colonies, favouring instead new economic and cultural relations with the EEC members, New Zealand has been obliged to look for a new position in the global scenario. *LOTR* provided an opportunity to modify the image of a country that had been globally perceived as a supplier of raw material, such as lamb and wool, for its former British motherland. At the beginning of the twenty-first century the New Zealand government was happy to rebrand the country and promote new 'environmentally safe' sectors of economy such as eco-tourism and the creative industries, in particular film-making. Upon the release in 2001 of the first part of the trilogy, *The Fellowship of the Ring*, tourism was immediately perceived as one of the main positive spin-offs of *LOTR*.

The association with the trilogy gave New Zealand a global exposure which, based on the attendances to the first two films, was estimated at approximately $US 42 million (Yeabsley and Duncan, 2002). The release of the third film, of the extended DVD versions and of a plethora of ancillary products in the following years mean this estimate has now been superseded. Clearer evidence of the tourist spin-off of the film is provided by Statistics New Zealand which in 2005 claimed that between 2001 and 2004, the years following the release of *LOTR*, New Zealand saw an increase in overseas visitors of nearly 23% (Statistics New Zealand, 2005), a figure which is all the more significant in light of the fact that after 9/11 the tourist industry suffered a crisis in most regions of the world.[1]

A 2002 study, commissioned by Tourism New Zealand to identify the post-production effects of films on the tourist image of New Zealand, revealed that 95% of the international visitors to the country were aware that *LOTR* had been filmed in New Zealand (NFO NZ, 2002 cited in Croy, 2004: 10) and for 9% of the respondents *LOTR* was one the reasons that prompted them to visit the country. The report showed a direct influence of the films upon tourist behaviour and, even though these figures might appear relatively small, they are still relevant for the country's economy, particularly if we consider that the tourism industry accounts for 10% of the country's GPD (Croy, 2004).

With more than 200,000 copies sold, *The Lord of the Rings Location Guidebook*, published in late 2002 by Ian Brodie, became a surprise bestseller, changing the life of the author who has since become a key spokesperson for Tourism New Zealand, one of the local tourist stakeholders along with Air New Zealand that had a crucial role in the elaboration of the 'New Zealand, Home of Middle Earth' campaign. Invoking Baudrillardian notions of hyper-reality and simulation, the conflation between New Zealand and the imaginary Middle Earth has proved to be fertile ground for cultural theorists[2] (Jutel, 2004; Mathijs, 2006; Mathijs and Pomerance, 2006; Lam and Oryshchuk, 2007; Margolis et al., 2009).

Furthermore, the seemingly intimate connection between *LOTR* and New Zealand has stimulated a widespread interest in the phenomenon of film-induced tourism, both from the commercial and academic point of view. As already indicated, several works have acknowledged the effect of film on tourism (Riley and Van Doren, 1992; Riley et al., 1998). Others, more specifically, have focused on the social and economical aspects of the phenomenon (Beeton, 2005) or, more specifically still, an analysis of tourists' behaviour at *LOTR* locations (Carl et al., 2007; Roesch, 2007).

Looking at the *LOTR* craze in retrospect, this chapter will attempt to identify the factors that led to the tourist construction of New Zealand as Middle Earth. My argument is that the prominent association between tourist activities and film gaze in the case of *LOTR*/New Zealand is the result of a complex series of interconnected factors. In particular, I claim that the historical context of the film's release contributed to the generation of a 'heterotopian impulse', which I would define as the tendency to react to a crisis or a traumatic event by moving across time and space from the 'real' into heterotopia. I draw this notion from the concept of heterotopia elaborated by Michel Foucault to describe places of otherness which are neither here nor there and are at once physical and mental. Heterotopia can be compared to a mirror as it represents, contests and inverts real social spaces (Foucault, 1986: 24). Heterotopias challenge traditional notions of time and space as they lie outside of real places, even though it may be possible to indicate their location within 'reality'. Typical examples of heterotopia are the cemetery, cyberspace or the boat. Foucault distinguishes between 'heteropias of deviation', for people cast outside mainstream society (such as rest homes and mental asylums), and heterotopias of crisis which are privileged, sacred or forbidden places, reserved for individuals who are in a state of crisis in relation to the human environment in which they live. New Zealand as Middle Earth is an example of the second kind of heterotopia.[3] *LOTR* and the traumatic context of its reception determine a state of crisis in the viewer which pushes him/her to move to an 'Other' space which is at once physical and imagined: New Zealand as Middle Earth. The heterotopian impulse is, therefore, inextricably linked to the notion of mobility as the subject moves across time and space from the real into the heterotopia.

### *The Lord of the Rings*: merchandising and film franchise

*LOTR* was an enormous international success: the three parts of the trilogy are respectively the second, eighth and fifteenth-highest grossing feature films of all time. The whole franchise earned $US 3 billion for the theatrical release alone. Taking into account the DVD releases and various ancillary products the total earnings of *LOTR* are estimated to be around $US 10 billion and rising. The worldwide diffusion of the movie boosted the international profile of the film director, actors and crew. Peter Jackson, Viggo Mortensen and Elija Wood, who previously played secondary roles in the world film industry, became very familiar faces to global audiences after the release of the films. Like the other characters of *LOTR*, the New Zealand landscape gained huge exposure which, in turn, resulted in increased flows of international tourism to the country. The effect of *LOTR* on New Zealand tourism is considered a typical example of film-induced tourism which, according to an early study in the field, is defined as the on-location tourism that results from the success of a film set or made in a certain region (Beeton, 2005). The pioneering work of Riley and Van Doren

(1992) in this field, has related film-induced tourism to the notion of 'hallmark event'.[4] The uniqueness and status related to its popular success make *LOTR* a prime example of a hallmark event. However, *LOTR* was not simply an extremely successful movie trilogy, it was also a cultural product anchored to the capitalist modes of production typical of the Hollywood system. In her extraordinarily detailed work about *LOTR*, Kristin Thompson defines the trilogy as a 'film franchise'. For Thompson, a franchise is "a movie that spawns additional revenue streams beyond what it earns from its various forms of distribution, primarily theatrical, video and television" (Thompson, 2007: 4). In the ideal franchise an important slice of the revenue stream comes from the licensing of ancillary products such as T-shirts, video games and other forms of merchandising. According to Thompson, the modern Hollywood franchise started in the late 1970s with *Jaws* (dir. Steven Spielberg, 1975) and particularly *Star Wars* (dir. George Lucas, 1977), films which provided a model for future franchises by linking the movies to an extensive range of merchandising. The emergence of the franchise was caused by the need of finding alternative revenue streams to recoup the big budget of massive blockbusters such as *Star Wars*, that required special effects and high-star salaries. The sequels and the seriality of the franchise play a crucial role in the creation of a brand that can be easily translated to other non-filmic products. In the case of *LOTR* the New Line Cinema studio built on the knowledge it had already gained in marketing and producing merchandise for its previous products such as *Nightmare on Elm Street* (dir. Wes Craven, 1984) and *Teenage Mutant Ninja Turtles* (dir. Steve Barron, 1990). The role of merchandise was even more important for *LOTR* because of the early connection between the novels and the fantasy gaming industry. According to Perry, "Merchandising is an important part of a film like this. Most Tolkien fans are either gamers, modellers, collectors or all three" (Perry cited in Conrich, 2006: 128). In his examination of the range of *LOTR* products and promotions Ian Conrich identifies at least four different consumer groups: mainstream consumers, family, children and 'cult' consumers (Conrich, 2006). The merchandise of *LOTR* ranged from traditional posters, books and figurines to trading cards, board games and video games. The cult collectibles extended to specially crafted full-size replicas of screen props. According to Conrich, "this superior movie merchandising is just one aspect of the fascinating series of high class products marketed for an executive consumer; materials of this sort have never been so well exploited in the selling of a film" (Conrich, 2006: 122). The equation of New Zealand with Middle Earth and the tourist commodification of the landscape in products such as Brodie's location guidebook could be seen as part of the effort to maximise the profitability of the franchise. Conrich comments on Jackson's exploitation of the spectacularity and sublimity of the New Zealand landscape thus: "a distant country which is on the edge of the world [is] cleverly manoeuvred and adjusted into a perceived Middle Earth which can be reached through mass culture and corporate packaging" (Conrich, 2006: 118).

The commodification of the New Zealand landscape for the tourist gaze is part of a strategy to maximise the lucrative potential of the *LOTR* franchise. Nevertheless, the wealth of ancillary products, in particular games and life-size props, associated with *LOTR* suggests the need for an explanation of the tourist appeal of the trilogy that goes beyond the simple socio-economic approach. In his essay 'The Myth of Total Cinema' (1971), Andre Bazin claims that the guiding myth of the cinema is the search for the complete and perfect illusion. In another prophetic work, *Le Cinema Total*, Rene Barjavel (2001) asserts that the technological evolution of the cinematic apparatus will eventually result in the total *enveloppement*, characterised by the multi-sensorial experience and the full interactivity of the spectator, within the movie itself. The *LOTR* franchise is concerned with the establishment of a 'believable', 'authentic' world in which the spectator can be immersed and with which s/he can eventually interact. Referring to Barjavel's definition of the total movie, it is therefore possible to consider *LOTR* as a sort of 'proto-total movie'. On the one hand, the filmic text itself produces a sense of *enveloppement* thanks to the realism of the special effects, the Dolby surround sound, the video-game-like aesthetics. On the other hand, the movies form the hub of a much wider network of *LOTR*-themed products and activities such as role-games, video games, full-size replicas, illustrations and internet communities that are all based on notions of immersion and interactivity. The cultural consumer easily shifts from one activity to the other and this imaginative investment enables the experience of living and acting in Middle Earth.

The films, video games and tours of the *LOTR* locations are characterised by immersion and interactivity within Middle Earth. In his analysis of *LOTR* games Brett Nicholls notices how, through claims such as "decide the fate of Middle-Earth", "be the hero of Middle Earth" or "live the power of the epic movies", the packaging of these products promise to deliver the pre-constituted world of the *LOTR* trilogy (Nicholls, 2009: 280). Similarly, the physical tourism to the film locations is the last stage of a Barjavelian *enveloppement* in the fantasy world created by *LOTR*: some tours to the film locations, in fact, offer the possibility of carrying the replicas of the weapons used in the films and performing 'photo-staged fights' in the actual location. The customers of Hassle Free Tours, for example, a company that proposes visits to Mount Sunday aka Edoras, have the chance to stand with Gimli's axe or the Rohirrim flag in the actual film locations. Queenstown-based Trail of Middle Earth, one of the most comprehensive tours dedicated to *LOTR*, provides a much wider range of film props. Tourists can wear or use $NZ 15,000 worth of replicas from the One Ring to the Elfish capes as well as Sting, Frodo's magic dagger. The brochure of the tour emphasises the possibility of immersion in Middle Earth by featuring pictures of ordinary tourists restaging scenes from the films (Figures 6.1 and 6.2).

During their tours, both companies make extensive use of the films' soundtracks and the DVDs which provide a constant background to the visits and enhance the sense of

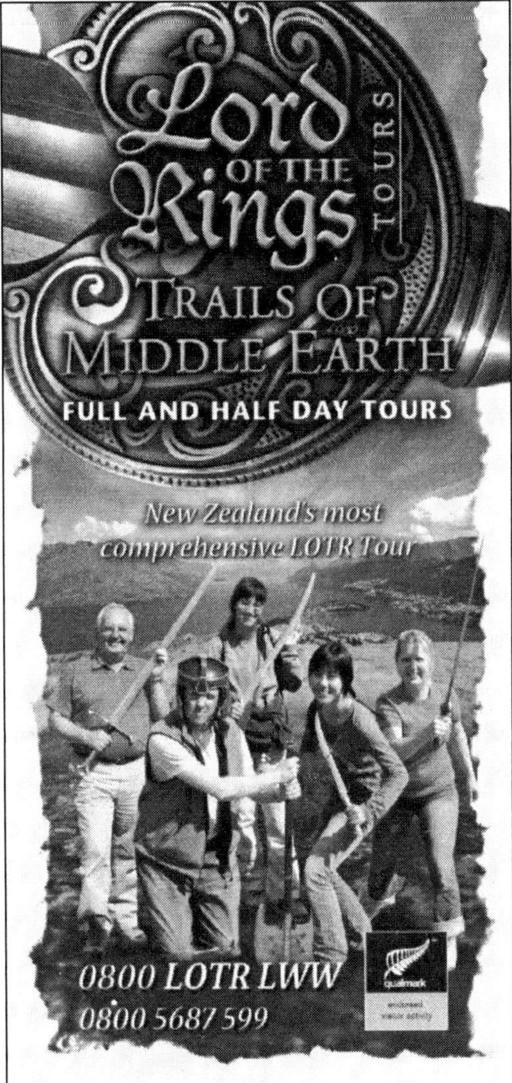


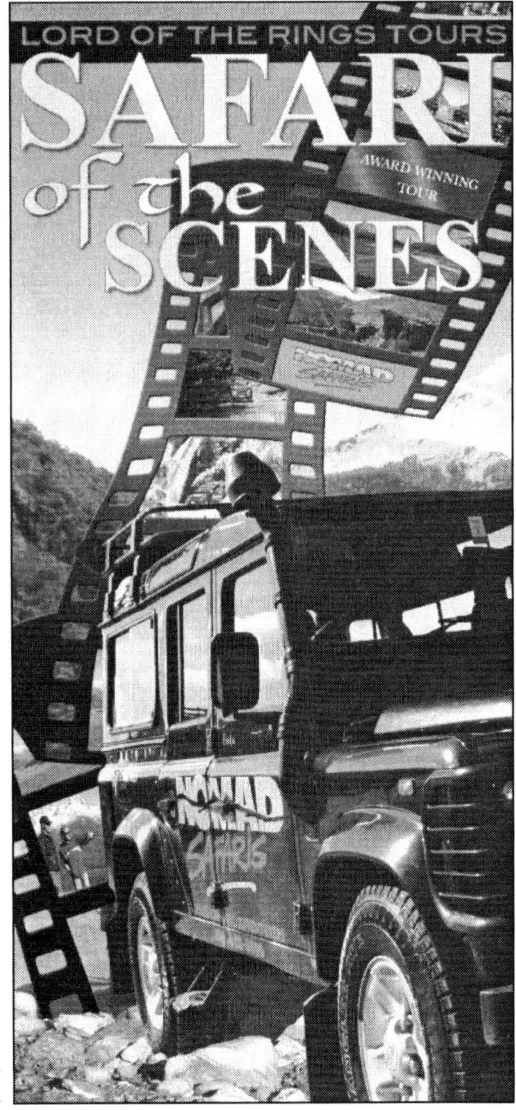


Figure 6.1.  Southern Lakes Sightseeing.
Brochure, 2008.

Figure 6.2.  www.nomadsafaris.co.nz.
Brochure, 2008.

*enveloppement* within Middle Earth. Furthermore, most of the *LOTR* dedicated tours use vans or 4×4 vehicles thus limiting the number of tourists visiting the location at the same time. Travelling in small groups, usually with other fans of the movies or the novel, increases the possibility of interaction and recreates the sense of belonging to a 'fellowship'. Other tourist operators, such as Minaret Lodge in Wanaka, go even further in the simulation of the fantasy world of the trilogy, proposing accommodation in Hobbit holes. The hyper-real experience of sleeping in a Middle Earth room is completed by the menu which includes lembas, the elfish bread baked according to the original Tolkien recipe. In these ways, *LOTR*-tourism contradicts Urry's thesis, according to which gazing is the main component of the tourist performance (Urry, 2002). On the contrary, most of the *LOTR* tourist experiences incorporate active bodily involvement. Apart from stimulating the hearing (movie soundtrack) or the taste (lembas breakfast), *LOTR* tours are also tactile and provide olfactory experiences as the tourists need sometimes to travel and walk long distances through the pristine New Zealand nature in order to access the remote film locations. Finally, the tourist experience also involves a cognitive activity: as most of the sets have been dismantled and the locations enhanced by digital effects, the tourists are often asked to make an imaginative effort in order to reconstruct the original movie scenes. *LOTR* tourism is marked by the notion of 'interactivity', since for *LOTR* tourists New Zealand is a huge adventure playground where it becomes possible to participate in interactive forms of tourist recreation.

The theming of New Zealand as Middle Earth, promoted by the tourism board, is a symptom of postmodernism. It offers a clear example of Jamesonian *pastiche* (Jameson, 1991), while somehow remaining consistent with the adventure tourism (bungee jumping, rafting, hiking) for which New Zealand has become well known around the world. From this point of view, *LOTR*-related tourism uncovers a tension between the effort to invest the location with a specific meaning, particularly apparent in the immersive attitude shown by *LOTR* tourists, and the blankness of the pastiche which implies that the location can receive multiple and contrasting meanings.

The official *LOTR* website represents another example of the wide network of interrelated consumption practices generated by the film franchise which help to reinforce the connection between New Zealand and Middle Earth. The site is, in fact, copyrighted by both New Line Productions and New Zealand Tourism and hosts computer games, toys and other cultural products related to the *LOTR* film trilogy. Drawing from the critical theory of exponents of the Frankfurt school such as Adorno and Horkheimer, Rodanthi Tzanelli uses the notion of cultural industry to highlight the correspondence between the film viewer and the general consumer. Adorno's and Horkheimer's theories, based on a Marxist analysis of capitalist societies, suggested that the corroding power of mass culture eventually causes the loss of individual identity. According to these critical theorists, mass culture, and cinema in particular, transforms individuals into "consumers in abstracto—that is, consumers who have lost their particularity and have become interchangeable and quantifiable" (Tzanelli, 2004: 24). Starting from these theoretical premises, Tzanelli attempts to relate cinematic consumption patterns to the development of film-induced tourism in New Zealand. Tzanelli claims in fact that "in films and film-induced tourist practices we never seem to consume specific objects but clusters of signs: we are invited to buy holidays to New Zealand because the country signifies Middle Earth; we are asked to buy replicas of Elfish ears because they appeared on the mythical creatures of the movie" (Tzanelli, 2004: 24). Tzanelli's main argument is that tourist production and film consumption are linked because one of the prominent characteristics of film is the fabrication of cultural messages. Both tourist and film industries participate in the circulation of what Jean Baudrillard has defined as symbolic 'sign values' (Baudrillard, 1973). The distinctions between film and tourism or production and consumption become irrelevant, as they are just different aspects of a broader sign industry. Hermeneutic activity is a central feature of this sign industry: during their holidays film viewers/tourists collect and appropriate signs that originated in films (Tzanelli, 2004: 24). New Zealand tourism marketing practices attempted to appropriate the *LOTR* sign industry for their own agenda. However, film viewers and prospective tourists do not always automatically consume what is produced by the tourist industry. In the case of New Zealand, in particular, the tourist products were based on an anticipation of the viewers' cinematic reception of the trilogy. According to Kristin Thompson, the community of virtual fans played a crucial role in the *LOTR* tourist development in New Zealand (Thompson, 2007). Fan websites such as www.theonering.net became communities of consumption (Hills, 2002) that acted as a *trait d'union* between the film production and the tourist industry.

According to Henry Jenkins, fan reading is "a social process through which individual interpretations are shaped and reinforced with other readers" (Jenkins, 1992: 45). The initial consumption of the original text is influenced by the virtual community. The *LOTR* fan websites represent the ultimate example of the dissolution of the dialectic between production and consumption. The international fan network created from the outset a strong association between Jackson's *LOTR* films and the New Zealand locations, regularly reporting about the making of the trilogy. The *LOTR* fan communities dispatched correspondents (spies according to New Line Cinema) to New Zealand in order to find out about the film locations and obtain news leaks or glimpses of the film-making. Before the release of the first film the central focus for many fans was the news about the film production, posted daily on websites such as TheOneRing.net. Most of these postings included photos of empty New Zealand landscapes, perhaps destined to become film locations. These pictures not only anticipated what the films might look like but, more importantly, introduced the scenic beauties of New Zealand to international fans who had never been exposed to images of the country before. Erica Challis, founder of the TheOneRing.net and one of those 'spies' also became one of the first *LOTR* tourist guides, leading small groups of hardcore fans to the top-secret film locations; in 2002 she was eventually employed by tourist operator Red Carpet to design a tour dedicated to *LOTR* (Thompson, 2007: 288). Later, several other *LOTR* fans moved around 'the hermeneutic circle', from sign consumption to sign production, becoming guides for the numerous *LOTR* tours that were conceived in New Zealand after the release of the films. The initial attitude of New Line Cinema towards *LOTR*-related tourism was characterised by explicit hostility. New Line put a legal trespass notice on Challis and felt threatened by the phenomenon of the fan spies. In particular, the producers were extremely reluctant to publicise the fact that the films were shot in New Zealand. However, the studio slowly learnt that fan websites could actually be an extremely valuable resource. The fan communities helped to generate the New Zealand tourist craze by dedicating discussion forums to the experience of fans visiting Middle Earth/ New Zealand. The interest shown by fans in the films' locations led to New Line's awareness of the great potential of a co-marketing strategy that would involve local tourist stakeholders such as Investment New Zealand, Tourism New Zealand and Air New Zealand. This collaboration, in turn, led to the famous 'New Zealand, Home of Middle Earth' campaign which, among other things, involved the temporary rebranding of Air New Zealand as the 'Airline to Middle Earth'. As mentioned, immediately after the release of the films many New Zealand tourist operators leaped at the chance to profit from *LOTR*. Many companies added tours dedicated to *LOTR* to their brochures, which proved to be extremely popular: the profit generated by the Wellington-based Rover Rings Tour, which originally offered tours of the capital city, represented 60% of the company's revenue. The owners of Nomad Safaris, one of the main Queenstown tourist operators that offers *LOTR*-themed packages, estimated that between 2002 and 2004 at the apex of the *LOTR* fever their business had risen a dramatic 500% (Thompson, 2007: 287). These tours attempted to boost the above-mentioned sense of the film viewer/tourist's *enveloppement* in the *LOTR* world, but they also provided access to the backstage of the making of the film. Most of the guides employed in *LOTR* tours participated as actors or crew members in one or more films of the trilogy. The 'authenticity' of the tourist experience is enhanced by the status of the guides as insiders who are able to reveal secrets and anecdotes about the film production.

An important component of the tourist experience of Middle Earth is the comparison between the actual New Zealand landscape and the stills of the films, in which the very same landscape has been at once emptied of its features and enhanced with new ones, particularly props, characters and digital effects. Reynolds et al. (2009) point out how, unlike typical tourist destinations that acknowledge their status via markers such as tourist signs or admission fees, *LOTR* sites are defined by markers which are not present at the location, but which are brought by the tourist themselves in the form of memory of the film or other resources such as Brodie's guidebook. The tourist/film viewer superimposes images of the film onto the physical landscape and this comparison involves a hermeneutic activity which eventually leads to the emergence of a new layer of meaning on the landscape. The process of recognising the real landscape as the film location activates the tourist memory of the film story which, if the discrepancy between the real and the virtual is not too obvious, could potentially alter the significance of the land (Reynolds et al., 2009: 243).

The comparison between the filmic landscape and the actual tourist site also points to the demystification of cinematic artifice. The tourist guide often comments on the film location, revealing the film-making techniques employed to modify the actual landscape and create the filmic image. The insights into the backstage region of the film production seem to contradict the experience of immersion in the fantasy world as it discloses the artifice necessary for its very existence. Nevertheless, the awareness of the artificial character of the filmic world does not seem to inhibit the immersive attitude of the tourists. They enjoy the pleasures of *enveloppement* while being extremely conscious and knowledgeable about the filming process that made it possible. The *LOTR* tours seem, therefore, to confirm MacCannell's formulation of the notion of 'staged authenticity', according to which tourists may be both aware of the lack of authenticity of a given cultural product and able to enjoy the pleasures associated with its consumption (MacCannell, 1999: 98).

The *LOTR* tours encourage immersion and provide insight into the secrets of the film production thus attracting the niche market of Tolkien's fans. Nevertheless, the percentage of international tourists in New Zealand for whom *LOTR* is the main attraction represents just a tiny minority of the incoming flow of tourists to the country. Five years after the release of the last episode of the trilogy the number of hardcore *LOTR* fans decreased; by contrast, according to tour guide Jason Bragg, the flow of tourists who have been inspired by the movies to visit the scenic beauties of New Zealand is steadily increasing (Bragg cited in Thompson, 2007: 289). As a result, apart from the traditional film locations, *LOTR* tours tend to focus, more and more, on the beauty of the New Zealand landscape. In fact, most of these tours include in their package visits to local attractions that did not feature in the movies. Trails of Middle Earth Tour, for example, offers the possibility of feeding animals and experiencing the 'Kiwi lifestyle' in one of the private farms where the films were shot. The conflation between New Zealand and Middle Earth goes beyond the specificity of the single film locations, suggesting that the country as a whole has benefited, in tourist terms, through its association with the *LOTR* franchise.

## Style, narrative and space in *The Lord of the Rings*

The narrative content, the stylistic features and the representation of space in the film text have greatly contributed to shaping a tourist reading of the trilogy. The emphasis on a tourist gaze external to the narration is one of the stylistic leitmotifs of the film. According to David Butler, the virtuoso camera movements which are a key aesthetic component in the trilogy reinforce the idea of an omnipotent observer while highlighting the scenic beauty of the country (Butler, 2007: 162). In *LOTR* the spectacular movements of the camera draw attention to its very existence and, by emphasising the presence of the camera/enunciator, Jackson attempts to highlight the real and authentic texture of the world the film is depicting. In the sequence of *The Fellowship of the Ring* where Frodo and friends paddle through the feet of the Argonaths the camera vertiginously swivels up and beyond the two massive statues disturbing some nesting birds. The statues, of course, do not exist as they are just 'bigatures', neither do the birds, which are digitally created: nonetheless, Jackson attempted to convey a documentary feeling to the scene emphasising the realism of the virtual landscape. As a result "these objective shots treat us spectators to a privileged [and yes, stunning] guided tour over middle earth the safari park" (Butler, 2007: 163).

Similarly, Kristin Thompson claimed that the *LOTR* films are based on an 'aesthetics of spectacle' which capitalises on visual attractions such as special effects and stunning landscapes (2006). The use of the varied New Zealand landscape was an essential element of the film narrative. Furthermore, the producers often used some of the country's most famous tourist sites such as the Southern Alps, Queenstown or Mount Ruapehu. Thompson's suggestion is confirmed by producer Barry Osborne who did not hesitate to admit that "throughout, we picked the most spectacular appropriate locations we could find" (Osborne cited in Duncan, 2002: 101). The aesthetics of spectacle cannot alone explain the conspicuous tourist spin-off generated by *LOTR*. Movie-going activity, and particularly certain genres such as pornography, horror and action movies, strongly foreground bodily pleasures. *LOTR* deploys high camera angles and movements that create at once vertiginous bodily orientations in the spectators and the simulation of physical mobility. The history of cinema has been characterised by its interconnection with technologies of mobility and tourism,[5] a link which is proven by the popularity, at the beginning of the history of cinema, of travel films, travelogues and film-travel rides.

The emphasis on mobility in proto-cinematic products could be considered as a reaction to the technological shift that questioned prior epistemological relations between the subject and the visual. According to Rabinovitz, "cinema challenged experiential norms for knowledge because (as an improved photographic technology) it ideally intensified perception through a focalisation and autonomisation of sight" (Rabinovitz, 2006: 43). Hale's Tours, a simulated entertainment train ride very popular at the beginning of the twentieth century, represented a reaction to the autonomisation of sight characteristic of cinema. Hale's tours and other ride films articulated a contradictory process for the spectator: they attempted to disembody the subjectivity of the spectator through his/her visual extension into the cinematic field, while emphasising his/her body as the centre of a sensory affect. In a way, by merging train and cinema, Hale's rides attempted to compensate for the excess of the visual that is typical of the cinematic medium by simulating the sensorial experience of physical mobility. From this perspective, all cinema could be read as the result of a complex interplay between embodied forms of subjectivity and arguments for the dematerialisation of the subject's body (Rabinovitz, 2006).

Similarly today, digital technologies threaten our acquired understanding of the cinematographic domain, in the same way in which, at the beginning of the last century, cinema and the new visual culture associated with it upset the viewers' existing conceptions of perceptual knowledge. The landscapes of *LOTR*, heavily modified by CGI, challenge the traditional perception of cinematic reality held by contemporary spectators. The film-induced tourism associated with *LOTR* represents a different reaction to the very similar epistemological crisis that affected cinema at its origins. The physicality and multi-sensorial experience of both simulated travel rides and film tourism compensate for the loss of a unified subjectivity and the omnipotence of the visual, binding vision to a wider range of sensory capacities.

The use of dizzying camera movements and spectacular locations are just some of the strategies employed by Jackson to reiterate the importance of space and movement in his films. Laurence Simmons observes that the story of *LOTR* is not plot-driven but spatial, told as "the extension outwards of space. Such a non-chronological narrative easily produces the sense of bewilderment of 'being lost in the wood' that is evoked so effectively in Jackson's film" (Simmons, 2007: 227). The film-makers organised the film space horizontally so that the positive characters consistently enter the frame from the left side and always move towards the right. By contrast, all the villains in the film enter from the right and move towards the left. Much of the film focuses on the fellowship's journey to Mordor and on the spatial opposition 'left versus right' which is particularly evident in the scenes where the armies clash on a great plain (Woodward and Kourelis, 2006: 196). According to Woodward and Kourelis, Jackson often resorted to the aesthetics of the sublime where spatial extremes express psychological polarities. The camera exploits other spatial binaries such as big/small, high/low, open/closed to convey the prominent role played by the landscape. The narrative is particularly concerned with the contrast in scale. Aerial shots are extremely common in the three films where they usually work to diminish the scale of the protagonists against imposing landscapes. According to Woodward and Kourelis, Jackson often places Frodo and his friends in an uneasy relation with the space that surrounds them: "We often discover the protagonists only after the camera has scanned along the ridges of sheer faced mountains or surveyed bleak frozen expanses" (2006: 196–97). This is the case in the sequence in which the fellowship attempts to find a pass across the Misty Mountains. Such scenes evoke again the notion of sublime nature, as the microscopic scale of the protagonists' silhouettes functions to emphasise the majesty of the environment. Interestingly, the popularity of the aesthetics of the sublime in European art corresponded to the emergence of tourism as an activity.[6] As Grant Major (*LOTR* Production designer) claimed in the audio commentary of the extended DVD versions, "the environments do become a character [in the story]" (Grant Major cited in Woodward and Kourelis, 2006: 189). The Misty Mountains, Mordor's marshland or the lava rock of Mount Doom actively oppose Frodo's quest, while at other times, nature and the environment play a positive role, like the river at the entrance of Rivendell which sweeps away the threatening Ringwraiths.

In their study of the influence of film on tourism, Van Doren and Riley note that the Australian movies that attracted some interest in the United States featured three common elements: the natural environment was used as background to the story, the protagonists interacted with that environment and, finally, the lifestyles portrayed in the movies were relatively uncomplicated (Riley and Van Doren, 1992). Later they claim that movies can present the backdrop of the film setting as more than mere 'scenery', producing icons that are central to the storyline. According to Riley et al., "Movie icons may not be visual as they may be storyline themes that become associated with locations" (Riley et al., 1998: 925). Icons can be recurrent and continuing images in the film or single, climatic events with which the viewers identify. Drawing upon the suggestions of Riley et al. and O'Regan (1988), Sue Beeton has analysed the tourist impact of some Australian films. Beeton found that in the case of *Crocodile Dundee*, for example, the iconic attractions were the laconic Australian identity, the Australian bush culture and the emotional relationship between the place and the characters. The film conveyed an imagined outback culture supported by few Australians; at the same time, the depiction of a frontier culture within a safe location accounted for its international appeal (Beeton, 2005).

*LOTR* produced a number of iconic attractions: a green and natural playground; the notion of community based on traditional and anti-modern values; the construction of a reassuring opposition between a white, European Self; and a threatening unfamiliar Other. Some of these iconic attractions, and the way in which they relate to the existing tourist imagery associated with New Zealand, are examined further in the following sections of the chapter. For the moment, it is important to focus on the notions of mobility and journey which are the central themes and icons of the films and the novels alike. The desire for exploration and the joy of discovery constitute the premises of the original story. Both Bilbo and Frodo leave the familiar place of the Shire to fulfil their desire of visiting new, exotic and adventurous places. Much of the narrative is articulated through the opposition between the harmonious, reassuring memory of Home (The Shire) and the spectacular but dangerous places visited by the members of the fellowship. This dialectic between familiar and unknown mysterious places is also at the core of the tourist experience. The tourist is bound to compare every new site s/he visits to the familiar space of home (Urry, 2002: 1). Both the films and the novel encourage the identification of the reader/spectator with the Hobbits. Unlike other characters in the story, the Hobbits have no special powers or skills and they are depicted as ordinary 'people' who love peace and tranquillity. The portrayal of the Hobbits matches the profile of the common reader/spectator who, through the identification with 'ordinary heroes', can vicariously travel through Middle Earth. The three films are, in fact, punctuated by close-ups or medium shots of Frodo's magnetic blue eyes gazing at the marvels of Middle Earth. According to Martin Phillips (2007: 152), much of the appeal of the original novel derived from its portrayal of place. Before writing the novel, Tolkien created a complex world whose geography, languages and inhabitants he would later meticulously describe. Similarly, the films attempted to convey the 'authenticity' of Middle Earth, accurately representing Tolkien's work. The cinematic fidelity to the literary construction of place, whose authenticity and realism enticed generations of readers, represented one of the main objectives set by the film-makers (Jones and Smith, 2005: 934).

Sean Cubitt notices how the production designers attempted to convey a sense of realism by emphasising the authenticity of every detail. Similarly, the realism of Middle Earth is reinforced by the staging of scenes in depth, the use of long shots and deep focus. The elaborate dolly, crane and helicopter shots that reveal huge expanses of land give Middle Earth a physical presence that the spectator could expect from a real geography (Cubitt, 2009: 191). A first-time theatrical viewing of *LOTR* leaves the spectator with the feeling of having missed much of the infinity of details that characterises the space of Middle Earth; this sense of dissatisfaction could explain the success of ancillary products such as the extended versions on DVD, real life-size replicas of the props or tours of the film locations. According to David Butler, when the first *LOTR* video game was released in the 1980s one of the main pleasures of the users was to wander off the beaten tracks and autonomously explore the different territories of Middle Earth (Butler, 2007). By recreating Middle Earth these *LOTR*-related products seek to satisfy the viewer's desire to grasp a reality which is essentially ungraspable.

The authenticity of the *LOTR* geography is reinforced by the recurring presence of the map. Tolkien designed very detailed maps of Middle Earth that were usually published in the first pages of the books. These maps play a crucial role in the immersion into the imaginary geography of Middle Earth, which represents one of the most important pleasures of reading *LOTR* (Simmons, 2007). According to Simmons, the landscape depicted by Tolkien "offers itself as both material and knowable, yet [it is] one that requires the imaginative investment of a reader to interpret and 'invent'"

(Simmons, 2007: 227). Drawing from the work of historian Christian Jackob, Tom Conley notices that *LOTR*, along with other British novels such as Stevenson's *Treasure Island*, belong to a literary genre that has been defined as 'cartographic fiction'. In such novels, the maps work to undo the narrative thread and inspire alternative itineraries to the extent of legitimising an interactive relation between text and reader (Conley, 2006: 225).

The map also features extensively in the cinematic version of the *LOTR*. *The Fellowship of the Ring* opens with a sequence in which the map features as the 'object of the tale', anticipating the narrative of displacement that characterises *LOTR*. Throughout the trilogy the physical dimensions of the fellowship's journey are emphasised by the foregrounding of the landscape as a map. According to Tom Conley, films often allude to maps in their opening sequences to situate their stories in time and space. For Conley, the state of being induced by the filmic maps is at once settling and unsettling:

> Settling insofar as the film produces geographical fantasies that lure into wanting to be [...] 'anywhere out of this world' [...] 'this world' is for us the movie theatre or what is exterior to the visual field of the screen. And our viewers' condition is unsettling in that we enjoy ourselves being tourists in the film, especially in a film that turns its milieu into a travel advertisement. (Conley, 2006: 216)

Maps, particularly in the case of *LOTR*, also have an authenticating power. As it organises the memory images of the space invented by the film, "the map in a movie is often the hidden guarantee of what it tells its spectator to be its truth" (Conley, 2006: 216). Like voice-offs, maps are often external to the diegesis and thus acquire a quasi-religious valence that can attest to the authenticity of the cinematic space.

The paraphernalia that accompanied the *LOTR* visual material was characterised by a proliferation of maps. Maps feature in the case of the extended DVD version of the film: the brochure of the DVD itself evokes the quasi-medieval script of Tolkien maps taking the form of a flow chart. At the 2001 Cannes film festival, Film New Zealand published a two-side promotional map of the country. One side featured the list of the facilities available in New Zealand while the other side displayed a Tolkienesque map of the country with film locations marked. Even though the aim of the map was to authenticate the slogan 'New Zealand, Home of Middle Earth', the attempt to virtualise the geography of New Zealand refers to notions of both hyper-reality and postcolonialism, which will be further discussed in the third section of this chapter.

## 9/11 and Western anxiety

In the introduction to one of the most extensive collections of academic responses to *LOTR*, *From Hobbits to Hollywood* (2006), Ernest Mathijs and Murray Pomerance, drawing upon Walter Benjamin, claim that the aesthetics and the politics of cinema are never separate entities. The two editors state that, like all other cultural artefacts, *LOTR* leads a double life as *objet d'art* and political statement about the contemporary world (Mathjis and Pomerance, 2006: 3). Since the release of the first part of the trilogy in December 2001, *LOTR* has been linked to the topical political and social subjects of the time. In particular, the films seemed to evoke political discourses widespread in the Western world at the beginning of the new century. *The Fellowship of the Ring*, in fact, was released in the immediate aftermath of an event that would have overwhelming consequences for the entire world: the 9/11 terrorist attacks on the World Trade Center. On the morning of 11 September 2001, nineteen suicide hijackers affiliated with the terrorist group Al-Qaeda took control of four United States commercial airplanes and crashed them, respectively, into the Twin Towers of the World Trade Center (WTC) in New York City, the Pentagon in Washington DC, and a field in Pennsylvania. Approximately 3000 people were killed in the attack, while the cost of the tragedy, in terms of rebuilding, was estimated at about $US 105 billion (CNN, 2001). The attack was immediately perceived as a turning point in world history; its significance went well beyond the direct losses that it had caused and affected all fields of society, from economics to politics and culture. As a consequence of the attack, the president of the United States, George Bush, launched the so-called War on Terror,[7] leading a Western coalition first against Afghanistan, accused of harbouring the terrorists responsible for the attacks, and then Iraq, ruled by dictator Saddam Hussein. The 9/11 attacks, the rise of Islamism and the military response of the Western world contradicted the 'end of history' thesis formulated in 1989 by Francis Fukuyama, who argued that the advent of Western liberal democracy may signal the end point of mankind's ideological evolution and the final form of human government (Fukuyama, 1992). By contrast, theories such as Samuel Huntington's 'Clash of Civilisations' (1996) gained popularity, particularly among conservative sectors of the Western world. Huntington claimed that in the new post-war scenario cultural and religious identity will be the source of global conflicts. He analysed trends in global conflict, predicting the clash between different civilisations, particularly between the Western and the Islamic world (Huntington, 1996). Huntington's thesis was also adopted by the American government, whose main slogan to recruit allies for the War on Terror was "with us or against us". The violent polarisation of the political debate, the rhetoric of war, the clear-cut opposition between good and evil, between white Western Self and coloured Other, resonate in the narrative of *LOTR* which screened in cinemas all over the world just three months after the startling events of 9/11. Even though Tolkien always denied the suggestion that his novels were an allegory of political or historical events, *LOTR*, both in its literary and cinematic versions, undoubtedly conveys a critique of industrial and technological modernity while celebrating the traditional values of social hierarchy such as war, race, organic community and attachment to the earth which, in turn, refer to a conservative ideology in which ethnicity is based on descent. Aragorn's heroism and claim to kingship, for example, is based on his noble lineage and the same is true for many other characters of the story. Douglas Kellner notices how the depiction of the Shire in both the novels and the films evokes the notion of *Gemeinschaft*. Hobbiton is, in fact, an organic community like those celebrated by conservative theorists against the influence of the modern *Gesellschaft*, the industrial society which advocates equality and democracy (Kellner, 2006: 26). Throughout the story, the characters always opt for violent military solutions and the enemy is nearly always easily recognisable. The conflict that tears apart Middle Earth is based on a clear opposition between white and black races. All the members of the fellowship are white and most of them embody stereotypical Aryan features such as blue eyes and blonde hair: good and purity are always associated with white, while evil is always linked to black. Orcs, Goblins, Ringwraiths and, of course, Sauron are all distinctively black, the evil Corsairs of Humbar wear outfits and armours that visually evoke the Middle East and the brutal Uruk-hai were played by strongly built Polynesian actors. Furthermore, the racial divide is nearly always clearly defined. Even though the white heroes can sometimes contravene their stereotypical features (a timid Hobbit can become a hero, a brave man can fall in temptation, a grumpy dwarf can be romantic) there is no such possibility of redemption on the other side: the black characters are consistently evil throughout the films and novels.

Smith-Rowsey (2007) has attempted to read *LOTR* as the story of a group of underdogs who manage to defeat a technocratic (capitalist) power, thus suggesting a reading of *LOTR* that could potentially appeal to Third World audiences. Nonetheless, given all the elements mentioned above, a conservative reading of the films seems much more plausible. Apart from reproducing the conservative, military ideology of the US government of the time, the narrative also resonates with millenarist fears of catastrophic destruction. As Kellner points out, "as the story proceeds it produces an aura of unease and fear, uncannily like the mood in the United States and other Western countries threatened by terrorism in the post 9/11 environment" (Kellner, 2006: 25). The very figure of Sauron, elusive but always threatening, uncannily suggests analogies with the phantasmagorical character of Osama Bin Laden.

Cathy Caruth writes that, because the experience of trauma is delayed and displaced, the location of trauma as physical event is complicated by its repetition as a psychic event (Caruth, 1995). Drawing on Caruth, Allen Meek claims that as media represent events in contexts that are always removed in space and time, they share the same problem of locatedness of the trauma: "media representations can become events in their own right, displacing access to any original context" (Meek, 2009: 215). Cinema can be therefore considered in terms of this logic of displacement and simulation of trauma.

Tolkien's novel was written during World War II as a result of the traumatic experience of the author in the trenches of World War I. Jackson's films were released on the eve of the War on Terror, meaning that the reception of the films has incorporated the Western anxieties of the time: terrorist menace, fear of the Other and concern about the prospects of an impending global catastrophe. The reality of the events that characterised the beginning of the twenty-first century seeped into the fantastic world of Middle Earth. The marketing of *The Two Towers*, for example, raised some controversy as, for some, the film (which features the collapse of one of the two evil towers) dramatically evoked the recent tragic events of 9/11. In both reality and fantasy the 'two towers' are at the centre of an epic struggle (Gelder, 2006).

9/11 itself has been perceived by some commentators as an event situated between the real and the fantastic. On the first anniversary of the attacks, in 2002, three of the most prominent voices of critical theory, Jean Baudrillard, Paul Virilio and Slavoj Zizek published simultaneously three texts about 9/11. Baudrillard's approach draws from that of his earlier texts. He assesses the interweaving of reality and fiction in the events of 9/11, describing the collapse of the Twin Towers as a hyper-real spectacle that is so extreme that it generates an extra degree of fictional supplementarity, the process of "reinventing the real as the ultimate and most redoubtable fiction" (Baudrillard, 2002: 22). In *Ground Zero* (2002) Virilio contextualises the terror attacks within large-scale genealogies of cultural and technological developments. He regards the transitions from total war to cold war to terrorism in terms of the evolution of a logic of the advancement of military technology. Similarly, 9/11 is a development within cultural forms that are themselves the product of militarisation. Reality TV, for example, is an 'image strategy' that is linked to the multimedia presentation of the Gulf War as well as it anticipates 9/11 (Virilio, 2002). Finally, in *Welcome to the Desert of the Real* (2002), which takes its title from a famous line in *The Matrix* (dir. Andy Wachowsky, 1999), Slavoj Zizek is concerned with the fantastic aspect of the 9/11 attacks. He articulates a similar interpretation of the events of 9/11 within the framework of Lacanian psychoanalysis. Zizek sees 9/11 as a dramatic intrusion of the Lacanian Real into the Symbolic world. The Western world has a "passion for the Real" as a site of otherness and authenticity, but, by failing to acknowledge how the Real is incorporated into our everyday Symbolic world, such a desire propagates a spectral social reality and represses more accurate interpretations of current events (Zizek, 2002: 5). In other words, in the late capitalist consumerist society, 'real social life' itself acquires the features of a staged fake. This is particularly true in terms of the dream of the USA as a safe haven and the representation of Osama Bin Laden as a cinematic villain (Gelder, 2006: 115). America has always fantasised about its own destruction, as is evident from the enormous popularity of the disaster movie genre. The association between 9/11 and Hollywood is that, in both cases, the unthinkable which happened was the object of fantasy, so that, in a way, as Zizek notoriously claims, "America got what it fantasized about" (Zizek cited in Bearn, 2004: 14). Similarly, Geoff King emphasises the 'fantastic' character of 9/11 when he claims that "the images [of 9/11 attacks] were, in some respects, uncannily similar to those offered by a number of Hollywood blockbusters produced in the previous decade" (King, 2005: 47). 9/11 and *LOTR* present a striking resemblance, as they are both epic visual events that dwell at the blurred border between fantasy and reality. The events of 9/11 seem to possess an almost fictional quality as they clearly evoke images of disaster movies such as *Towering Inferno* (dir. John Guillermin, 1974), *Independence Day* (dir. Roland Emmerich, 1996) or *Fight Club* (dir. David Fincher, 1999), that anticipated by just a few years the destruction of the twin towers.

By contrast, the fantastic world of *LOTR* persistently attempts to enter the domain of the real by emphasising the authenticity of the world it depicts. The film-makers repeatedly claimed that they wanted to make Middle Earth as believable, realistic and authentic as possible. The authenticity of the costumes, weapons and 'bigatures' created by Weta Workshop (the company responsible for the production of the special effects) was based faithfully on Tolkien's world. Jackson personally authenticated his home country as the perfect site upon which to recreate Tolkien's world by claiming that since he was a child he had been "struck by the similarities between New Zealand's unspoilt terrain and Tolkien's depiction of a 'rugged Middle Earth'" (Jackson cited in Tzanelli, 2004: 22). On another occasion, he defined Middle Earth as "more like history than fantasy" (Jackson cited in Brodie, 2002: 6). Jones and Smith aptly describe the peculiar process of 'fabricating authenticity' at work in *LOTR*, claiming that in the production of the trilogy "the believability of a real, recreated, world is based on a combination of exhaustively researched 'historical' details […] and twenty-first century high technology special effects" (Jones and Smith, 2005: 934). Jones and Smith borrow the concept of 'fabricating authenticity' from Richard Peterson, who proposes that the appearance of authenticity is central to the success of cultural industries and its fabrication is therefore linked to commercial purposes (Peterson and Anand, 2004). The *LOTR* franchise was a huge commercial hit and the detailed reproduction of Tolkien's world, which satisfied even the most long-standing fans of the novel, accounts for one of the factors of its success.

On the eve of the release of *The Fellowship of the Ring*, the screens of the whole world were saturated with both images of the impact of the hijacked planes on the twin towers and glimpses of the spectacular special effects of *LOTR* offered by its commercial trailer. The physicality and realism of the fantastic world shaped by Jackson and Tolkien compensated for the fantastic quality of reality.[8] In his analysis of the televisual coverage of 9/11 Geoffrey King points out how the images of the attack were heavily mediated and constructed through a complex process of editing (King, 2005: 54). The televisual construction of catastrophe has a therapeutic effect, as by knitting video fragments into continuity sequences it reduces the indeterminacy of the catastrophic event itself. As a media event 9/11 distorted the difference between fantasy and reality by rendering the events of real spectacle in a form closer to that of fictional productions. Nevertheless, even the media construction of real events is not able to completely tame the threatening power of reality; the video footage of the attacks on the World Trade Center does not in fact provide the spectator with the conventional roles and practices of fictional works, such as a recognisable hero or the predictable triumph of 'good'. This state of crisis determines the heterotopian impulse of the spectator who attempts to resolve this trauma in an Other space.

Jackson's *LOTR* did not merely provide an escape from the real world. It went as far as replacing it and constituting itself as a heterotopia: on the one hand, articulating conservative political discourses that were popular among the Western audiences of the time, on the other, proposing the immersion in a consistent cultural and geographical space—Middle Earth—in which conflicts between good and evil are clearly structured and successfully resolved. This could explain the paradoxical impact of the trilogy on tourism. The terrorist attacks of 9/11 had an immediate and devastating impact on the global tourist industry. Sonmez et al. note that among other negative events such as natural calamities, economic recessions and epidemics, the risk of terrorism is the factor that most severely impacts on tourism (1998: 13). In the immediate aftermath of the attacks, US domestic tourist flows fell by 15%, with hotel rates simultaneously softening by 10% (Litvin and Alderson, 2002: 188). 9/11 caused a 30% global drop in tourist demand: airlines experienced $US 2.1 billion losses while hotels suffered a $US 2 billion loss in room revenue (9/11 Meetingsnet, 2008). The destinations most affected were those situated in regions perceived as particularly at risk of terrorist attack, such as the Middle East and Third World countries. However, even Europe was not immune to the global crisis as in 2001 international arrivals declined for the first time since 1982 (IPK, 2002). 9/11 inhibited travel to 'real' destinations marked by social conflicts, such as the Middle East or Europe, but even hyper-real places such as theme parks located within 'real' countries suffered the global tourist slowdown. According to estimated figures released by Amusement Business, attendance was down between 3% and 15% at most American amusement parks in 2001 (Ultimate Rollercoaster, 2002).

By contrast, in 2002 New Zealand was one of the few countries where the tourist flow was not affected—indeed, it actually increased (Statistics NZ, 2005). After the release of the first *LOTR* film New Zealand gained an extraordinary level of exposure, to the extent that the very phenomenon of film-induced tourism attracted the interest of tourist stakeholders, national governments and researchers. In 2004 a survey conducted by Thomson Holidays found that eight Britons out of ten find ideas about their holiday destinations from films. The research revealed that 40% of British tourists voted New Zealand their top holiday movie spot (Guardian, 2004). The success of New Zealand in terms of film tourism does not simply relate, as suggested by Gelder, to the fact that the country is generally perceived as a 'safe destination' in an otherwise unsafe world; "an innocent place, untouched by terrorism, much like the Hobbit's Shire just prior to the events of *The Lord of the Rings*" (Gelder, 2006: 110). The reasons that allowed New Zealand to escape and even flourish as a tourist destination in the gloomy period that followed 9/11 are related to the uncanny similarity between the heterotopia of Middle Earth and 'real' New Zealand, an analogy which in turn can be traced back to the colonial history of the country. The conflict between British settlers and the Māori, in fact, evokes and short-circuits the opposition between a Western Self and a dark-skinned Other which is characteristic of both the War of the Ring and the War on Terror. In the last section of the chapter I will focus on the local historical, social and cultural preconditions that enabled the successful identification of New Zealand with the "transposable 'otherness'" (Jutel, 2004: 55) of Middle Earth.

## New Zealand

The New Zealand government recognised, very early on, the significant benefits that *LOTR* could potentially bring to the country. In 2001 Prime Minister Helen Clark, referring to the films, claimed that:

> [s]et against the spectacular and diverse New Zealand landscape *The Lord of the Rings* trilogy has the potential to be a major tourist promotion and investment tool for the years to come, by highlighting the country's natural beauty and the creative talents of its people across a wide range of knowledge based industries. (Clark, 2001)

Clark allocated several million dollars to leverage the association between the country and *LOTR* and also appointed associate minister Pete Hodgson to manage the involvement of the New Zealand government in *LOTR*-related activities. Hodgson was quickly nicknamed 'The Minister of the *Lord of the Rings*', a designation that somehow demonstrates the importance of the project in the governmental agenda (Thompson, 2007: 311). Hodgson and Paul Voigt, one of the directors of Investment New Zealand, coordinated the involvement of governmental agencies such as Investment New Zealand, Film New Zealand, New Zealand Film Commission and Tourism New Zealand in the 'New Zealand, Home of Middle Earth' campaign. Air New Zealand was included in the team, even though at that time it was not a public institution. New Line Cinema collaborated on the promotional campaign granting the licensing fee for free (Thompson, 2007: 311).

New Zealand governmental agencies emphasised the national authenticity of the *LOTR* project, profiting from every opportunity to reiterate the claim that the trilogy was a local product and a perfect expression of national identity (Jones and Smith, 2005: 927). The promotion of the films by the government as a unique legacy of the celebrated 'Kiwi ingenuity' was part of a wider project of rebranding of the country. Until the 1960s New Zealand maintained a privileged relation with its former 'mother country' Britain, the main buyer of New Zealand's raw material such as lamb and wool. Up until this era, the colonial umbilical cord that linked the two countries had never been cut, as New Zealand still regarded Britain as its main political, cultural and social reference. From the end of the 1960s, however, with the emergence of the EEC, Britain chose to reframe its economic, political and cultural activities within Europe and as a consequence it loosened its ties with former colonies such as New Zealand. New Zealand in turn was obliged to find a new position within the global scenario. Since the mid-1970s new government policies have encouraged the promotion of sectors of the economy that are environmentally sustainable, such as new technologies, tourism and creative industries, and in particular film-making.[9] The subsequent tax cuts and financial support granted to *LOTR* and other foreign productions were precisely part of a conscious attempt to boost the profile of the local film industry and promote the country as a perfect film-making location.

Through slogans such as 'the world in one country', Film New Zealand, the agency responsible for the promotion of the country as a film-production site, encouraged potential film producers to remove the landscape from its socio-historical context and to use it as an undefined and transposable setting for international productions. The Film New Zealand campaign echoes the slogans of the early local film productions funded by the tourist department. The credits of *Romantic New Zealand*, for example, defined the country as a 'world in a nutshell'. The early tourist films about New Zealand featured a long series of scenic views of the country's pristine nature, empty landscapes devoid of inhabitants. These empty New Zealand landscapes were raw material that could be imaginatively and materially processed and consumed by the tourist/spectator or the settler. The land was possessed, cleared physically and metaphorically of its features and eventually invested with meaning originating from the mother country.[10] Thus, New Zealand became the 'Britain of the South Seas', Christchurch the 'English city' and Dunedin an antipodean piece of Scotland. The same mechanism is at work in contemporary New Zealand, which once again provides raw material to be creatively processed by foreign agents (Tolkien and Hollywood production). The tourist industry that revolves around *LOTR* capitalises on this reconstruction of New Zealand spatial identity. An extreme example of this is provided by the brochure of Nomad Safaris, the Queenstown based company that offers *LOTR* tours (Safari of the Scenes). As the brochure is unfolded it reveals what seem to be two spectacular 180-degree views of New Zealand nature (Figure 6.3).

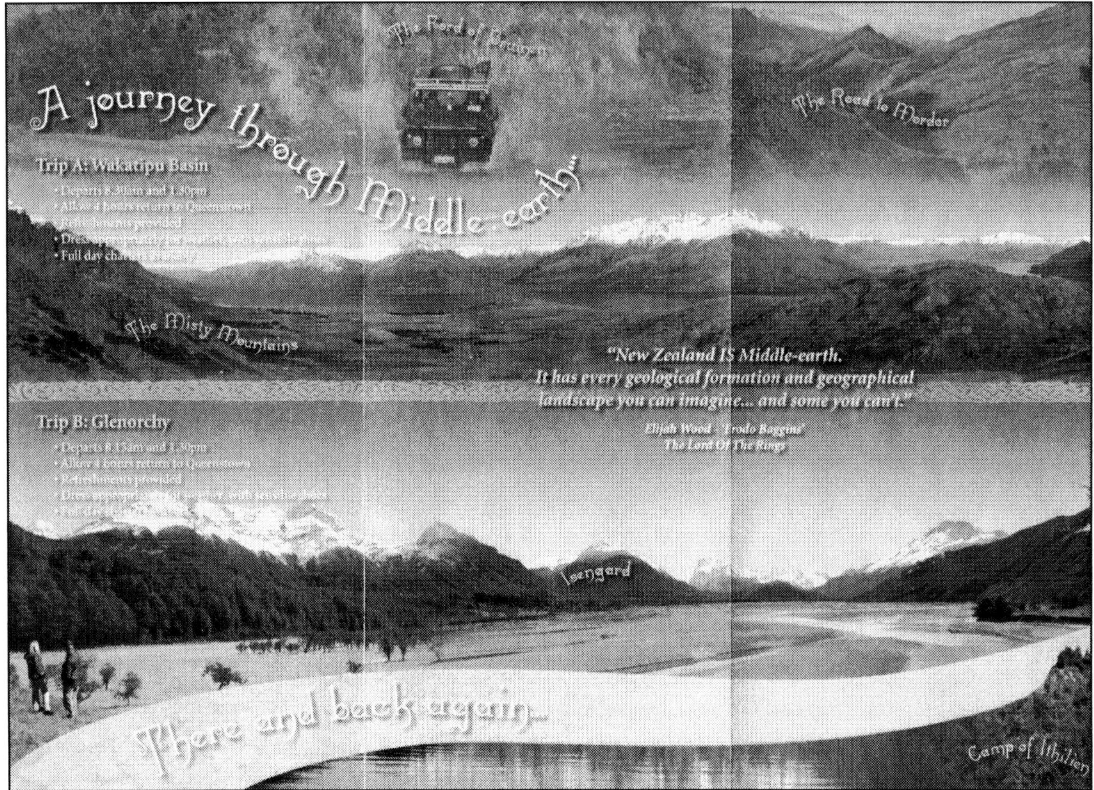


Figure 6.3. www.nomadsafaris.co.nz. Brochure 2008.

The different corners of the landscape are marked with the names of the film locations, such as Isengard, Camp of Ithilien or Forest of Lothlorien, that will be visited in the tour. A closer inspection of the photograph, however, reveals that it is actually a photomontage where the different locations have been superimposed to form a consistently connected landscape.

The specific identity of the tourist sites is ignored, as they have been rearranged to form a new virtual geography based on the *LOTR* narrative. This is somehow at odds with the claim of the same tourist brochure: "the tours are based around several places of the specific sites where filming took place. These are real places—there are no film sets—they are areas of outstanding natural beauty that need no enhancement". Curiously, while the tourist operators are eager to emphasise the reality and authenticity of the locations, at the very same time they remove them from their context, omitting to mention even their actual topographical names. For Jutel, the extensive use of CGI, bigatures and other effects in *LOTR* produced 'virtual cartographies', rendering it impossible for the viewer to distinguish between real and artificial landscapes (Jutel, 2004: 61). The virtual landscapes in *LOTR* do not simply erase the colonial legacy of the country, they go so far as to create a new heritage. As Reynolds et al. point out, the associative link between Middle Earth and New Zealand is so strong that "the whole country becomes a potential 'unmarked site' that can become Middle-earth at the tourist's will—particularly in remote areas" (Reynolds et al., 2009: 246). The identity of New Zealand as home of Middle Earth could be better defined as a form of heterotopia. According to Stan Jones, the heterotopia represented by 'New Zealand, Home of Middle Earth' is a space whose authenticity is based on the perceived correspondence between New Zealand's physical reality and the imported myth (Jones, 2006: 292). A Disney-like theme park would counteract the tourist dissatisfaction sometimes reported while visiting a *LOTR* location, in particular the deception related to the disjunction between the filmic landscapes enhanced by CGI and the actual ones (Carl et al., 2007: 58). By contrast, the creation of a physical site would limit the potential of *LOTR* as national epic and cultural heritage, a potential founded on the intermingling between the virtual and the real (Jones, 2006: 297).

The production of *LOTR* is not the only agent responsible for the fusion of Middle Earth with New Zealand. The conflation of the fantasy land with the real one was predicated on the pre-existing cinematic and touristic imagery of the country. As Smith-Rowsey points out, "in Jackson's films the presumption of familiarity with medieval Europe is counter-balanced, to a significant extent, by a presumption of unfamiliarity with New Zealand itself" (Smith-Rowsey, 2007: 142). Before the trilogy New Zealand was a place as imaginary as Middle Earth for many viewers. Epithets like 'down under' or the 'edge of the world' convey the idea of a land kept pristine and unspoilt due to its distance from the First World. The physical remoteness of the country from the centre of the Western world (Britain or United States) played a crucial role in the development of colonial fantasies about New Zealand. This is evident particularly in British or American film productions set in Aotearoa, such as *The Seekers* or *Green Dolphin Street*, where the distance between centre and periphery is the most prominent element of the narrative.

Similarly, the settler rhetoric, evident in definitions of New Zealand as 'Godzone' or 'Country of the Golden Weather', paradoxically conflates notions of familiarity and exoticism, purity and abundance, thus incorporating a religious valence which points to the utopian character of the country. In the nineteenth and twentieth century New Zealand was therefore constructed as a promised land, an egalitarian society that could offer prospective British settlers the chance of a new life. In their analysis of the perception of New Zealand by overseas *LOTR* audiences, Barker and Mathjis noticed that for the viewers 'New Zealand' as depicted in the films is an abstract, distanced and ideal location which naturally embodies goodness and purity (2007). For these viewers and potential tourists, New Zealand represents a perfect destination for a pilgrimage of self-rediscovery. Barker and Mathjis draw the notion of pilgrimage from Zygmunt Bauman, who in turn describes this concept as the act of distancing one's self from the familiar home in order to achieve a clearer perception of one's personal identity (Bauman cited in Barker and Mathjis, 2007: 125). New Zealand as Middle Earth, inheriting the colonial fantasy of the settler culture, provides metropolitan audiences with a radical 'there'. The title of Bilbo's book, 'There and Back Again', that features at the beginning of the trilogy is, in this respect, particularly significant. The film constructs itself as a narrative of travel whose destination is a utopia elsewhere at the border between fantasy and reality. The opening sequence of *The Two Towers* (Figure 6.4), a spectacular aerial view of the Misty Mountains/Southern Alps set against the epic soundtrack of the film, bears a striking resemblance to the final scene of *This is New Zealand*, a travelogue produced by the National Film Unit which achieved a huge popularity both in New Zealand and overseas during the 1970s (Figure 6.5). *This is New Zealand* was a spectacular three-screen film made for the Japan Tourist Expo to promote the scenic beauty of the country. The last scene of the film, which features a bird's-eye view of the Southern Alps accompanied by the climatic build of Sibelius' *Karelia Suite*, became the most famous part of this travelogue. Interestingly, both in *LOTR* and *This is New Zealand* film technological innovations work to emphasise the sublime 'naturalness' of the landscape.

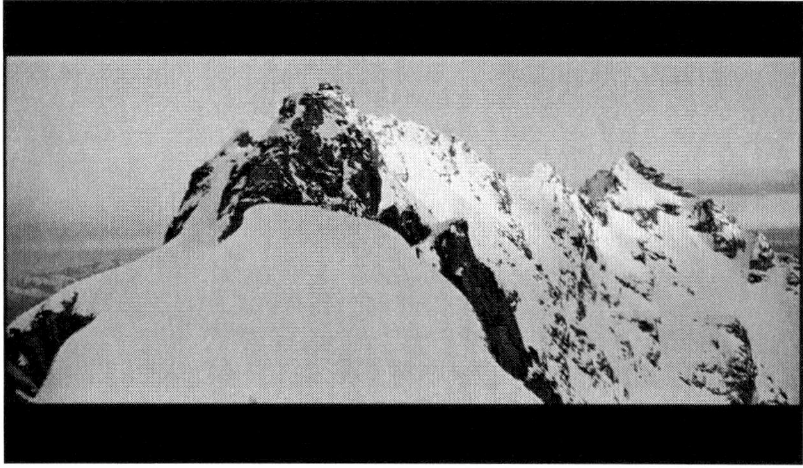

Figure 6.4. *The Lord of the Rings-The Two Towers*, New Line Cinema.

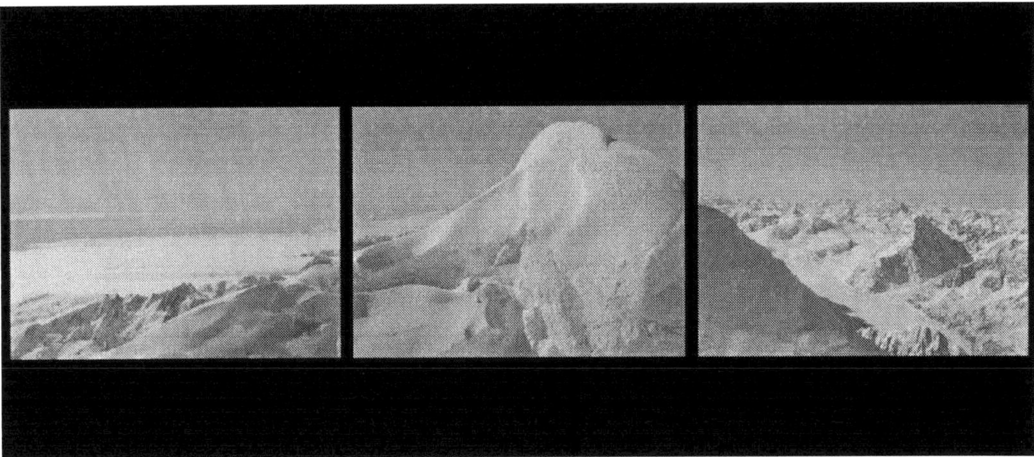

Figure 6.5. *This Is New Zealand*, NZFU.

The touristic representations of New Zealand as a '100% pure, green and clean' destination positioned the country in radical opposition to the metropolitan centres of the First World. Similarly, in several New Zealand films the country's empty landscapes are used to signify wilderness, remote spaces and primordial nature untamed by the modern world. This mythical representation of New Zealand as a natural paradise clearly resonates in *LOTR*. The ecological aesthetics of the films in fact reflect the marketing campaign of the national tourism board. In both cases the message is clear: New Zealand/Middle Earth is the only place in which 'the green' resists and triumphs over an evil, invisible and polluting power. Sean Cubitt notices a clear analogy between discourses of nature in *LOTR* and New Zealand: "respect for boundaries is critical to the stability of Middle Earth, a respect mirroring the bio-security measures of the Department of Conservation, the environmental agency charged with protecting the island environments of Aotearoa New Zealand" (Cubitt, 2006: 67). Furthermore, the eco-political subtext present in both the films and the novel, with their implicit attacks on modernity and industrialisation, echo the engagement of New Zealand governments in the environmental realm. New Zealand, which has declared itself nuclear-free since 1987, supported Greenpeace's protest against the French nuclear tests in the Pacific, in the mid-1980s. The uneven struggle between New Zealand and one of the major political powers of the world bears comparison with the conflict between Merry and Pipin and Saruman's hordes in *The Two Towers*. The two Hobbits eventually gain the support of the Ents, defeating the evil wizard. In the same way, New Zealand has managed to attract worldwide support by holding France accountable for its actions.

The contemporary appeal of 'nature' could also be explained via the notion of 'biophilia', a term coined by Edward O. Wilson to define "our innate tendency to focus on life and lifelike forms and in some instances to affiliate with them emotionally" (Wilson, 2002: 134). According to this theory, for most of their history humans have lived in the wilderness as hunters-gathers, making their shift to urban environments relatively recent. As a consequence, contemporary human beings that live in cities tend to be attracted to spaces that simulate their ancestral home (in particular the African savannah, dotted by groves and scattered trees). This could possibly explain the appeal of gardens and pets, or the significant popularity of aquariums and zoos as forms of entertainment. According to Dissanayake (1992: 136), only the most 'civilised' and artificial groups and societies glorify nature. This hypothesis is confirmed by the powerful appeal of New Zealand landscape for (what the tourist board has defined as) 'interactive travellers'.[11] The representation of 'natural' environments, which is a constant presence throughout *LOTR*, is an essential component of its appeal for urban dwellers potentially attracted by New Zealand's pristine nature. In the films, the natural world often acts as a substitute for human values. Some commentators (Barker and Mathjis, 2007; Wilson, 2007) have noticed that the representation of 'green' in *LOTR* is inextricably linked with moral attributes such as 'goodness'. Phillips (2007), by contrast, suggests a less simplistic hypothesis when he claims that in many instances the cinematic landscapes of Middle Earth recreated by Jackson may have other influences, particularly in terms of what has been defined as New Zealand or antipodean Gothic (Tincknell, 2000; Kavka et al., 2006).[12] The Kiwi Gothic, which is a stylistic feature that characterises films such as *Vigil* (dir. Vincent Ward, 1984), *The Piano* or *Rain* (dir. Christine Jeffs, 2001), constructs New Zealand not as a place of some pastoral idyll but rather as an environment where danger and horror lurk everywhere. During the 1950s, in his seminal essay '*Fretful Sleepers*' (1974) Bill Pearson described New Zealanders as living anxious lives haunted by their own conformism. A few decades later, in his exploration of New Zealand culture entitled *Mapping Godzone* (1998), American critic William Schaffer was struck by the 'Gothicism' of most of the country's self-representation. The Kiwi Gothic is generally considered to be an expression of the settler anxiety derived from the confrontation with a hostile and alien environment, such as the native New Zealand bush. *LOTR* carries the residues of the colonial past and in particular the Pākehā fear of the indigenous element. Significantly, the dark-skinned, savage and cruel Uruk-hai are played by Māori actors. Uruk-hai are literally autochthonous, as they pop out of the earth, and the scene in which the first Uruk-hai breaks an amniotic sack made of mud and soil evokes, in a grotesque way, the Māori notion of *whenua*, the placental afterbirth which

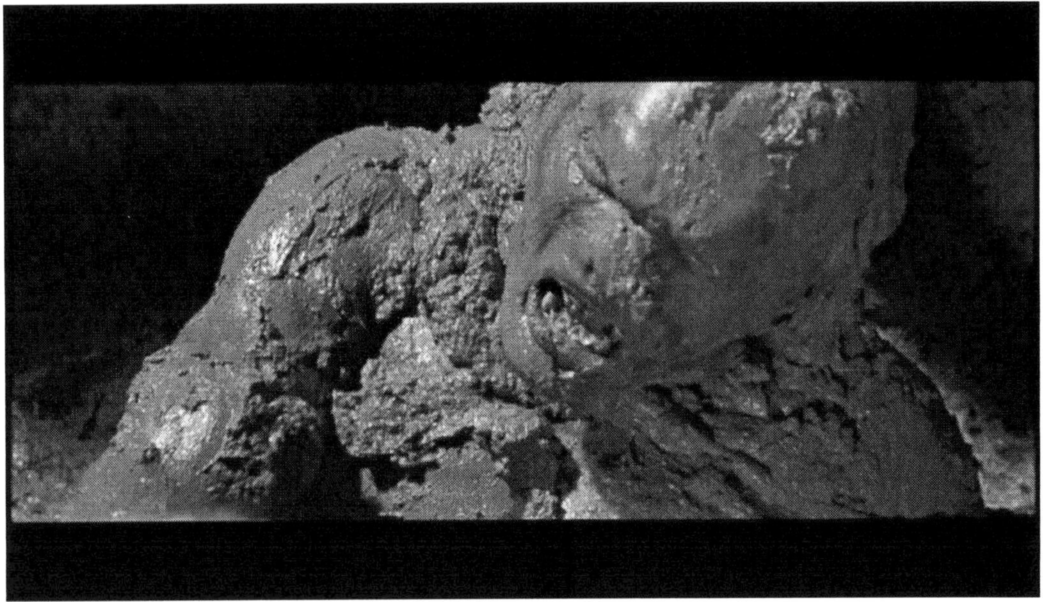

Figure 6.6. *The Lord of the Rings-The Fellowship of the Ring*, New Line Cinema.

is inextricably connected to the land (Figures 6.6). Apart from being invariably black, the forces of evil are also often associated with mud and dirt and, significantly, some of the most perilous obstacles confronted by Frodo and the fellowship are unstable or shaky ground, such as marshlands or lava flows. Similarly, in colonial fantasies such as *The Seekers*, Māori are associated with volcanoes and mudpools in ways which convey the destructive and threatening power of a 'young' people in a 'young' land without a past and therefore implicitly prone to the process of colonisation. Frodo leaves the most domesticated environment of the story, the Shire, and embarks on a quest to the least civilised space of all: the crater of Mount Doom. Located in the middle of Mordor, the volcano is at once the most untameable and the most evil place of all, as it is there that the One Ring was forged. At the climax of the story, when the ring is destroyed, the volcano explodes and disappears. Thus, Frodo has tamed the potentially destructive power of the uncivilised land. Martin Phillips, deriving his analysis from Propp's structuralist approach, argues that adventure stories, such as *LOTR*, map constructions of identity and geography. He notices how these kinds of stories usually involve "spatial movement from a home environment [...] into a distant unknown and life-threatening environment which, after much struggle, becomes known, domesticated and civilised" (Phillips, 2007: 105). The narrative of *LOTR* evokes the process of the colonial enterprise, as the story is based on the opposition between a rural but highly civilised space, that is, the Shire, which was explicitly modelled on the 'Olde England', and a dangerous and threatening wilderness that needs to be tamed. The Uruk hai is a stereo-trope, a refraction of New Zealand history which articulates the settler dread of the savage indigenes (Kavka and Turner, 2009: 232). By contrast, the Hobbits display clothes, accents and a tendency to walk barefoot that equate them with displaced Britons or, in other words, Pākehā. From a New Zealand perspective, *LOTR* could be read as the story of peaceful but strong-minded Pākehā (Hobbits) who are obliged to confront barbaric indigenous peoples who threaten islands of civilisation, such as the Shire, remade in the image of England. This possible colonial reception of *LOTR* as opposition between Pākehā and Māori short-circuits the more contemporary reading of the film as an allegory of the war launched by the Western world against terror. New Zealand colonial history reproduces, on a smaller scale, the opposition between a Western Self and a dark-skinned Other. A great part of the tourist imagery of the country is represented by depictions of coded and ritualised violence: Māori warriors, the Haka and rugby. Even the 'accelerated sublime' (Bell and Lyall, 2002) of adventure tourism, associated with Aotearoa in more recent years, incorporates a component of staged danger and violence. The New Zealand tourist experience does not offer mere escapism but rather restages the Western anxiety caused by the War on Terror. Significantly, Tolkien carefully constructed Middle Earth as the mythical land of origin of the Anglo-Saxon race and this element re-emerges in the films where the architecture of Rohan evokes the Viking civilisation while Gondor bears a resemblance to the English Middle Ages. In a time characterised by the popularity of discourses about the clash of civilisations, the meta-political valence of Middle Earth/New Zealand as legendary source of the Western race should not be ignored. New Zealand as Middle Earth is a land where the libidinally invested threat of the Other (indigenous people/dark forces) is eventually defeated and the story is concluded by the victory of the Western Self (Frodo/British settler).

Middle Earth is essentially a space of violence as it is dotted with numerous battlegrounds. Tourists visiting *LOTR* film locations often look for the places where the virtual battles between the fellowship and Mordor took place. According to A. V. Seaton (1999), the stimulus of war has been one of the main energisers in the history of tourism. In particular, Seaton notices how the Grand Tour, the historical precursor of modern tourism, was partially shaped by war, in that the classical literature which underpinned its structural itinerary was epic history and poetry which celebrated war, particularly in the works of classical authors such as Homer and Tacitus (Seaton, 1999: 132). Tourism to battlefields can acquire political significance in particular historical moments. For example, increased visits to the site of the battle of Stirling Bridge in Scotland have been associated with the resurgence of the Scottish nationalist movement.

New Zealand landscapes are characterised by overlapping layers of meaning: for the overseas visitor they evoke at once pre-colonial conflicts between the British and the Māori and the phantasmatic battles between the armies of Middle Earth. The tourist journey to Middle Earth, which significantly was imagined by Tolkien as the legendary land of Anglo-Saxon origin, is therefore a cathartic return to the mythical cradle of Western civilisation, where conflicts with the Other have been, at least from the symbolic point of view, successfully resolved.


## Conclusions

*LOTR* has been unanimously acclaimed as one of the most significant and revolutionary films in the history of cinema in terms of the scale of the project, the extensive use of CGI and because it was one of the first Hollywood blockbusters to be entirely produced in another country. *LOTR* had a dramatic impact on New Zealand from an economic, social and cultural point of view. This small antipodean country has, in fact, incorporated *LOTR* into its national identity to the extent that the films have become an acknowledged component of the country's heritage. The most obvious example of the impact of *LOTR* on the country's self-perception has been the marketing campaign launched by several government agencies, 'New Zealand, Home of Middle Earth'. The successful application of the campaign for purposes of tourist promotion generated much anticipation about the tourist spin-offs of the film. The alleged influence of *LOTR* on visitor numbers to New Zealand has attracted the interest of stakeholders and academics alike and, since the release of the last episode of *LOTR*, a wide array of research on the impact of the films on New Zealand tourism is available. In this chapter I have attempted to review the different approaches taken by these works to formulate a more encompassing theory of the relation between *LOTR* and tourism in New Zealand. While there is clear evidence that the tourist flow to New Zealand increased after the release of the films, it has been difficult for researchers to measure the actual role played by *LOTR*. It is difficult to pinpoint a single cause to explain the enormous impact of the film on the country's tourism. Rather, this phenomenon is the result of a complex interplay of factors that concern the modes of production, the style and the narrative of the film text, the context of its reception and finally the history of the film-tourist location, New Zealand.

First, the trilogy was conceived from the outset as a franchise and this played a crucial role in the commodification of Middle Earth for tourist purposes: *LOTR* tourism represented just one of many ancillary products produced to maximise the lucrative power of the franchise. The logic of capitalism is responsible for the creation of a consistent heterotopia, an alternative world consisting of games, websites, full-size prop replicas and *LOTR* tourism in which cultural consumers can completely immerse themselves. *LOTR* therefore becomes a 'total movie', in the Bazinian sense of the term, as it envelops the spectator inside its world. Secondly, the cinematographic style of the film is based on an aesthetics of spectacle, characterised by vertiginous and spectacular camera movements, that highlights the visual pleasure associated with the visual consumption of special effects and scenic views of the land. From this point of view, *LOTR* belongs to a well-established New Zealand film tradition which separates the landscape from its history and people, thus preparing it for commodification and export. Unlike other New Zealand films, however, *LOTR* attempts to inscribe the fantastic geography of the film over the 'real' New Zealand as a consistent cultural and physical space: Middle Earth. The accuracy and realism of the depiction of Middle Earth reinforced the tactile quality of the relation between the viewer and the world of the films. *LOTR* tourism to New Zealand, like some of the video games based on the franchise, offers precisely the possibility to complete the *LOTR* experience by actually grasping the world which is only hinted at in *LOTR* maps and films. Finally, the constitution of the heterotopia New Zealand/Middle Earth was paradoxically amplified by the excess of reality represented by the 9/11 attacks. The first episode of the *LOTR* saga was released just three months after the tragic events of 9/11 and the reading of the film was influenced by the political discourses that circulated in the Western world at the time. Significantly, the *LOTR* trilogy is an Anglo-Saxon enterprise (English writer, American production, New Zealand director) and carries the traces of a Western-settler anxiety exacerbated by the War on Terror. After all, the trilogy tells the story of a group of white warriors who, in a time of impending catastrophe, fight a desperate war against an invisible and terrorist enemy. *LOTR* translates and rearticulates the trauma of global war and interracial conflicts within a fantastic and controlled space  New Zealand/Middle Earth—where these conflicts are successfully resolved.

The status of New Zealand as officially standing in for Middle Earth seems to be reinforced by the decision to film the prequel of *LOTR*, *The Hobbit*, in the same country. The mechanism of the film franchise, which proved to be so successful in the *LOTR* trilogy, seems to be at work once again in this production. Unlike Bilbo, who went 'there and back again' the journey does not seem to stop for film viewers/prospective tourists, who will be offered another chance to return to Middle Earth.


**Notes**

1.  Serendipitous contingencies, such as the launch of the Louis Vuitton Cup in Auckland or the implementation of new tourist policies including the working holiday visa scheme could partially explain the popularity of New Zealand as a tourist destination at the beginning of the millennium.

2. Commenting on the Tourism New Zealand advertisement promoting the country as the 'Best supporting Country in a Motion Picture', some scholars (Wong, 2007) have gone as far as to declare a Baudrillardian 'death' of New Zealand.

3. Significantly, Foucault claims that the colony is an extreme type of heterotopia as, like the boat, it is "a place without a place, that exists by itself, that is closed in on itself and at the same time is given over to the infinity of the sea" (Foucault, 1986: 27).

4. For a definition of the notion of 'hallmark event' see page 150 in Chapter 5.

5. See Chapter 1.

6. See Chapter 3.

7. In the immediate aftermath of the attacks and the launch of the War on Terror many Western governments reinforced anti-terrorist measures. The new safety regulations did not stop a new series of terrorist attacks: on 11 March 2004 Madrid was the site of a train bombing that killed nearly 200 people while on 7 July 2005 a bomb blast in London claimed more than 50 lives.

8. I would suggest that, paradoxically, fantasy as a literary genre is itself strictly connected to reality: the popularity of fantasy increased significantly during the two World Wars as an escape and a reaction to the prevalent anxiety of the time.

9. See page 37 in Chapter 2 for a history of earlier policies and tax breaks that aimed to support the New Zealand film industry.

10. See Chapter 1.

11. For a definition of 'interactive travellers' see page 88 in Chapter 3.

12. Gothic literature emerges at the end of the eighteenth century in correspondence with the emergence of Romanticism and as a reaction to the Enlightenment values. The Gothic should be considered as a mode rather than as a genre, as the latter term does not account for the ability of the Gothic to mutate and adapt to a variety of cultural and geographical contexts. The traditional content of Gothic novels, which included haunted castles and graveyards, gradually shifted

to explore the issue of a divided consciousness, as in Mary Shelley's famous *Frankenstein* (1818). It is precisely this focus on psychological horror that most influenced the Kiwi version of the Gothic which often deals with alienation, family traumas and the uncanny. For a recent analysis of gothic literature see Brown (2005).

# CONCLUSIONS

This book has attempted to analyse the relation between the representation of the landscape in New Zealand cinema and the construction of the country's tourist imagery. New Zealand has recently become world famous as a tourist destination because of its association with the *LOTR* trilogy by Peter Jackson. However, this is not the first time New Zealand has benefited from the exposure generated by a feature film. In 1994, the success of *The Piano* introduced the rugged landscapes of the country to global audiences, and, in the following years, New Zealand tourist guidebooks promoted Karekare beach as the main film location and one of the most important attractions of the Auckland region. In reality, the connection between film and tourism in New Zealand dates back to the very origins of the cinematographic medium in this country. In fact, the emergence of the early New Zealand film industry cannot be divorced from the national institutions responsible for the promotion of tourism. Since the beginning of the twentieth century, the New Zealand Tourist Department has funded most of the early New Zealand films that were consequently used to promote the country as a potential tourist destination. One of the main objectives of this book has been, precisely, to determine the extent to which the legacy of this mode of landscape representation is still active, in different forms, in contemporary New Zealand cinema.

Knowing that no single study could exhaust such a broad field of study, I have focused on the analysis of the film texts and, in particular, the representation of the landscape in four principal films that have had (or were expected to have) a considerable impact in terms of tourism. Nevertheless, the book has often gone beyond this semiotic approach, focusing on the analysis of the historical, economic and social factors that led to the explosion of the film-tourism craze in New Zealand. In particular, the first two chapters of this work look closely at the development of the local film industry to see how the specificity of those early New Zealand productions influenced the representation of space in more recent films. Further research might examine the reception of these films and the influence of the context of reception on travel decisions to New Zealand. I hope that by prioritising the analysis of the film texts I have provided a useful starting point for future researchers wishing to substantiate the analysis of this subject with other approaches.

This book has pursued four major lines of argument to explain the tendency to promote New Zealand as a tourist destination through films: first, the representation of New Zealand at the border between nature and culture; secondly, the construction of the country in its cultural production as the 'appealing object of the tourist gaze'; third, the consequent use of the country as a transposable otherness and, finally, the evolution of the country into a 'film-tourist heterotopia'.

The core of the recent '100% Pure New Zealand' campaign, launched by the national tourist board, is the marketing of the country as a green, clean and safe, Edenic garden. The myth of a primeval nature in New Zealand has been particularly powerful because it has performed three different functions. First, the representation of a pure nature implicitly suggested that the country was a good terrain for the colonial enterprise. Purity is equated with emptiness and, in turn, emptiness justifies the settler enterprise. The early New Zealand films represented an infinite series of empty landscapes waiting to be filled by tourists and/or prospective settlers. From this point of view, discourses of film, tourism and colonialism cannot be separated from each other. The very films that suggested the emptiness of New Zealand were at the same time concerned to display the technological advancement of the country, particularly in terms of mobility. New Zealand is not simply the domain of 'nature'; the emphasis on technologies of mobility reveals that the primeval forces of the land have been tamed and are ready to be physically and metaphorically appropriated (through the gaze). Second, the myth of nature provides settlers coming from different cultural and social backgrounds with a common identity. The shared experience of struggle against a hostile nature represents the foundation of New Zealand's egalitarian society. Nature, of course, does not solely perform a negative function, as it is precisely this struggle that allows the eventual redemption of the settler. The history of New Zealand cinema is characterised by over-representations of natural settings, in particular the beach and the bush. The beach is the liminal place between nature and culture; all the settlers arrive from the sea and have to cross the beach in order to access the heart of the country. In many of the films analysed in this study (*Memory and Desire*, *The Piano*, *Whale Rider*), the beach is a crucial component in the development of the narrative. The beach also represents the synthesis of a New Zealand identity, combining a mythical unspoilt nature personified by the Māori and the British legacy of culture and civilisation. The surreal image of the piano on the beach in Campion's film has proven to be so successful because it embodies an iconic power that points towards the country's cultural identity.

Unlike the beach, the bush as a filmic place is clearly positioned within the domain of 'nature'. The narrative of most New Zealand films is based upon the opposition between nature and culture. Culture is embodied by the city, the centre of the empire

(Britain), or even by a more general threat of corruption which is never fully realised. In contrast, the bush represents the extreme expression of nature and film characters often escape into the bush from the oppression of an authoritarian figure. The bush represents at once an alien and uncanny environment and the promise of a mythical reconnection with an unspoilt nature. Māori are often represented as at ease in the bush and they contribute to the promise (and the threat) represented by this environment.

The third function of the myth of nature is the creation of an appealing 'otherness' in terms of both temporal and geographical distance for potential European tourists/settlers. The emergence of tourism as a form of leisure is linked to the revaluation of the rural as a reaction to the industrialisation of Western cities that is familiar to the great majority of workers and potential tourists. In Britain, for example, tourist discourses have focused on the celebration of a supposedly authentic 'Olde England' generally associated with the countryside. The construction of a New Zealand identity cannot be separated from the tourist rhetoric of the pastoral paradise; thus, New Zealand is defined as 'Britain of the South Seas' or 'Britain's Farm'. The promise of both an untamed land and an egalitarian society, that constituted one of the major appeals of the country, refers to the purity of origins, represented by a land unspoilt by industrialisation and centuries of class privilege. Paradoxically then, the 'Newness' of New Zealand points towards an idealised past. From this perspective it was almost inevitable that New Zealand should become a tourist destination as an embodiment of Middle Earth and the Shire, a place Tolkien conceived precisely as the mythical place of British origin. New Zealand represents an 'otherness' located in a different temporal dimension. In this way, New Zealand at the antipodes *is* 'Olde England', the same idealised destination celebrated by early British tourists who, during the nineteenth century, escaped industrial cities seeking the authenticity of the rural. Interestingly, the narratives of all the case studies discussed in this book (*LOTR*, *The Last Samurai*, *The Piano*) are situated in the past. Even though *Whale Rider* is set in contemporary New Zealand, there are no obvious signs of 'civilisation' in Whangara (no cars or advanced technology) and the villagers seem to live in a pre-modern time. Most importantly, all the films are set in a time of epochal change where the original purity of the place is at stake. This is quite apparent in *LOTR* and *The Last Samurai* where the tranquillity of the shire and the traditional values of the Samurai village are threatened respectively by Sauron and by Western reforms. In *The Piano* this opposition is more veiled but still in evidence: the purity of the land represented by the sexually liberated Māori and the lush bush, is under the attack from an oppressive settler authority, embodied by Stewart. The threat is dissolved when Ada chooses Baines, who is perceived as being 'closer to nature', and thus forming the foundation of a settler household more respectful of the peculiarity of the land. In *Whale Rider*, it is the Māori tradition that guarantees Whangara the status of 'lost paradise' which is threatened by the modern phenomenon of women's rights. Once again, the menace is foiled as modernity is reconciled with tradition and the village is allowed to maintain its idyllic existence.

In all these narratives, New Zealand features as a 'pure' place threatened by an incumbent menace, and in all cases the original status of the preoedipal space is partially, or completely, saved. The otherness of New Zealand does not only refer to its construction as a different temporal dimension or 'lost paradise'. The emphasis of New Zealand films on the natural assets of the country also signifies the physical remoteness of the country from the world's major urban centres. New Zealand represents the perfect alternative to the steady increase of urban populations and the heightened concerns about environmental issues, at least in Western countries. The New Zealand myth of nature is constructed in order to satisfy the escapist desires of urban dwellers. The insularity and the geographical distance of the country from the main tourist markets represents the main appeal of Kiwi land, as it offers the illusion that New Zealand is detached from globalisation, a 'safe haven' forgotten by the unstoppable advancement of late capitalism. Paradoxically, it is precisely this geographical remoteness that helped to clearly position New Zealand in the global tourist market. It is these notions of insularity and geographical distance that lead to my second line of argument, according to which New Zealand is 'the seductive object of the tourist gaze'.

Most New Zealand films focus on the physical distance that separates New Zealand from the metropolitan centre of the world. New Zealand is often represented as the final destination of a journey of personal or collective redemption. The notion of travel features prominently in all the films examined in this book and filmic characters travel ceaselessly from an urban or civilised space (overseas, or New Zealand cities) to a utopian landscape which is sometimes threatening, but often liberating, even in tragic ways. Travel is the main narrative element of New Zealand feature films from *Runaway* to *The Piano* as well as *LOTR*. These films represent the legacy of the connection between film and tourism, firmly established in New Zealand since the beginning of the twentieth century. Early travel films commissioned by the Tourist Department inscribed the simulacrum of the viewer in these texts, filling the empty landscapes with the occasional tourist/traveller. Similarly, later feature films encouraged the identification of the spectator with a protagonist who is often also a traveller. Furthermore, these films often activate what Martin Lefevbre, drawing on the work of Laura Mulvey (1989), defines as a 'spectacular mode' of reception which is often opposed to the 'narrative' one (Lefebvre, 2006). The spectacular mode focuses on the visual pleasure which, in the case of New Zealand films, is represented by a surplus of landscape. The film gaze often coincides with the tourist gaze of the protagonist which tends to linger on the natural scenery. In these productions, the landscape is freed from the narrative constraints of the film, becoming more than a simple setting. Even though these landscapes sometimes carry a symbolic meaning, and are thus reincorporated to the narrative logic of the film, they are principally distractions that open up new narrative possibilities. As the narrative temporarily stops, the film invites the visual consumption of the landscape by appealing to the tourist gaze of the spectator. As mentioned in Chapter 2, the critics of one of the first New Zealand feature films, *Runaway*, noticed the unnecessary, at least from the narrative point of view, focus on scenic views of the landscape. The over-representation of the landscape conceived as a manifestation of the 'uniqueness' of the country is part of an attempt to define a clear national identity. This mechanism was eventually coded and reinforced by the regulations of the national film-funding agency. In fact, the New Zealand Film Commission favoured projects with a relevant 'New Zealand content'. The setting and the landscape often constituted the New Zealand content mentioned in the Film Commission guidelines. This emphasis on landscape is also consistent with another of the commission's strategies: the marketing of New Zealand as a tourist destination through feature films. The New Zealand film industry used the uniqueness and exoticism of the country's locations to position itself in the global market. Similarly, because of its limited budget, the national tourist board increasingly used film features as a marketing tool and this strategy culminated in the branding of the country as Middle Earth following the filming of *LOTR*.

New Zealand film landscapes are framed by a tourist gaze for two reasons. First, early settlers were confronted with an alien environment which they represented and tamed using the European artistic conventions of the time: the New Zealand landscape was framed by the canons of the sublime and picturesque that in turn fed the tourism industry of the time. In his book *The Search for the Picturesque* (1989) Malcolm Andrews claims that since the end of the eighteenth century British travellers stormed the countryside, and indeed the whole of Europe, seeking picturesque and sublime sites. He states that the peculiar nature of 'picturesque tourism' was "to find scenery which resembled familiar paintings or poetic descriptions" (Andrews, 1989: 76). Picturesque tourism implies a tension between the search for new and thrilling experiences and the familiarity of traditional artistic practices. The aesthetic experience of the picturesque and the sublime resonates with the dialectic between risk and safety that characterises the tourist practice. Early New Zealand travel films, produced to promote the country to both tourists and settlers, inherited the traditional canons of visual art. This legacy is also apparent in much later cultural productions such as *The Piano*. Second, the limited opportunities offered by the New Zealand domestic market meant that most of the country's cultural products were conceived for export overseas. Tourism has always been a precious asset for the country, but it has recently gained even more importance, overtaking dairy production and becoming the country's first export industry. The subsistence of New Zealanders relies on the selling of their country, so that Aotearoa is first and foremost a tourist destination before being home or *whenua*. This validates Minette Hillyer's definition of New

Zealanders as "both tourists and themselves proud pioneers" (Hillyer, 1997: 18). The construction of a national identity is inextricably linked to the shared imagining of the land as a tourist commodity. Even though it did not generate any relevant form of film tourism, one of the texts analysed in this book is quite revealing in this sense. In *Memory and Desire*, the film gaze is consistently mediated by a tourist gaze and the story is in fact told from the perspective of a couple of Japanese tourists visiting the country for their honeymoon. The tourists' encounter with both an appealing and an unfamiliar landscape has dramatic consequences for the life of the couple. The tragedy at the centre of the narrative disguises a deep settler anxiety in relation to the alien environment.

The tourist gaze implies a relation of power over the object of the gaze, thus tourist practices cannot be divorced from the commodification of the land that is typical of the settler enterprise. The tourist gaze allows one to frame and therefore tame the landscape represented. Furthermore, the object of the gaze is domesticated because it is always compared to the familiar. The tourist gaze always has a transformative power over the landscape, as this latter becomes the focus of the projected fantasies of the gazer. In many instances, the tourist site/sight physically changes in order to meet the expectations of the tourist gaze. The New Zealand landscape is historically constructed and understood through a comparison with the familiar, represented by Britain and Europe. Early settlers physically redefined the local landscape, clearing the land of native flora and replacing it with an imported one. As has already been mentioned, early settler discourses of New Zealand make sense of the local space by comparing it to the familiar, thus transforming Aotearoa into a 'Britain of the South Seas'. These narratives often opposed New Zealand to the familiar, the country cannot exist outside this relation. In other words, it cannot subsist beyond the dichotomy 'sameness versus otherness'. The tourist gaze inevitably constructs the object of the gaze as 'otherness'. When the tourist gaze meets a settler culture whose subsistence relies on the production of raw material to be processed and consumed somewhere else, the landscape becomes a 'blank otherness', ready to be filled with meaning produced elsewhere. This leads to the definition of New Zealand as a 'transposable otherness' that has constituted one of the main arguments of this book. Historically, New Zealand has been one of the favourite destinations for runaway productions seeking cheaper labour and locations. The national government has always been particularly attentive to the potential benefits offered by film productions in this country. This support has become even more explicit in connection to the recent redefinition of New Zealand's political economy: the government has in fact formulated special grants, film funds and financial schemes in an effort to attract film productions to the country. This strategy has regularly been followed by the attempt to capitalise on the potential tourist spin-offs of these productions, mainly based on the association between the landscape and the aura of the Hollywood 'circus'. The enthusiasm and the efforts of local authorities in promoting film-tourist sites has thus been marked by disillusion, from the case of *The Rescue* in 1987 to the more recent example of *The Last Samurai* in 2003.

In most cases, the attempt to capitalise on the potential tourism generated by these films failed, and this was linked to the difficulty for viewers of recognising New Zealand as the actual film location. Even though the geographical defamiliarisation that characterises these texts prevents them from producing direct benefits for the local tourist industry, they contributed in the redefinition of the New Zealand landscape. Landscape is an artificial construct and films actively contribute to redefine its meaning. In the great majority of the runaway productions filmed in this country, the landscape is the background to narratives of adventure and heroism. From *Without a Paddle* to *Vertical Limit*, as well as the TV series *Xena* and *Hercules*, most of the productions that exploit New Zealand landscapes are action movies where nature plays the actantial role of 'Opposer'. There is a clear connection between the use of landscape both in these films and in the adventure tourism that has made the country world famous, in terms of the representation of space, construction of cultural identity and economics. Displaying the intense stimulation and emotion of cinematic bodies, action movies can harness the system of physical and emotional excess of the spectator which constitutes, in itself, one of the pleasures of movie-going activity. Similarly, recent studies of adventure tourist attractions revealed how most of these recreational activities are based on a complex person-environment relation, thus creating "mildly unpleasant feelings of nervousness and apprehension that can also be exciting" (McIntyre and Roggenbuck, 1998: 401). The degree to which activities are pleasant or not is influenced by perceptions of risk.

The action films shot in New Zealand, like adventure tourism, are founded on the commodification of both the place and the bodily responses that it generates directly (tourism) or indirectly (through the vicarious identification with a film character). The transaction with the environment becomes the focus of the escapist pleasures of tourists/spectators. The establishment of New Zealand as a place where the scenery provides a backdrop for heroic adventures represents an evolution of the notion of the sublime that was sought by early tourists. For the viewers aware that New Zealand is the actual film location these movies could simply anticipate the adventurousness of the country. But, more importantly, this use of the landscape goes as far as influencing the country's national identity. In a country where the great majority of the population lives in urban areas, the construction of an 'adventurous landscape' is an attempt to emphasise its alterity, thus positioning it in the new global scenario. Like runaway producers, tourists visiting New Zealand are more interested in the adventurousness of the landscape rather than its biological uniqueness. The construction of the national myth of an unspoilt and sublime nature cannot, therefore, be divorced from its commodification as an adventure playground to be sold to domestic and international tourists and producers. In both adventure tourism and runaway productions, New Zealand nature is a 'transposable otherness' subjugated to the imperatives of consumption. The success of adventure tourism is due to the threatening power of nature, but most of all due to the technological advancement that allows the minimising of risks and guarantees the safety of the tourist experience. Similarly, in runaway productions nature is tamed, controlled and modified by film technology.

Attempts to promote film locations to tourists can indirectly shed new light on the true meaning of the slogan '100% Pure New Zealand'. In this context, 'pure' is the antonym of 'corrupted' as the national tourist board attempts to position the country in radical opposition to the urban and industrial environment inhabited by the prospective tourists. However, in these tourist campaigns pure is also a synonym for 'empty'. The constant efforts to market film locations, even those used by runaway productions, as tourist destinations, suggest that local landscapes have to be filled with meaning produced elsewhere. '100% Pure New Zealand' is a blank canvas which is appealing precisely because of its emptiness. However, the uniqueness of this landscape is guaranteed via layers of meaning superimposed onto the original ones and created by the centre of the empire for its own audiences. Tourist discourses related to *The Last Samurai*, for example, marketed the region as 'the place where Tom Cruise stayed' or as a 'Little Japan'. This example provides an interesting counterpoint to New Zealand colonial identity—evident in the very name of the country. Early British settlers attempted to counter New Zealand's out-of-nationess by emphasising the Englishness of Canterbury or the Scottishness of Otago. Now that New Zealand's allegiance to the British motherland has been in doubt for a number of decades, the country is undergoing a redefinition of its identity. In this context, films seem to be deployed to generate a coherent national narrative and forge new meanings of place. Most of the productions that have used New Zealand as a transposable alterity failed to either generate tourist flows to the film locations or redefine a new national identity. *LOTR*, nevertheless, forms a notable exception.

Jackson's trilogy is different from other runaway productions in many respects. First of all, the production of the film took place all over the country and therefore the films could be associated with the country as a whole and not just a region, as is the case with *The Last Samurai*. Second, in *LOTR* New Zealand is the stand-in for an imaginary land, Middle Earth, which uncannily resembles it. While the identification between New Zealand and the real countries it was meant to portray in runaway productions was highly implausible, simply because those countries actually existed elsewhere, the association with Tolkien's imaginary land was facilitated by the fact that the former had no prior physical existence. Interestingly, as New Zealand is increasingly questioning its former relation to Britain, Kiwis are keen to emphasise the relation between their country and Middle Earth, which in turn had been imagined by Tolkien as the mythical land of Anglo-Saxon origin. There is an eerie resonance between New Zealand as Middle Earth and the colonial rhetoric of New Zealand as 'Britain of the South Seas'. In both cases, New Zealand is conceived and defined as heterotopia, a place which is simultaneously present and absent.

Both the colonial and the filmic heterotopias share three common elements. First, they both emerge as a response to the crisis represented by war: colonial New Zealand is founded on the conflict between Māori and British settlers while the good-versus-evil dichotomy that tears apart Middle Earth resonates in discourses about the post 9/11 War on Terror. Second, the existence of both heterotopias is justified by economic imperatives of the capitalist mode of production. The subsistence of colonial New Zealand was based on the production of raw materials for the centre of the empire, while New Zealand as Middle Earth could not exist outside of the Hollywood franchise system. Finally, in both cases, cultural discourses about these two heterotopias configure them essentially as tourist destinations. The main concern for early New Zealand governments was to attract enough settlers to sustain the colonial enterprise. One of the main arguments of this book has been that New Zealand activates the conflation between tourist and colonial gazes. The colonial imagery of an exotic but tamed land and indigenous people titillated the imperialist ambitions of prospective tourists/settlers. In a similar fashion, New Zealand as Middle Earth is functional to the mythology of the Western empire. It provides a safe and imaginary tourist destination, as opposed to the real and perilous sites animated by social and political conflicts. New Zealand as Middle Earth uses the veiled threat of the Other, the Māori-Orc, to celebrate the superiority of a mythical Anglo-Saxon race in a historical moment in which this domination is forcefully challenged.

Colonial New Zealand was famous for its loyalty to the British crown and, ironically, in the postcolonial era the same enthusiasm once generated by the royal tours is now created by the premiere of a film called *The Return of the King*. New Zealand, as a socio-political orphan, has replaced the mother country with Hollywood, the new seat of power in the Anglo-Saxon world. Peter Jackson's trilogy has become part of the cultural fabric of the nation, at once reshaping New Zealand's sense of 'imagined community', becoming a component of the country's heritage and attracting foreign tourists to the country. This research has examined the cultural, historical and economic conditions that eventually led to the *LOTR*-related tourist craze. Particular attention has also been dedicated to the analysis of the film text, which has revealed how the construction of space and the influence of the New Zealand tradition in the representation of landscape impacted on, what I have defined in Chapter 6 as, the 'tourist heterotopian impulse'.

A number of questions remain unanswered. How will the different filmic representations of New Zealand interact in the long term and how will they impact on the tourist imagery of the country? How long will the film effects on a tourist destination last? Will Karekare always be the beach of *The Piano* or will new layers of meaning supersede the old ones? Will New Zealand always be home of Middle Earth? Will the mutated historical conditions increase or attenuate the impact of the film on tourism? Is any other film production likely to replace the heterotopian dominance of *LOTR* in the country? The production of *The Hobbit* in New Zealand is expected to reinforce the connection between the *LOTR* franchise and New Zealand, thus attracting new contingents of spectators/visitors to the country. And so, while local films will continue to shape New Zealand's virtual geography, global audiences will still undertake both imaginary and physical filmic tours of the country.

**Primary films**

***The Piano*** (1993)
Director: Jane Campion
Production: Jan Chapman
Screenplay: Jane Campion
Photography: Stuart Dryburgh
Editing: Veronika Jenet
Music: Michael Nyman
Art Direction: Andrew McAlpine
Cast: Holly Hunter (Ada McGrath), Harvey Keitel (George Baines),
    Sam Neill (Alisdair Stewart), Anna Paquin (Flora McGrath)
Company: CIBY 2000, Jan Chapman Productions, The Australian
    Film Commission
Running time: 120 mins.

***Whale Rider*** (2002)
Director: Niki Caro
Production: Tim Sanders, Frank Hubner and John Barnett
Screenplay: Niki Caro (from a novel by Witi Ihimaera)
Photography: Leon Narbey
Editing: David Coulson
Music: Lisa Gerrard
Art Direction: Grace Mok
Cast: Keisha Castle-Hughes (Paikea), Rawiri Patene (Koro), Vicky Haughton
    (Nanny Flowers), Cliff Curtis (Porourangi)
Company: South Pacific Pictures, Pandora Filmproduktion, ApolloMedia,
    New Zealand Film Commission, New Zealand On Air
Running time: 101 mins.

***The Last Samurai*** (2003)
Director: Edward Zwick
Production: Paula Wagner, Tom Cruise and Edward Zwick
Screenplay: John Logan, Marshall Herskovitz and Edward Zwick
Photography: John Toll
Editor: Victor Du Bois
Music: Hans Zimmer
Art Direction: Chris Burian Mohr
Cast: Tom Cruise (Nathan Algren), Ken Watanabe (Katsumoto),
    Billy Connoly (Zeb Gant), Timothy Spall (Simon Graham),
    Mr. Omura (Masato Harada)
Company: Warner Bros. Pictures, The Cruise/Wagner Productions,
    Radar Pictures, Bedford Falls Company
Running time: 160 mins.

***The Lord of the Rings* trilogy**:
***The Fellowship of the Ring*** (2001)
***The Two Towers*** (2002)
***The Return of the King*** (2003)
Director: Peter Jackson
Production: Barry M. Osborne, Peter Jackson, Fran Walsh, Tim Sanders
Screenplay: Fran Walsh, Philippa Boyens, Peter Jackson (from a novel by
    J. R. R. Tolkien)
Photography: Andrew Lesnie
Editing: John Gilbert
Music: Howard Shore
Art Direction: Joe Bleakley, Rob Outterside, Phil Ivey, Mark Robins
Cast: Elijah Wood (Frodo Baggins), Ian McKellen (Gandalf), Liv Tyler
    (Arwen), Viggo Mortensen (Aragorn), Sean Austin (Sam Gamgee),
    Orlando Bloom (Legolas), Christopher Lee (Saruman), Sean Bean
    (Boromir), Andy Serkis (Gollum)
Company: New Line Cinema, WingNut Films
Running time: (theatrical) 558 mins., (extended edition) 663 mins.

## Secondary films

*Across the Mountain Passes of New Zealand* (dir. Franklyn Barrett, prod. Pathé Freres, 1910).

*Alien 3* (dir. David Fincher, prod. Twentieth-Century Fox, 1992).

*Amokura* (dir. J.C. Morton, prod. Filmcraft Ltd, 1928).

*Aorangi: In New Zealand's Alpine Playground* (dir. & prod. New Zealand Publicity Office, 1929).

*Ben Hur* (dir. William Wyler, prod. M.G.M., 1959).

*Black Sheep* (dir. Jonathan King, prod. Live Stock Films Ltd, 2006).

*Braveheart* (dir. Mel Gibson, prod. Icon Entertainment International, 1995).

*Broken Barrier* (dir. John O'Shea, prod. Pacific Films Ltd, 1952).

*Crocodile Dundee* (dir. Peter Faiman, prod. Rimfire Films, 1986).

*Daughter of Dunedin* (dir. Rudall Hayward, prod. "Hollywood-on-Tour" Company, 1928).

*Deep Sea Thrills* (dir. & prod. Government Motion Pictures, 1934).

*Don't Let It Get You* (dir. John O'Shea, prod. Pacific Films Ltd, 1966).

*Fight Club* (dir. David Fincher, prod. Fox 2000 Pictures, 1999).

*Glacier* (dir. & prod. Filmcraft Ltd, 1938).

*Glorious New Zealand* (dir. Arthur H. Messenger, prod. New Zealand Government Publicity Office, 1925).

*Goodbye Pork Pie* (dir. Geoff Murphy, prod. A.M.A., 1980).

*Green Dolphin Street* (dir. Victor Saville, prod. M.G.M., 1947).

*Happy Altitudes in New Zealand Southern Alps* (dir. & prod. Filmcraft Ltd, 1933).

*Heavenly Creatures* (dir. Peter Jackson, prod. WingNut Films, 1994).

*Hei Tiki* (dir. Alexander Markey, prod. Markey Films, 1935).

*Hercules: The Legendary Journey* (TV series, prod. Universal Pictures, 1995-1999).

*Holiday Haunts* (dir. & prod. New Zealand Film, 1935).

*Holiday Sounds* (dir. & prod. Government Motion Picture, 1937).

*Illustrious Energy* (dir. Leon Narbey, prod. Mirage Entertainment Corporation Ltd, 1988).

*In Spring One Plants Alone* (dir. & prod. Vincent Ward, 1980).

*Independence Day* (dir. Roland Emmerich, prod. Twentieth-Century Fox, 1996).

*Japanese Story* (dir. Sue Brooks, prod. Gecko Films Pty. Ltd, 2003).

*Jaws* (dir. Steven Spielberg, prod. Universal Pictures, 1975).

*L'Avventura* (dir. Michelangelo Antonioni, prod. P.C.E., 1960).

*Mauri* (dir. Merata Mita, prod. Awatea Films, 1988).

*Memory and Desire* (dir. Niki Caro, prod. Frame Up Films, 1997).

*Midnight Run* (dir. Martin Brest, prod. Universal Pictures, 1988).

*Minority Report* (dir. Steven Spielberg, prod. Twentieth-Century Fox, 2002).

*Mr. Wrong* (dir. Gaylene Preston, prod. Preston Laing Productions Ltd, 1985).

*Natalie of Napier* (dir. Rudall Hayward, prod. "Hollywood-on-Tour" Company, 1929).

*New Zealand Charm: A Romantic Outpost of the Empire* (dir. & prod. Filmcraft Ltd, 1935).

*Ngati* (dir. Barry Barclay, prod. Pacific Films, 1987).

*Nightmare on Elm Street* (dir. Wes Craven, prod. New Line Cinema, 1984).

*Off the Edge* (dir. Mike Firth, prod. Pentacle Films Production, 1977).

*Once Were Warriors* (dir. Lee Tamahori, prod. Communicado, 1994).

*Pan's Labyrinth* (dir. Guillermo del Toro, prod. Tequila Gang, 2006).

*Patu!* (dir. Merata Mita, prod. Awatea Films, 1983).

*Picnic at Hanging Rock* (dir. Peter Weir, prod. Picnic Productions Pty. Ltd, 1975).

*Rabbit Proof Fence* (dir. Philipp Noyce, prod. Showtime Australia, 2002).

*Rain* (dir. Christine Jeffs, prod. Communicado Productions, 2001).

*Rain Man* (dir. Barry Levinson, prod. United Artists, 1988).

*Rewi's Last Stand* (dir. Rudall Hayward, prod. Māori War Films Ltd, 1925).

*River Queen* (dir. Vincent Ward, prod. Silverscreen Films, 2005).

*Romantic New Zealand* (dir. & prod. Filmcraft Studios, 1934).

*Runaway* (dir. John O'Shea, prod. Pacific Films Ltd, 1964).

*Scenes at the Rotorua Hui* (dir. James MacDonald, prod. Dominion Museum, 1920).

*Scenes in Māori Camp* (dir. James MacDonald, prod. Dominion Museum, 1920).

*Send a Gorilla* (dir. Melanie Read, prod. Pinflicks Productions, 1988).

*Shortland Street* (TV series, prod. South Pacific Pictures, 1992-2009).

*Sione's Wedding* (dir. Chris Graham, prod. South Pacific Pictures, 2006).

*Sleeping Dogs* (dir. Roger Donaldson, prod. Aardvark Films, 1977).

*Smash Palace* (dir. Roger Donaldson, prod. Aardvark Films, 1981).

*Snakeskin* (dir. Gillian Ashurts, prod. CowGirl Productions, 2001).

*Snows of Aorangi* (dir. Brian Brake, prod. National Film Unit, 1955).

*Somebody Else's Horizon* (dir. Hugh MacDonald, prod. National Film Unit, 1976).

*Star Wars* (dir. George Lucas, prod. Twentieth-Century Fox, 1977).

*Tangata Whenua* (dir. Barry Barclay, prod. Pacific Films, 1974).

*Te Rua* (dir. Barry Barclay, prod. Pacific Films, 1991).

*Teenage Mutant Ninja Turtles* (dir. Steve Barron, prod. New Line Cinema, 1990).

*The Adventures of Priscilla Queen of the Desert* (dir. Stephan Elliot, prod. Specific Films, 1994).

*The Bounty* (dir. Roger Donaldson, prod. Dino de Laurentis Company, 1984).

*The Chronicles of Narnia* (dir. Andrew Adamson, prod. Walt Disney Pictures, 2005).

*The Cinema of Unease* (dir. Sam Neill and Judy Rymer, prod. British Film Institute, 1995).

*The Leading Edge* (dir. Mike Firth, prod. Everard Films, 1987).

*The Lord of the Rings* (dir. Ralph Bakshi, prod. Saul Zaentz Production Company, 1978).

*The Māori: Everyone Bathes on Washing Day at Rotorua* (dir. & prod. Movietone News, 1937).

*The Matrix* (dir. Andy Wachowsky, prod. Village Roadshow Pictures, 1999).

*The Navigator* (dir. Vincent Ward, prod. Arena Film, 1988).

*The Price of Milk* (dir. Harry Sinclair, prod. John Swimmer Productions, 2000).

*The Prince of Wales at Rotorua* (dir. James MacDonald, prod. Dominion Museum, 1920).

*The Quiet Earth* (dir. Geoff Murphy, prod. Cinepro/Pillsbury Productions, 1985).

*The Rescue* (dir. Ferdinand Fairfax, prod. Walt Disney Pictures, 1988).

*The Return of the King* (dir. Jules Bass & Arthur Rankin Jr., prod. Rankin/Bass Productions, 1980).

*The Seekers* (dir. Ken Annakin, prod. Group Film Productions, 1954).

*The Southern Alps of New Zealand* (dir. S. B. Taylor, prod. New Zealand Agriculture Department, 1916).

*The Te Kooti Trail* (dir. Rudall Hayward, prod. Whakatane Films, 1927).

*This is New Zealand* (dir. Hugh MacDonald, prod. National Film Unit, 1970).

*Titanic* (dir. James Cameron, prod. Twentieth-Century Fox, 1997).

*Top Gun* (dir. Tony Scott, prod. Paramount Pictures, 1986).

*Tourist Train Leaving Livingston, Mont.* (dir. & prod. Edison Manufacturing Co., 1897).

*Towering Inferno* (dir. John Guillermin, prod. Irwin Allen Productions, 1974).

*Under the Southern Cross* (dir. Lew Collins, prod. Universal, 1929).

*Utu* (dir. Geoff Murphy, prod. Utu Productions Ltd, 1983).

*Vertical Limit* (dir. Martin Campbell, prod. Mountain High Productions, 2000).

*Vigil* (dir. Vincent Ward, prod. John Maynard Productions, 1984).

*Wake* (dir. & prod. Annie Goldson, 1994).

*Whakarewarewa* (dir. C.J. Morton, prod. New Zealand Government Publicity Office, 1927).

*Willow* (dir. Ron Howard, prod. Lucasfilm, 1988).

*Without a Paddle* (dir. Steven Brill, prod. De Line Pictures, 2004).

# BIBLIOGRAPHY

9/11 Meetingsnet. 2008. An Ongoing Report on the Impact of the Events of September 11 2001. [Online]. Available: http://911.meetingsnet.com/travel_updates. [Accessed 23 December 2008].

Aitken, S. and Zonn, L. [eds]. 1994. *Place, Power, Situation, and Spectacle: A Geography of Film*. Lanham: Rowman & Littlefield.

Anderson, B. 1991. *Imagined Communities: Reflections on the Origin and Spread of Nationalism*. London: Verso.

Ateljevic, I. and Doorne, S. 2002. Representing New Zealand: Tourism Imagery and Ideology. *Annals of Tourism Research*, 29(3): 648–67.

Babington, B. 2007. *A History of the New Zealand Fiction Feature Film*. Manchester: Manchester University Press.

Barclay, B. 1988. The Control of Ones Own Image. *Illusions*, 8: 8–14.

Barclay, B. 1990. *Our Own Image*. Auckland: Longman.

Barclay, B. 2003a. Celebrating Fourth Cinema. *Illusions*, 35: 7–11.

Barclay, B. 2003b. Exploring Fourth Cinema. *Summer School lectures, Reimagining Indigenous Cultures: The Pacific Islands*. Summer Institute: Hawaii, 23 July.

Barjavel, R. 2001. *Cinema Totale*. Roma: Editori Riuniti.

Barker, M. and Mathjis, E. 2007. Seeing the Promised Land from Afar, in *How We Became Middle Earth* edited by A. Lam and N. Oryshchuk. Zurich: Walking Tree Publisher: 107–28.

Barrett, P. 2006. Nice Work. *The Auckland Guide*, 2 (Summer): 120–21.

Batchen, G. 1997. *Burning with Desire: The Conception of Photography*. Cambridge, MA: MIT Press.

Baudrillard, J. 1973. *Toward a Critique of the Political Economy of the Sign* (Trans. C. Levin). St. Louis: Telos.

Baudrillard, J. 1983. *Simulations* (Trans. P. Foss). New York: Semiotexte.

Baudrillard, J. 2002. *The Spirit of Terrorism* (Trans. C. Turner). London: Verso.

Baum, L. F. 1996. *The Wizard of Oz* (Illustr. L. Zwerger). New York: North-South Books. First published 1900.

Bazin, A. 1971. The Myth of Total Cinema, in *What is Cinema?* (Trans. H. Gray). Berkeley: University of California Press.

Bearn, M. 2004. On the Rampage. *The New Statesman*, 2 (August): 16.

Beeton, S. 2005. *Film-Induced Tourism*. Buffalo: Channel View Publications.

Bell, C. 1996. *Inventing New Zealand*. Auckland: Penguin Books.

Bell, C. and Lyall, J. 1995. *Putting our Town on the Map*. Auckland: Harper Collins Publishers.

Bell, C. and Lyall, J. 2002. *Accelerated Sublime: Landscape, Tourism and Identity*. Westport: Praeger.

Benjamin, W. 1977. *The Origin of German Tragic Drama* (Trans. J. Osborne). London: NLB.

Benjamin, W. 1979. *Illuminations* (Trans. H. Zohn). Glasgow: Fontana.

Bernardi, S. 2002. *Il Paesaggio nel Cinema Italiano*. Venezia: Marsilio.

Bilborough, M. 1993. The Making of *The Piano*, in *The Piano* edited by J. Campion. London: Bloomsbury: 135–53.

Bingham, D. 2004. Kidman, Cruise and Brecht: A Brechtian Pastiche, in *More than a Method* edited by C. A. Baron, D. Carson and F. P. Tomasulo. Detroit: Wayne State University Press, 247–74.

Blythe, M. 1988. From Maoriland to Aotearoa: Images of the Māori in New Zealand Film and TV, Ph.D. Thesis. Los Angeles: University of California.

Blythe, M. 1990. The Romance of Maoriland: Ethnography and Tourism in New Zealand Films, *East-West Film Journal*, 4(2): 90–109.

Blythe, M. 1994. *Naming the Other: Images of the Māori in New Zealand Film and Television*. Metuchen: Scarecrow Press.

Boorstin, D. J. 1962. *The Image: A Guide to Pseudo-Events in America*. Harmondsworth: Penguin.

Bourdieu, P. 1984. *Distinction: A Social Critic of the Judgement of Taste* (Trans. R. Nice). London: Routledge.

Bregent-Heald, D. 2007. Primitive Encounters: Film and Tourism in the North American West. *Western Historical Quarterly*, 38(1): 47–67.

Brodie, I. 2002. The Lord of the Rings *Location Guidebook*. Auckland: Harper Collins.

Brown, C. 2003. The Representation of the Indigenous Other in *Daughters of the Dust* and *The Piano*. *NWSA Journal*, 15(1): 1–19.

Brown, G. and Keith, H. 1982. *An Introduction to New Zealand Painting 1839–1980*. Auckland: Collins.

Brown, M. 2005. *The Gothic Text*. Stanford: Stanford University Press.

Bruno, G. 1997a. Site-seeing: Architecture and the Moving Image. *Wide Angle*, 19(4): 8–24.

Bruno, G. 1997b. City Views: The Voyage of Film Images, in *The Cinematic City* edited by D. Clarke. London: Routledge: 47–60.

Bruzzi, S. 1993. Bodyscape. *Sight and Sound*, 3(October), 10.

Burke, E. 1998. *A Philosophical Enquiry into the Origins of our Ideas of the Sublime and the Beautiful*. New York: Oxford University Press. First published 1759.

Busby, G. and Klug, J. 2001. Movie-Induced Tourism: The Challenge of Measurement and Other Issues. *Journal of Vacation Marketing*, 7(4): 316–32.

Bushline Lodge. 2008. Bushline, Lodge, Treks and Tours. [Online]. Available: http://www.bushlinelodge.co.nz/tours/local_features.html. [Accessed 20 April 2009].

Butler, D. 2007. One Wall and No Roof Make a House: The Illusion of Space and Place in Peter Jacksons *The Lord of the Rings*, in *How We Became Middle Earth* edited by A. Lam and N. Oryshchuk. Zurich: Walking Tree Publisher: 149–68.

Byrnes, G. 2001. *Boundary Markers: Land Surveying and the Colonisation of New Zealand*. Wellington: Bridget Williams Books.

Cairns, B. and Martin, H. 1994. *Shadows on the Wall: A Study of Seven New Zealand Feature Films*. Auckland: Longman Paul.

Campbell, N. 2005. Producing America, in *The Media and the Tourist Imagination* edited by D. Crouch, R. Jackson and F. Thompson. London: Routledge: 198–214.

Capp, R. 2003. Romancing the Stone: Outback Adventures of a Different Kind in *Japanese Story*. *Metro Magazine*, 138: 28–32.

Carl, D., Kindon, S. and Smith, K. 2007. Tourists Experiences of Film Locations: New Zealand as *Middle Earth*. *Tourism Geographies*, 9(1): 49–63.

Caruth, C. 1995. *Trauma: Explorations in Memory*. Baltimore and London: Johns Hopkins University Press.

Casetti, F. 1998. *Inside the Gaze: The Fiction Film and its Spectator* (Trans. N. Andrew). Bloomington: Indiana University Press.

Churchman, G. 1997. *Celluloid Dreams: A Century of Films in New Zealand*. Wellington: PL Books.

Clark, H. 2001. Facts about The Lord of the Rings. [Online]. Available: http://www.executive.govt.nz/minister/clark/lor/lor.htm. [Accessed 20 December 2008].

Clover, C. 1989. Her Body, Himself: Gender in the Slasher Film, in *Fantasy and the Cinema* edited by J. Donald. London: British Film Institute: 91–133.

CNN 2001. New York: Television News Report. 5 October.

Conley, T. 2006. *The Lord of the Rings* and The Fellowship of the Map, in *From Hobbits to Hollywood* edited by E. Mathijs and M. Pomerance. Amsterdam: Rodopi: 215–30.

Conor, B. 2004. "Hollywood, Wellywood or the Backwoods?": A Political Economy of the New Zealand Film Industry. Masters Thesis. Auckland: Auckland University of Technology.

Conrich, I. 2006. A Land of Make Believe: Merchandising and Consumption of *The Lord of the Rings*, in *From Hobbits to Hollywood* edited by E. Mathijs and M. Pomerance. Amsterdam: Rodopi: 119–36.

Coombs, F. and Gemmell, S. [eds]. 1999. *Piano Lessons: Approaches to* The Piano. Sydney: John Libbey.

Coventry, N. 2003. We Are in the Right Path, Minister. *Inside Tourism*, 451: 1–2.

Cresswell, T. and Dixon, D. [eds]. 2007. *Engaging Film: Geographies of Mobility and Identity*. Oxford: Rowman & Littlefield.

Crofts, S. 2000. Foreign Tunes?: Gender and Nationality in Four Countries Reception of *The* Piano, *Jane Campions* The Piano edited by in H. Margolis. Cambridge: Cambridge University Press: 135–61.

Crouch, D., Jackson, R. and Thompson, F. [eds]. 2005. *The Media and the Tourist Imagination*. London: Routledge.

Croy, W. G. 2004. *The Lord of the Rings*, New Zealand, and Tourism: Image Building with Film. *Working Paper Series of the Department of Management*. Melbourne: Monash University.

Cubitt, S. 2006. The Fading of the Elves: Eco-Catastrophe, Technopoly, and Bio-Security, in *From Hobbits to Hollywood* edited by E. Mathijs and M. Pomerance. Amsterdam: Rodopi: 65–80.

Cubitt, S. 2009. Realising Middle Earth: Production Design and Film Technology, in *Studying the Event Film* edited by H. Margolis, S. Cubitt, B. King and T. Jutel. Manchester: Manchester University Press, 185–94.

De la Roche, C. 1988. *Performance*. Palmerston North: Dunmore Press.

Dennis, J. [ed.]. 1981. *The Tin Shed*. Wellington: Clive Sowry Editions.

Dennis, J. 1993. *Making Films in Australia and New Zealand in the Silent Period*. Wellington: Moa Films.

Derrida, J. 1997. *De LHospitalité*. Paris: Calmann-Levy.

Dissanayake, E. 1992. *Homo Aestheticus: Where Art Comes from and Why*. New York: Macmillan.

Downey, P. J. 1964. Runaway. *Comment*, October–November: 5–6.

Duncan, J. 2002. Ringmasters. *Cinefex*, 89: 64–131.

During, S. 1992. Postcolonialism and Globalisation. *Meanjin*, 48(2): 339–53.

Durr, E. 2007. Island Purity as Global Imaginary: New Zealand and German Perspectives. *Seminar Series of the Centre for Communication Research*. Auckland: Auckland University of Technology.

Dyer, R. 1986. *Heavenly Bodies: Film Stars and Society*. London: Routledge.

Eco, U. 1986. *Travels in Hyperreality*. Trans. W. Weaver. San Diego: Harcourt.

Edensor, T. 2005. Mediating William Wallace, in *The Media and the Tourist Imagination* edited by D. Crouch, R. Jackson and F. Thompson. London: Routledge: 105–18.

Edwards, S. 1989. Cinematic Imperialism and Māori Cultural Identity. *Illusions*, 10: 17–21.

Edwards, S. and Martin, H. 1997. *New Zealand Film: 1912–1996*. Auckland: Oxford University Press.

Eisenstein, S. M. 1987. *Non-Indifferent Nature*. Trans. H. Marshall. Cambridge: Cambridge University Press.

Evans, M. 1997. Plugging into TV Tourism. *Insights*, March: D35–D38.

Featherstone, M. 1988. In Pursuit of the Postmodern: An Introduction. *Theory, Culture and Society*. 5(2): 195–215.

Feifer, M. 1985. *Going Places: The Ways of the Tourist from Imperial Rome to the Present Day*. London: Macmillan.

Film New Zealand. 1999. *The Production Guide to the World in One Country*. Wellington: Film New Zealand.

Foucault, M. 1973. *The Birth of the Clinic*. Trans. A. M. Sheridan Smith. London: Tavistock.

Foucault, M. 1986. Of Other Spaces. *Diacritics*, 16: 22–7.

Franklin, H. 1978. *Trade, Growth and Anxiety*. Wellington: Methuen.

Friedberg, A. 1993. *Window Shopping: Cinema and the Postmodern*. Berkeley: University of California Press.

Fukuyama, F. 1992. *The End of History and the Last Man*. New York: Maxwell Macmillan International.

Gelder, K. 2006. Epic Fantasy and Global Terrorism, in *From Hobbits to Hollywood* edited by E. Mathijs and M. Pomerance. Amsterdam: Rodopi: 101–18.

GoAustralia 2006. Taranaki, New Zealand: ThePlace of *The Last Samurai*. [Online]. Available: http://goaustralia.about.com/od/northislandsightseeing/a/taranaki.htm. [Accessed 7 July 2006].

Goldson, A. 2006. *Memory, Landscape, Dad & Me*. Wellington: Victoria University Publications.

Greimas, A. J. 1983. *Structural Semantics*. Trans. D. McDowell Lincoln: University of Nebraska Press.

Greimas, A. J. 1987. *On Meaning*. Translated P. Perron. Foreword by Fredric Jameson. London: Frances Pinter.

Greimas, A. J. and Courtes, J. 1982. *Semiotics and Language: An Analytical Dictionary*. Trans. L. Crist. Bloomington: Indiana University Press.

Grierson, J. 1981. The Face of a New Zealander, in *The Tin Shed* edited by J. Dennis. Wellington: Clive Sowry Editions: 21–22.

Guardian [The] 2004. Movies that give Brits the Travel Bug. [Online]. Available: http://www.guardian.co.uk/film/2004/sep/28/news. [Accessed 10 May 2006].

Gunby, D. 1977. Sleeping Dogs. *Islands*, 6(2): 134–36.

Gunning, T. 1990. The Cinema of Attractions: Early Cinema, its Spectator, and the Avant-Garde, in *Early Cinema: Space Frame Narrative* edited by T. Elsaesser. London: British Film Institute: 56–62.

Gunning, T. 2006. The Whole World within Reach: Travel Images without Borders, in *Virtual Voyages* edited by J. Ruoff. London: Duke University Press: 25–41.

Hahm, J. 2004. Assessing the Impact of Movies upon an Individuals Image Formation concerning a Given Destination, Masters Thesis. Orlando: University of Central Florida.

Hammond, B. 2004. Whale Rider and Gisborne/Eastland: An Investigation into the Effects of the Film Whale Rider on Gisborne/Eastland, Honours Dissertation. Auckland: University of Auckland.

Hannigan, J. 1998. *Fantasy City: Pleasure and Profit in the Postmodern Metropolis*. London: Routledge.

Harvey, B. 1994. *The Piano*: Virtual Reality of the Real Thing. *The National Business Review*, 15 April: 16.

Harvey, B. and Bridge, T. 2005. *White Cloud, Silver Screen*. Auckland: Exisle Publishing.

Hayes, M. 2002. Photography and the Emergence of the Pacific Cruise: Rethinking the Representational Crisis in Colonial Photography, in *Colonialist Photography* edited by E. M. Hight and G. D. Sampson. London: Routledge: 172–87.

Heidegger, M. 1977. *The Question Concerning Technology and Other Essays*. Trans. W. Lovitt. New York: Harper and Row.

Hill, D. 1994. Beatson doesn't Play *The Piano*. *Admark*, 31 March: 48.

Hills, M. 2002. *Fan Cultures*. London: Routledge.

Hillyer, M. 1997. We Calmly and Adventurously Go Travelling: New Zealand Film, 1925–35, Masters Thesis. Auckland: University of Auckland.

Hokowhitu, B. 2008. The Death of Koro Paka: Traditional Māori Patriarchy. *The Contemporary Pacific*, 20(1): 115–41.

Holmes, B. 1953. *The World is Mine*. Culver City: Maurice and Gee.

Hopkins, J. 1994. A Mapping of Cinematic Places, in *Place, Power, Situation, and Spectacle: A Geography of Film* edited by S. Aitken and L. Zonn. Lanham: Rowman and Littlefield, 47–67.

Horrocks, R. 1989. The Creation of a Film Feature Industry, in *Te Ao Marama* edited by S. Toffetti and J. Dennis. Torino: Le Nuove Muse: 100–03.

Horrocks, R. 1999. New Zealand Cinema, in *Twin Peeks: Australian and New Zealand Feature Films* edited by D. Verhoeven. Melbourne: Damned Publishing: 129–38.

Hudson, S. and Ritchie, J. R. B. 2005. Film Tourism and Destination Marketing: The Case of *Captain Corellis Mandolin*. *Journal of Vacation Marketing*, 12(3): 256–68.

Hughes, O. 2008. Interview with the author. 17 September 2008. Auckland.

Huntington, S. 1996. *The Clash of Civilizations and the Remaking of World Order*. New York: Simon & Schuster.

IPK 2002. The Latest Global Travel Trends: 2002–2003. [Online]. Available: http://www.etc-corporate.org/resources/uploads/GTENGLISH%20VERSION.pdf. [Accessed 13 October 2008].

Jackson, R. 2005. Converging Cultures; Converging Gazes; Contextualizing Perspectives, in *The Media and the Tourist Imagination* edited by D. Crouch, R. Jackson and F. Thompson. London: Routledge: 183–97.

Jameson, F. 1991. *Postmodernism, or the Cultural Logic of Late Capitalism*. Durham: Duke University Press.

Jenkins, H. 1992. *Textual Poachers: Televisions Fans and Participatory Culture*. New York: Routledge.

Jesson, B. 1984. Money Talks. *Onfilm*, 1(4): 19–20.

Jones, D. and Smith, K. 2005. Middle-earth Meets New Zealand: Authenticity and Location in the Making of *The Lord of the Rings*. *Journal of Management Studies*, 42(5): 923–45.

Jones, S. 2006. Fixing a Heritage: Inscribing Middle Earth onto New Zealand, in *The Lord of the Rings: Popular Culture in Global Context* edited by E.Mathjis. London: Wallflower Press: 285–300.

Jutel, T. 2004. *Lord of the Rings*: Landscape, Transformation, and the Geography of the Virtual, in *Cultural Studies in Aotearoa* edited by C. Bell and S. Matthewman. Auckland: Oxford University Press: 54–65.

Kavka, M., Lawn, J. and Paul, M. 2006. *Gothic NZ: The Darker Side of Kiwi Culture*. Dunedin: Otago University Press.

Kavka, M. and Turner, S. 2009. This is not New Zealand: An Exercise in the Political Economy of Identity, in *Studying the Event Film* edited by H. Margolis, S. Cubitt, B. King and T. Jutel. Manchester: Manchester University Press: 230–38.

Kearney, R. 1999. Aliens and Others: Between Girard and Derrida. *Cultural Values*, 3(3): 251–62.

Kellner, D. 2006. *The Lord of the Rings* as Allegory: A Multiperspectivist Reading, in *From Hobbits to Hollywood* edited by E. Mathijs and M. Pomerance Amsterdam: Rodopi: 17–40.

Kennedy, G. 2003. Taranaki Cruises to Stardom. *The National Business Review*, 24 April: 34.

Kim, H. and Richardson, S. L. 2003. Motion Pictures Impacts on Destination Images. *Annals of Tourism Research*, 25(2): 216–327.

King, B. 2008. Stardom, Celebrity and the Para-Confession. *Social Semiotics*, 18(2): 115–32.

King, G. 2005. "Just Like a Movie"?: 9/11 and Hollywood Spectacle, in *Spectacle of the Real* edited by G. King. Portland: Intellect Books: 47–57.

Kirby, L. 1997. *Parallel Tracks: The Railroad and Silent Cinema*. Devon: University of Exeter Press.

Kristeva, J. 1980. From One Identity to an Other, in *Desire in Language: A Semiotic Approach to Literature and Art* edited by L. S. Roudiez and translated by T. Gora, A. Jardine and L. S. Roudiez. New York: Columbia University Press: 124–47.

Kristeva, J. 1985. The Speaking Subject, in *On Signs* edited by M. Blonsky. Oxford: Basil Blackwell: 210–20.

Lacan, J. 1978. *The Four Fundamental Concepts of Psycho-Analysis*. Trans. Alan Sheridan. New York: Norton.

Larsen, J. 2001. Tourism Mobilities and the Travel Glance: Experiences of Being on the Move. *Scandinavian Journal of Hospitality and Tourism*, 1(2): 80–98.

Lasch, C. 1979. *The Culture of Narcissism*. New York: Norton.

Lash, S. 1990. *Sociology of Postmodernism*. London: Routledge.

Lash, S. and Urry, J. 1994. *Economies of Signs and Space*. London: Sage.

Le Heron, E. J. 2002. Translating Place: Landscape, Film and Film Landscape. Masters Thesis. Auckland: University of Auckland.

Lee, S., Scott, D. and Kim H. 2008. Celebrity Fan Involvement and Destination Perceptions, *Annals of Tourism Research*, 35(3): 809–32.

Lefebvre, M. [ed.]. 2006. *Landscape and Film*. New York: Routledge.

Litvin, S. W. and Alderson, L. L. 2002. How Charleston Got Her Groove Back: A Convention and Visitors Bureaus Response to 9/11. *Journal of Vacation Marketing*, 9(2): 188–97.

Lotman, J. 1976. *Semiotics of Cinema*. Trans. M. E. Suino. Ann Arbor: University of Michigan Press.

Lyotard, J. F. 1984. *The Postmodern Condition: A Report on Knowledge*. Trans. G. Bennington and B. Massumi. Minneapolis: University of Minnesota Press.

Lyotard, J. F. 1991. *The Inhuman: Reflections on Time*. Trans. G. Bennington and R. Bowlby. Stanford: Stanford University Press.

Macassey, O. 2008. Gramophones Taken for Wonders: The Aesthetic of Superimposition in Colonial Heritage Film. *Screen Studies Conference*. Glasgow: University of Glasgow, July 2008.

MacCannell, D. 1999. *The Tourist: A New Theory of the Leisure Class*. Berkeley: University of California Press.

Margolis, H. [ed.]. 2000. *Jane Campions* The Piano. Cambridge: Cambridge University Press.

Mathijs, E. and Pomerance, M. [eds]. 2006. *From Hobbits to Hollywood*. Amsterdam: Rodopi.

Matthews, P. 2003. The Making of *The Whale Rider*: Turning a New Zealand Classic into an International Hit Movie. *New Zealand Listener*, 1 February, 18–25.

McNaughton, T. 1986. *Countless Signs: The New Zealand Landscape in Literature*. Auckland: Reed Methuen.

Meek, A. 2009. Fantasising History as Trauma, in *Studying the Event Film* edited by H. Margolis, S. Cubitt, B. King and T. Jutel. Manchester: Manchester University Press: 214–21.

Message, K. 2003. *Whale Rider* and the Politics of Location. *Metro Magazine*, 136 Spring: 86.

Metz, C. 1975. The Imaginary Signifier. *Screen*, 16(2): 14–76.

Metz, C. 1983. *Psychoanalysis and Cinema: The Imaginary Signifier*. Trans. C. Britton. London: Macmillan Press.

Mirams, G. 1945. *Speaking Candidly*. Hamilton: Pauls Book Arcade.

Mita, M. 1992. The Soul and the Image, in *Film in Aotearoa New Zealand* edited by J. Dennis and J. Bieringa. Wellington: Victoria University Press: 39–54.

Modleski, T. 1982. *Loving with a Vengeance: Mass-Produced Fantasies for Women*. London: Methuen.

Morgan, N. J., Pritchard, A. and Piggott, R. 2003. Destination Branding and the Role of the Stakeholders: The Case of New Zealand. *Journal of Vacation Marketing*, 9(3): 285–99.

Morin, E. 2005. *The Stars*. Trans. R. Howard. Minneapolis: University of Minnesota Press.

Morris, P. 2003. Review of *Whale Rider*, directed by Niki Caro, *Cineaste*, 29, 18.

Mulvey, L. 1989. *Visual and Other Pleasures*. Bloomington: Indiana University Press.

Murray, S. 2007. Images of Dignity: The Films of Barry Barclay, in *New Zealand Filmmakers* edited by I. Conrich and S. Murray. Detroit: Wayne State University Press: 88–102.

Musser, C. 1985. *A Guide to Motion Picture Catalogues by American Producers and Distributors, 1894–1908: A Microfilm Edition*. Frederick: University Publications America.

Neill, A. 1999. A Land without a Past: Dreamtime and Nation in *The Piano*, in *Piano Lessons: Approaches to* The Piano edited by F. Coombs and S. Gemmell. Sydney: John Libbey: 136–47.

Neill, S. and Rymer, J. 1995. *BFI Century of Cinema Series—New Zealand Cinema: Cinema of Unease* [Videorecording].

New Zealand Film Commission 2008. NZ Theatrical Releases. [Online]. Available: http://www.nzfilm.co.nz/FilmCatalogue/Statistics.aspx. [Accessed 11 July 2008].

Nicholls, B. 2009. The Ludic Integration of the Game and Film Industries, in *Studying the Event Film* edited by H. Margolis, S. Cubitt, B. King and T. Jutel. Manchester: Manchester University Press: 280–90.

NZembassy 2006. New Zealand Fast Facts—The World in One Place. [Online]. Available: www.nzembassy.com. [Accessed 4 June 2006].

NZOYB 1976. Tourism: The Invisible Export. *New Zealand Official Yearbook.* Wellington: Department of Statistics.

NZPA 1994. Piano Gives NZ World Springboard. *New Zealand Herald.* 24 March: 24.

O'Regan, T. 1988. Fair Dinkum Fillums: *The Crocodile Dundee* Phenomenon, in *The Imaginary Industry: Australian Films in the late 80s* edited by S. Dermody and E. Jacka. Sydney: Australian Film, Television and Radio School and Media Information: 155–75.

O'Regan, T. and Goldsmith, B. 2005. *The Film Studio.* Lanham: Rowman & Littlefield.

O'Shea, J. 1999. *Dont Let It Get You.* Wellington: Victoria University Press.

Park, G. 2006. *Theatre Country: Essays on Landscape and Whenua.* Wellington: Victoria University Press.

Pearson, B. 1974. *Fretful Sleepers and Other Essays.* Auckland: Heinemann Education Books.

Pearson, B. 1984. *Rifled Sanctuaries: Some Views of the Pacific Islands in Western Literature to 1900.* Auckland: Auckland University Press.

Perry, N. 1994. *The Dominion of Signs.* Auckland: Auckland University Press.

Perry, N. 1998. *Hyperreality and Global Culture.* London: Routledge.

Perry, N. 2001. On Forging Identities, in *Baudrillard: West of the Dateline* edited by V. Grace, H. Worth and L. Simmons. Palmerston North: Dunmore Press: 102–16.

Peters, G. 2007. Lives of their Own: Films by Merata Mita, in *New Zealand Filmmakers* edited by I. Conrich and S. Murray. Detroit: Wayne State University Press: 103–20.

Peterson, J. L. 2006. "The Nations First Playground": Travel Films and the American West, 1895–1920, in *Virtual Voyages* edited by J. Ruoff. London: Duke University Press: 79–98.

Peterson, R. A. and Anand, N. 2004. The Production of Culture Perspective. *Annual Review of Sociology*, 30: 311–34.

Phillips, M. 2007. *The Lord of the Rings* and Transformations in Socio-Spatial Identity in Aotearoa/New Zealand, in *Cinematic Countrysides* edited by Robert Fish. Manchester: Manchester University Press: 147–74.

Pihama, L. 2000. Ebony and Ivory: Constructions of Māori in *The Piano*, in *Jane Campions* The Piano edited by H. Margolis. Cambridge: Cambridge University Press: 114–34.

Pound, F. 1982. The Real & the Unreal in New Zealand Painting. *Art New Zealand*, 25: 42–47.

Pound, F. 1983. *Frames on the Land: Early Landscape Painting in New Zealand*. Auckland: Collins.

Pratt, A. C. 2007. Imagination can be a Damned Curse in this Country: Material Geographies of Filmmaking and the Rural, in *Cinematic Countrysides* edited by Robert Fish. Manchester: Manchester University Press: 127–46.

Pratt, M. L. 1992. *Imperial Eyes: Travel Writing and Transculturation*. London: Routledge.

Prentice, C. 2006. Riding the Whale?: Postcolonialism and Globalization in *Whale Rider*, in *Global Fissures: Postcolonial Fusions* edited by C. Joseph and J. Wilson. New York: Rodopi: 247–68.

Propp, V. 1968. *Morphology of the Folktale*. Trans. L. Scott. Austin: University of Texas Press.

Rabinovitz, L. 2006. From Hales Tours to Star Tours: Virtual Voyages, Travel Ride Films and the Delirium of the Hyper-Real, in *Virtual Voyages* edited by J. Ruoff. London: Duke University Press: 42–60.

Radcliff, S. 2006. Interview with the author. 25 November 2006. Uruti.

Rauwerda, A. M. 2004. *The Whale Rider*—Book and Film Review, *Postcolonial Text*, 1:1. [Online]. Available: http://postcolonial.org/index.php/pct/article/viewArticle/292/779. [Accessed 10 October 2008].

Reynolds, R., Bial, H. and Keramidas, K. 2009. Tourist Encounters, in *Studying the Event Film* edited by H. Margolis, S. Cubitt, B. King and T. Jutel. Manchester: Manchester University Press: 239–48.

Riley, R. and Van Doren, C. S. 1992. Movies as Tourism Promotion: A Pull Factor in a Push Location. *Tourist Management*, 13: 267–74.

Riley, R., Baker D. and Van Doren, C. S. 1998. Movie-Induced Tourism. *Annals of Tourism Research*, 25(4): 919–35.

Ritchie, B. 1984. Assessing the Impact of Hallmark Events: Conceptual and Research Issues. *Journal of Travel Research*, 23(1): 2–11.

Ritzer, G. 1996. *The McDonaldization of Society*. Thousand Oaks: Pine Forge Press.

Roesch, S. 2007. There and Back Again: Comparative Case Studies of Film Location Tourists On-Site Behaviour and Experiences. Ph.D. Thesis. Dunedin: University of Otago.

Rojek, C. 1993. *Ways of Escape: Modern Transformation of Leisure and Travel*. London: Macmillan.

Sayle, J. 1999. The Gendered Sublime in *Memory and Desire*. *Illusions*, 28: 17–23.

Schafer, J. W. 1998. *Mapping the Godzone: A Primer on New Zealand Literature and Culture*. Honolulu: University of Hawaii Press.

Schivelbusch, W. 1986. *The Railway Journey: The Industrialisation of Time and Space in the Nineteenth Century*. Berkeley: University of California Press.

Screen Production Industry Taskforce. 2003. Taking on the World: The Report of the Screen Production Industry Taskforce. [Online]. Available: http://www.nzte.govt.nz/common/files/screen-taskforce-report.pdf. [Accessed 5 January 2007].

Seaton, A. V. 1999. War and Thanatourism: Waterloo 1815–1914. *Annals of Tourism Research*, 26(1): 130–59.

Sellors, P. 2000. The Nature of Film Spectators, *Film-Philosophy*, 4:19. [Online]. Available: http://www.film-philosophy.com/vol4-2000/n19sellors. [Accessed 6 June 2008].

Shaw, G. and Williams, A. 2004. *Tourism and Tourist Spaces*. London: Sage.

Shelton, L. 2005. *The Selling of New Zealand Movies*. Wellington: Awa Press.

Shepard, D. 2000. *Reframing Women: A History of New Zealand Film*. Auckland: Harper Collins.

Shohat, E. and Stam, R. 1994. *Unthinking Eurocentrism: Multiculturalism and the Media*. London: Routledge.

Simmons, L. 1995a. "Take Them Out of the Crate Joe": The Surface of Detail in John O'Shea's *Runaway*. *Interstices*, 1995: 55–70.

Simmons, L. 1995b. Track Record: Trains in New Zealand Film. *New Zealand Journal of Media Studies*, 2(2): 50–7.

Simmons, L. 1999a. From Land Escape to Bodyscape: Images of the Land in *The Piano*, in *Piano Lessons: Approaches to* The Piano edited by F. Coombs and S. Gemmell. Sydney: John Libbey: 122–35.

Simmons, L. 1999b. Distance Looks Our Way, in *Twin Peeks: Australian and New Zealand Feature Films* edited by D. Verhoeven. Melbourne: Damned Publishing: 39–50.

Simmons, L. 2007. The Lord of the Rings: The Fellowship of the Ring, in *The Cinema of Australia and New Zealand* edited by G. Mayer and K. Beattie. London: Wallflower: 223–32.

Simmons, L. 2008. Forming the Image from a Distance. *Illusions*, 40: 15–20.

Smith, B. 1960. *European Vision and the South Pacific*. New Haven: Yale University Press.

Smith, B. 1992. *Imagining the Pacific: In the Wake of the Cook Voyages*. Melbourne: Melbourne University Press.

Smith-Rowsey, D. 2007. Whose Middle-Earth is it?: Reading *The Lord of the Rings* and New Zealands identity from a Globalized, Post-Colonial Perspective, in *How We Became Middle Earth* edited by A. Lam and N. Oryshchuk. Zurich: Walking Tree Publisher: 129–45.

Solanas, F. and Gettino, O. 1986. Toward a Third Cinema, in *Movies and Methods: An Anthology* edited by Bill Nichols. Berkeley: University of California Press: 44–64.

Sonmez, S. F., Apostolopoulos, Y. and Tarlow, P. 1999. Tourism in Crisis: Managing the Effects of Terrorism. *Journal of Travel Research*, 38(1): 13–18.

Stafford, J. and Williams, M. 2006. *Maoriland: New Zealand Literature 1872–1914*. Wellington: Victoria University Press.

Statistics New Zealand 2005. Tourism and Migration 2004. [Online]. Available: www.stats.govt.nz/tables/tables-tourism-2004. [Accessed 7 July 2006].

Stevenson, R. L. 1993. *Treasure Island*. New York: Dover Publications. First published 1883.

Stewart, B. 2008. Memory and Desire *Summary Review*. [Online]. Available: http://movies.nytimes.com/movie/162734/Memory-Desire/overview. [Accessed 17 September 2008].

Stuart, I. 2003. *Whale Rider* Beguiles Influential US Audience. *New Zealand Herald*, 20 May: B6.

Te Punga Somerville, A. 2009. Asking that Mountain: An Indigenous Reading of *The Lord of the Rings*?, in *Studying the Event Film* edited by H. Margolis, S. Cubitt, B. King and T. Jutel. Manchester: Manchester University Press: 249–58.

Thompson, K. 2006. Scale, Spectacle and Movement: Massive Software and Digital Special Effects, in *From Hobbits to Hollywood* edited by E. Mathijs and M. Pomerance. Amsterdam: Rodopi: 283–300.

Thompson, K. 2007. *The Frodo Franchise:* The Lord of the Rings *and Modern Hollywood*. Berkeley: University of California Press.

Thompson, W. 2000. Disney Heads to Henderson. *New Zealand Herald*, 17 August: 10.

Thorner, S. G. 2007. Changing the Rules of Engagement. *Visual Anthropology Review*, 23(2): 137–50.

Tierney, S. M. 2006. Themes of Whiteness in *Bulletproof Monk, Kill Bill*, and *The Last Samurai. Journal of Communication*, 56: 607–24.

Tincknell, E. 2000. New Zealand Gothic?: Jane Campions *The Piano*, in *New Zealand: A Pastoral Paradise?* edited by I. Conrich and D. Woods. Nottingham: Kakapo Books: 107–19.

TNZ 2004. Interactive Travellers: Who are They?. [Online]. Available: http://www.newzealand.com/travel/library/y42301_23.pdf. [Accessed 7 July 2006].

TNZ 2006. The Last Samurai *New Zealand Film Location*. [Online]. Available: http://www.newzealand.com/travel/destinations/regions/taranaki/last-samurai-feature/last-samurai-feature-home.cfm. [Accessed 12 July 2006].

Tolkien, J. R. R. 2001. *The Lord of the Rings*. Boston: Houghton Mifflin. First published 1954.

Tooke, N. and Baker, M. 1996. Seeing is Believing: The Effect of Film on Visitor Numbers to Screened Locations. *Tourism Management*, 17(2): 87–94.

Tourism Auckland 2008. Karekare. [Online]. Available: http://www.aucklandnz.com/index.php/content_B/?L1=223&L2=229&id=1333. [Accessed 17 September 2008].

TRCNZ 2005. *New Zealand Regional Tourism Forecasts*. Wellington: TRCNZ.

Turner, S. 2000. Colonialism Continued: Producing the Self for Export, in *Race, Colour and Identity in Australia and New Zealand* edited by J. Docker and G. Fischer. Sydney: University of New South Wales Press: 218–29.

Turner, S. 2002. Cinema of Justice: The Feathers of Peace. *Illusions*, 33: 9–11.

Turner, S. 2007. Inclusive Exclusion: Managing Identity for the Nations Sake in Aotearoa/New Zealand. *Arena Journal*, 28: 87–106.

Tzanelli, R. 2004. Constructing the Cinematic Tourist: The Sign Industry of *The Lord of the Rings. Tourist Studies*, 4(1): 21–42.

Tzanelli, R. 2007. *The Cinematic Tourist*. New York: Routledge.

Ultimate Rollercoaster 2002. Amusement Park Attendance Down Overall Last Year. [Online]. Available: http://www.ultimaterollercoaster.com/news/ stories/012102_02.shtml. [Accessed 23 December 2008].

Urry, J. 2002. *The Tourist Gaze*. London: Sage.

US Department of Commerce 2001. The Migration of US Film and Television Production: Impact of Runaways on Workers and Small Business in the US Film Industry. [Online]. Available: http://www.ita.doc.gov/media/filmreport. html. [Accessed 5 January 2007].

Venture Taranaki 2002. *The Last Samurai* at Last!. [Online]. Available: www.taranaki. info/news/samurai.htm. [Accessed 12 July 2006].

Venture Taranaki 2004. *Economic Impact Assessment for the Filming of* The Last Samurai *in Taranaki*. New Plymouth: Venture Taranaki.

Venture Taranaki 2005. *Taranaki Visitor Trends 2004*. New Plymouth: Venture Taranaki.

View: The Aucklanders Guide to Auckland 2008. Karekare Beach. [Online]. Available: http://www.viewauckland.co.nz/karekare_beach_waitakere_auckland_index. html. [Accessed 17 September 2008].

Virilio, P. 2002. *Ground Zero*. London: Verso.

Walker, D. R. 2001. Queenstown and Film Friendliness: Tourism, Film, Local Government and the Community. Masters Thesis. Dunedin: University of Otago.

Walker, D. 2006. Representing the Self, Representing the Other: Ethics and Ethnicity in the Contemporary Cinema of Aotearoa. *International Yearbook of Aesthetics*, 10: 99–106.

Ward, V. 2009. Personal communication with the author. 18 May 2009. Auckland.

Warner Bros. 2004. *The Last Samurai* Making Of: The Set. [Online]. Available: www. lastsamurai.warnerbros.com. [Accessed 11 July 2006].

Webwombat 2006. Interview with Vincent Ward. [Online]. Available: http://www.webwombat.com.au/entertainment/movies/vincent-ward-int.htm. [Accessed 12 September 2008].

Wells, P. 1991. *Dangerous Desires*. Auckland: Reed Books.

West, R. 2003. Set up for Prime Viewing. *New Zealand Herald*, 6 March.

Wevers, L. 1994. A Story of Land: Narrating Landscape in some Early New Zealand Writers or: Not the Story of a New Zealand River. *Australian and New Zealand Studies in Canada*, 11 June: 1–11.

Wilson, E. O. 2002. *The Future of Life*. London: Little Brown.

Wilson, J. K. T. 2006. The Cinematic Economy of Cliff Curtis. Masters Thesis. Auckland: University of Auckland.

Wilson, T. M. 2007. Blockbuster Pastoral, in *How We Became Middle Earth* edited by A. Lam and N. Oryshchuk. Zurich: Walking Tree Publisher: 185–96.

Wong, L. 2007. Theme/Film Tour: The Disappearing of Illusion into Integral Reality, in *How We Became Middle Earth* edited by A. Lam and N. Oryshchuk. Zurich: Walking Tree Publisher: 87–106.

Woodward, S. and Kourelis, K. 2006. Urban Legend: Architecture in *The Lord of the Rings*, in *From Hobbits to Hollywood* edited by E. Mathijs and M. Pomerance. Amsterdam: Rodopi: 189–214.

Wright, A. 2000. Realms of Enchantment: New Zealand Landscape as Tolkienesque, in *New Zealand: A Pastoral Paradise?* edited by I. Conrich and D. Woods. Notthingam: Kakapo Books: 52–59.

Yeabsley, J. and Duncan, I. 2002. *Scoping the Lasting Effects of* The Lord of The Rings: *Report to the New Zealand Film Commission*. Wellington: NZ Institute of Economic Research.

Zizek, S. 2002. *Welcome to the Desert of the Real*. London: Verso.